EDWARD BOYKIN, whose *Ghost Ship of the Confederacy* was a Civil War Book Club selection in 1957, is an untiring scholar in the field of American history. Born in Petersburg, Virginia, he attended the United States Military Academy at West Point. After several years as a reporter and Assistant City Editor with the famous New York *Evening Journal*, he turned to public relations, with the Edison Company, and advertising, with the nation's leading agencies. During all these years, however, Mr. Boykin's interest in American history never waned. He wrote two historical plays and six books. Among his works are *Congress and the Civil War, The Wisdom of Thomas Jefferson, Living Letters from American History*. His motion picture, *Thomas Jefferson and Monticello*, has been seen by about 5,000,000 school children, and his radio program, *Americana Quiz*, which he originated and conducted for ten years, earned him the title, "Radio Professor of American History." Mr. Boykin also acted as Master of Ceremonies for the coast-to-coast program, *National Radio Forum*. He headed the Thomas Jefferson Bicentennial Commission in Washington and was Director of the National Capital Sesquicentennial Celebration. Mr. Boykin now resides in Charlottesville, Virginia.

John Newland Maffitt
From a photograph taken shortly before the Civil War, when he was
still a lieutenant in the United States Navy.

Sea Devil of the Confederacy

The story of the Florida and her captain, John Newland Maffitt

by

EDWARD BOYKIN

FUNK & WAGNALLS COMPANY

NEW YORK

© 1959 Funk & Wagnalls Company
Library of Congress Catalog Card Number 59-10897
Printed in the United States of America

1

TO CAPTAIN EDWARD BOYKIN, JR.

EIGHTH AIR FORCE

1917–1943

Preface

JOHN NEWLAND MAFFITT occupies a unique place in the annals of the Civil War. He was the only Confederate naval officer to play the dual role of high-scoring commerce raider and blockade runner.

As captain of the far-famed raiding cruiser *Florida* he blazed off the biggest prize ever captured by the South on the high seas, while at the same time racking up a record of seizure and destruction of Northern shipping only slightly less than that of Raphael Semmes and the *Alabama*. Under Maffitt's command, the *Florida* and her tenders incinerated a tonnage of Yankee vessels that ran into millions of dollars. A total of fifty-five ships. Admiral Porter maintained that Maffitt was even more feared by Yankee skippers than Semmes.

As blockade runner, Maffitt's adventures stagger the imagination. His hairbreadth escapes amounted to sheer genius. Captain of four government-owned runners plying their trade in this bitter offshore conflict, he was fired at, chased, and "sunk" so often as to defy the telling. In the dying moments of the Confederacy, when her battle lines were finally crumbling, John Maffitt turned in the acknowledged blockade-running classic of the war. His run of the helpless *Florida* through cataracts of gunfire into Mobile Bay still stands unparalleled. To complete the picture, add his masterly seamanship, at which he may have had peers, but never one better.

Maffitt's exploits as a commerce raider were at times overshadowed by those of his teammate, Raphael Semmes, but they were, none the less, remarkable. Not until now has the *Florida* received her fair share of attention. These two, the *Florida* and the *Alabama*, both ships built stealthily in England and spirited through the barricade of Britain's Foreign Enlistment Act, became the most hated and successful sea-raiders the world has known. Called "pirates" by the North, they wrote the brightest page of Confederate naval history. The *Shenandoah*, a steamer bought in England and converted to war usage, was the Johnny-come-lately of the Confederate raiders, though her blazing pounce on the whaling fleet in the far-off Pacific never acquired the luster and prestige to match that investing the *Alabama* and the *Florida*, whom the Union Navy pursued with virulence. Actually, the *Florida* was never caught. She chanced into a neutral port, where a Federal warship, by a violation of international law, maimed and captured her at night.

Maffitt's Papers and Journals—the only considerable collection of his memoirs—were presented to the Southern Historical Collection of the University of North Carolina Library several years ago by the surviving members of his family, now living at Wilmington. Pithy comment and apt expression came as naturally to Maffitt as the sea itself. Yet his papers reveal barely a fraction of his incredible adventures.

Of his postwar literary efforts, the best was *Nautilus, or Cruising Under Canvas*, where a breezy narrative thinly disguises his own experiences as midshipman on "Old Ironsides" on the Mediterranean station during the 1830's.

Maffitt's contributions to various magazines have been helpful; but the actual story of his amazing blockade-running feats had to be laboriously gathered and pieced together bit by bit. His third wife, Emma Martin Maffitt, whom he married after the war, sought to recreate the great episodes of his career in a documentary published in 1906, which was helpful. The first author in comparatively modern days to give Maffitt his due was Joseph Hergesheimer. A brief chapter in his *Swords and Roses* (1928) brings Maffitt to the fore, though it is doubtful that Hergesheimer ever consulted Maffitt's papers, or knew they existed. Aside from a short piece or two, Maffitt has since been neglected, as, until recently, was the whole naval panorama of the Civil War. It is high time that Maffitt appears in a book all his own.

The log of the *Florida*, which Maffitt had graced with descriptions of his raiding adventures, was tossed overboard off Charleston when it looked as if his blockade runner *Owl* was about to be captured. It was a great loss. The best that is left is an abstract of that log, minus the coruscations of Maffitt's pen.

The chief source books available today are the Official Records of the Union and Confederate Navies, published by the Federal government in 1894. This massive contribution to our nation's military and naval history is studded with reports of the long, fruitless chase after one of the most elusive figures ever to set sail, John Newland Maffitt.

The writer is much indebted to many who have given help or pointed the way to it. Among these are Mrs. Clarence D. Maffitt, widow of John Maffitt's last surviving son, and his granddaughter, Mrs. Kate Maffitt Woollcott, both of Wilmington. Most helpful was Mr. Louis T. Moore, Chairman of the New Hanover Historical Commission, at Wilmington, North Carolina.

Mr. James Patton, Director of the Southern Historical Collection at the University of North Carolina Library, gave the writer unstinted assistance in examining John Maffitt's Journals and Papers deposited with that fine institution. Miss India Thomas, regent of the Confederate Museum at Richmond, kindly offered various suggestions and tidbits of research that found their way into this book.

The Alderman Library at the University of Virginia was, as always, most generous to the writer. The same can be said for the Library of Congress at Washington, the Navy Department, and the National Archives. The writer's thanks go also to the Rosenberg Library, at Galveston; the Department of Archives and History, Jackson, Mississippi; the Texas State Historical Association, Austin; the Maine Historical Society, Portland, Maine.

Nor should the writer forget Mrs. Virginia Corey and Mrs. Robert Hoskins, of the Alderman Library's photostatic department, for many courteous favors. Lastly, there is the debt the author owes Lois De Bell of Charlottesville, Virginia, for whose excellent work as copyist he is happy to acknowledge his gratitude.

EDWARD BOYKIN

Charlottesville, Virginia
January, 1959

Contents

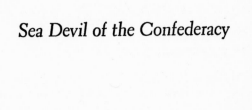

Sea Devil of the Confederacy

CHAPTER I

Gunfire on the Gulf Stream

"Heave to, or I'll sink you!"

The stern command was barked across the dark waters, every word distinct, loaded with menace.

Back sped a brisk reply, "Aye, aye, sir!", followed by the sharp, loud-voiced order, "Stop the engine!"

Suddenly, with hiss and sparkle, rockets began jetting up from the Federal blockaders, to blossom like massive poppies overhead, coating the waters with red brilliance. Drummond lights reached out cold fingers that tore the dark to tatters. The scene was eerie; the sea bright as noonday. Any moment gunfire might crash through the night and canister begin spattering iron hail on the Confederate blockade runner. The Yankee gunners on the blockade took no chances. They shot to kill.

Moments before, the *Cecile's* pilot had whispered, "Captain, it seems to me from our soundings we should be stumbling on them varmints. Maybe we've slipped by 'em."

"Maybe we haven't," snapped John Maffitt. "Listen! There's a ship's bell. One, two, three, four, five, six, seven—half past eleven. Good timing. It's high water on the bar."

"My God! There's two of 'em," blurted the pilot. "Right on top of us."

"Dive between them," ordered Maffitt quietly.

His nightglasses had failed to reveal two huge objects that sud-

3

denly loomed out of the gloom, dead ahead, anchored cable-lengths to port and starboard. The *Cecile* was sliding into their very jaws. Nondescript, converted merchantmen they were, but packing enough artillery to cut the slim *Cecile* in two with a single broadside. To Maffitt it seemed that the Union ships were close enough to touch with his hand. How could they miss at less than pistol range? If they caught the *Cecile* in their crossfire? By this time every whistle in the Federal fleet was screaming, drums beating, rockets going up, and the very devil to pay. Trembling, her whole frame shuddering with the sudden shutdown of her engine, the *Cecile's* headway lugged her along. Maffitt could hear the shrill pipe of a Federal boatswain's whistle, the falling away of the cutters, the tramping of boat crews. Boarders were coming.

Again the stern voice hailed, "Back your engine, sir! Stand by to receive my boats!"

This was the big, dread moment in the life of a blockade runner, and Maffitt knew it well enough. There was no time to think it out. Whatever he did must be done as fast as God and steam would let him.

He raised his trumpet, "Aye, aye, sir!" His voice was smooth, compliant as silk. The words were hardly out of his mouth when a Confederate officer, who had recently escaped from a Northern prison and was returning by way of Nassau and the *Cecile*, appeared at Maffitt's side.

"My God! Captain Maffitt!" he implored, wringing his hands. "You, of all men, can't surrender this ship without making an effort to escape!"

Maffitt turned on him fiercely. "Get back to your cabin, sir!" he ordered sternly. "I need no interference from you."

Almost in the same breath Maffitt roared into the speaking tube to his engineer, "Full speed ahead! Open your throttle wide! Give her all you've got. We're running for it!"

No whisper this time. What difference could it make? The *Cecile* was a sitting duck. Her boilers were ready to explode, and right under the broadsides of two would-be captors. John Maffitt had his choice: Old Capitol at Washington (or maybe Fort Warren, Boston) or Davy Jones's locker. The blockaders shot fast, but at night they missed more often than they hit. Maffitt had taken chances before. This was just another. The Union crews would cut no prize-money melon for capturing the *Cecile*. The life of Lieutenant John Newland Maffitt, Confederate States Navy, had been bright with danger—hairbreadth escapes and hazard—since he took command of the *Cecile* at Wilmington on January 7, 1862.

All but invisible at one hundred yards, even by day, the *Cecile* was skimming over the dark waters like a phantom, shaping her course for the eastern bar of the Cape Fear River, threshold to Wilmington, fabulous paradise of this dangerous undercover traffic. She was a long, rakish, low-masted sidewheeler, camouflaged lead gray, with telescoping funnels. One of hundreds of eely, lightdraft craft, she slithered back and forth through the triple cordon of watchdogs prowling the Southern coast intent on corking up every inlet and port through which overseas supplies could reach the beleaguered Confederacy.

Outbound, these slippery, elusive daredevils ferried cotton, the Confederacy's white gold, to buy cannon and rifles, gunpowder and sulphur, saltpetre and bayonets, quinine, lead pigs, morphine, chloroform for a brand new nation that had staked her fate and fortune on pluck, endurance, hard fighting, and hope. Nor should the knickknacks be forgotten: the silks, satins, fine wines, and patés that ran that blockade along with the necessities of war. The risks were legion, but the rewards magnificent. Southern ports were gold mines for the man who could slip in and come out with a whole skin and his ship bulging with the fluffy staple that was anointed King of the South.

The *Cecile* was on the last lap of the 570-mile gantlet from neutral Nassau, in the Bahamas, fabulous relay station to Liverpool, where five-cent cotton brought sixty. At dusk, the Cape Fear bar loomed up thirty miles distant. At half past eleven it would be high water, the witching hour for crossing. The sun had gone down in a blaze of gold and crimson. Night had fallen serene and dark. No waiting tonight for the moon to set. The *Cecile* had on her fourteen-knot running shoes. She was fleet, for in her business it was run like hell or get caught. Slow-pokes stood little chance. Her paddles were beating the water like frenzied flails. Steam pressure had mounted to twenty-six pounds, paddle revolutions to thirty-six a minute, racking her whole frame. Soon she would be near enough to hear the roar of the surf on the beach. Maybe it would drown out the noise of her paddles. She couldn't do much better, but at that she could outfoot anything on the patrol.

The run from Nassau was a Scylla-Charybdis affair. Federal gunboats were everywhere. If one didn't pounce on you, another might. A gritty lot, the captains of these runners, able to stand fire without returning it. The *sine qua non*'s of their business were: nerves that could stretch taut without snapping; a ship that could knife through the water like a swordfish; and a gambling impulse to take every chance in the book. It was hare-and-hound stuff with a vengeance—with death and destruction always lurking for the hare, seldom for the hound.

The *Cecile* had left Nassau at dusk two days before. At break of day off Abaco Light, turning point for Wilmington and Charleston, three Federal cruisers had sighted her. It was a favorite hangout for these busybodies. For hours they clung on like steam-driven leeches. Eating up the miles, the *Cecile* gave them the go-by, but not before they paid long-range obeisance with a few shots that fell short. By noon the Union ships had faded under the horizon.

Crossing the Gulf Stream she easily eluded the dragnet that patrolled this river of the sea. Maffitt had decided to run in by the New Inlet of the Cape Fear River, which meant he still had to negotiate the Federal inshore cordon. Once clear of this last barrier, a quick dash would bring him to the channel and under the friendly guns of Fort Fisher, the formidable bastion whose big-caliber pieces kept Federal sea-dragons at respectful distance. Once in reach of the fort's iron snouts, the vessel could slow down her engine and haul twenty-eight miles upriver to Wilmington to receive the customary greeting for a successful run, every steam whistle on the river caterwauling like a calliope.

But now—not the tiniest glimmer of light showed on the *Cecile*. She was blacked out. On each quarter stood a leadsman quietly calling his soundings. Save for the splash of her paddles, absolute silence prevailed. Orders were given in whispers. Sound traveled like magic over the waters. A single word was enough to warn a blockader. They were sharp-eyed, sharp-eared rascals. The fire-room hatch was doused with a tarpaulin, the binnacle hooded, leaving only a peephole for the pilot to see the compass. On the paddle boxes, on the bow, crouched behind the bulwarks, lookouts strained to see into the murk. Five miles now to go to the white line of breakers and smooth water. Yet, between her and sanctuary lay the crescent-shaped inner cordon of Federal blockaders, whose horns by night drew inshore so close that a rowboat could hardly mouse by without discovery.

No blockade runner commanded by a Confederate naval officer had as yet been captured, and Lieutenant Maffitt, master of the *Cecile*, had no intention of setting a bad precedent. He knew every inch of the coast by heart. Back in the Fifties in the old navy he had charted it for the government—every league, fathom, channel, current, shoal, and harbor. But now the warning lighthouses had ceased to exist. War had dimmed these beacons on dunes and headlands from the Capes of the Chesapeake to Matamoras on the Mexican border. Yet, night or day, he could almost pick his way without a leadsman; that is, had there been no Federal foe waiting on the dark waters. Coming in by night one had to rely on exact navigation, cold nerve, and speed. The Carolina shoreline was dotted with hulks whose pilots had guessed wrong.

Now, the *Cecile*, in the glare of the Federals' lights, responded with a leap to Maffitt's full-speed lash. Her paddle wheels beat the water to foam. For a moment the Federal commander was deceived into thinking his threatening "Heave to!" had taken effect, then he realized his prize was taking to her heels. Coolly taking his station on the port paddle box, Maffitt ordered every man below deck save himself and the pilot. A salty oath hurtled out of the dark. Then one word—"Fire!"

Maffitt described the next brutal moments: "Then commenced the old music of shot and shell. The explosive thunder of artillery that rent the atmosphere and convulsed the ocean until the *Cecile* rocked to and fro with the ponderous concussions."

The red hurricane came with a roar and shock. John Maffitt felt its hot breath sweep the deck. Caught under the converging fire of two blockaders, the *Cecile* fled through a pandemonium of exploding iron demons that splintered spars and bulwarks, pitted the deck, severed rigging. But luck herself paced the *Cecile* that night, as she had seven times before. Nor had faint heart any place on the deck with John Maffitt and his pilot. Yet the *Cecile's* escape was a freakish matter. The Drummond lights that stripped her naked under the muzzles of the Federal guns so radiated the mist that her hull appeared far higher than it was—and broadsides that might have raked her to pieces went screeching through the rigging. Now her funnels gushed dense streamers of smoke that were caught by the wind and swept aft, blurring the Federal sights and blacking out the fleeing vessel. Shots stabbed after her, but firing into smoky darkness seldom paid off. And the *Cecile* had the speed of anything in the cordon.

Maffitt wrote humorously in his Journal, "We paused not recklessly, but at the rate of sixteen knots absolutely flew out of unhealthy company, who discourteously followed us with exploding shells, and for some time kept up such a fusillade as to impress us with the belief that the blockaders had inaugurated a 'Kilkenny cat muddle,' and were polishing each other off; a supposition I afterward learned was partially true."

The pilot took a deep breath. "A close shave, Captain Maffitt."

"It was, sir. Too close."

"I was just thinking what might have happened if one of those things had landed in the hold."

So was John Maffitt. Below deck were nine hundred barrels, consigned to the Confederate government—ninety thousand pounds of gunpowder, the best British manufacturers could produce. Ten times as much as U. S. Grant would one day use to rip a hole in Lee's fortified lines at Petersburg. The Confederacy needed every pound she could get her hands on. Her own mills had not yet begun grinding, and big battles were coming up in Virginia. McClellan's one hundred thousand men were tramping bloodily up the Peninsula toward Richmond. In the West the tempo was rising: a bloody shambles called Shiloh was near at hand. Albert Sidney Johnston's graybacks were famishing for powder. Yet, had a single shell lunged through the *Cecile's* hull, the whole caboodle, hunters and hunted, blockaders and runner, John Maffitt & Company, would have gone up in a blast that would sprinkle the ocean with blackened wreckage.

Somewhere in the greyhound's wake, two Federal watchdogs were glumly retracing their steps back to their nautical "kennels" in the cordon. In the morning the two crestfallen captains would write their apologetic reports to the Flag Officer of the North Atlantic Blockading Squadron. They would begin no doubt with the customary, "I regret, sir, to inform you that last night about eleven-thirty a ship suddenly appeared out of the mist. We opened fire at point-blank range, but . . ."

Breakers ahead warned of shoaling water, and the *Cecile* slowed down to pick her way into the channel. She had made it again. Bulking darkly off to starboard Maffitt sighted the welcome pile of Fort Fisher, whose wide-awake gunners, hearing gunfire afar, were standing by just in case the wayfarer needed a helping shot. A blue light flashed from the Mound Battery near the New Inlet. It was the fort's welcome.

At one A.M. the *Cecile* dropped anchor off Federal Point and banked her fires. In the morning she could continue her run up to Wilmington. Tomorrow at mess call the crew would splice the main brace—in champagne, if you please. Maffitt's round trip to Nassau had taken exactly seven days. In an upsurge of relief he sought his cabin. The jack-tars had already tumbled below. Running the bloc racked nerves, exhausted bodies to dead weariness. The oil lamp shed a pleasant glow over the captain's cubicle. A cubicle only, for living quarters on runners were meager. Flooded with the delightful sense of repose that follows hours of peril and vigil, John Maffitt caught himself repeating lines he long had loved:

> *If after every tempest come such calms,*
> *May the winds blow till they have wakened death;*
> *And let the laboring barks climb hills of seas*
> *Olympus high! and duck again as low*
> *As hell's from heaven!*

It was time to turn in, but old habit was strong, even in John Maffitt at forty-three. He must have a nightcap of fresh air. Fetching an antique naval cloak from his locker, he tossed it about his shoulders and stepped out on deck. The sky was resplendent with stars. They were old friends and he could name them by scores. Often had he looked to them for guidance on faraway waters.

The night air was chilly. In the excitement of running the gantlet he had not noticed it, but now his old cloak felt good. He thought: if only it could talk, what tales it could tell. Memory would out, harking him back to a night on the Mediterranean long, long ago, when the Queen of Greece had worn the cloak about her shoulders. "Midshipman John Maffitt had gallantly thrown his cloak around her Majesty to protect her from the spray." So ran the log of that memorable night. But away with reveries! With a goodnight to the deck-watch John Maffitt went to his cabin, dimmed the lamp and turned into his bunk.

CHAPTER II

White Gold and Revelry

DAY WAS DAWNING when the *Cecile* hove anchor and steamed up-river to Wilmington. At her peak the Stars and Bars snapped in the breeze. Presently, amid a bedlam of steam-whistles, she sidled up to the once-drowsy, now-bustling old town. On her bridge, jaunty and chipper, as if the night before had been one of deep, dreamless sleep, stood John Maffitt, laying his ship smartly alongside the government dock.

On the pier to greet her was a sizable early-bird reception committee: busybody officials with impressive airs, buzzing about as if the whole Confederacy hung on their words; officers conversing in top-secret whispers, looking very military in their neat gray tunics that had not yet seen a battle; unassuming clerks waiting to check the *Cecile*'s manifesto and channel her cargo to battle areas, hospitals, warehouses, or wherever the rash of war demanded it. A score of Negro stevedores, grinning broadly, stood waiting to roll out the barrels and load them onto freight cars parked on a nearby sidetrack. What if it was gunpowder? It hadn't exploded yet.

To the citizenry of Wilmington the arrival of one of these ships gave a lift like a glass of champagne. Excited throngs gathered, whatever the hour. If nothing else, it meant contact with the outside world which the Yankee strait jacket sought to bar. Besides, these ships were invested with a romantic aura of do-and-dare that appealed to young and old alike, so closely were they allied with the adventurous business of flouting death and danger on the seas nearby. But even more exciting was what the runners brought. There was no predicting what they might yield—what riots of dress, edibles, liquors, toiletries—what fabulous delights denied a people starved for the niceties and necessities of life by the stringency of the blockade—all to be auctioned off and avidly bid for at highwayman prices, in Confederate money.

The runner captains themselves were daredevils sans pareil, awesome figures who commanded great respect. John Maffitt was one of them. His name was already a household word in Wilmington. To the sprinkling of small fry who squirmed through the crowds, he was a demigod.

Maffitt's eye skimmed across the scores of faces on the dock to the wharves groaning under barrels of turpentine and rosin, and hogsheads of tobacco slated for fast trips to Nassau, where they would be exchanged for gold. Across the Cape Fear River, on the marshy flat near the Market Street ferry, the steam cotton press ran without stopping. Beside it rose a huge mound of cotton bales. Policing the area were sentries carrying bayonet-tipped muskets to collar deserters who would try to sneak aboard runners and stow away between the tightly compressed bales. Anchored in midstream were half a dozen runners taking on cotton from barges moored alongside. Seldom were they kept waiting. Time meant money, big money.

The Cecile was chartered by the government at two hundred dollars a day. Her freight was largely war matériel, though too often luxuries were smuggled aboard. It was the giant blockade-breaking corporations, financed by English and often Northern capital, that monopolized the luxury business. They were to grow so greedy that the government would soon take half their cargo space for munitions.

After safely mooring his ship, Maffitt went to his cabin to welcome the boarding officers who were already crossing the gangplank to shake his hand, gape at the evidences of the hot reception given the Cecile on her last night's dash and consume a few rounds of drinks. A successful run warranted breaking out the bottle. Champagne was already icing; brandy was handy, as well as rum swizzles. Richmond was lenient in this respect. It was a necessary perquisite, a means of letdown after days of high tension, and corks popped fast. Maffitt kept his locker (and his decanters) well stocked with the best Nassau could offer, and it was "on the government."

After the delegation had departed, he wrote a terse report to Secretary of the Navy Mallory: "Sir, I have the honor to report my successful arrival at this port. Cargo is already being unshipped. If all is propitious, I hope to get off again day after tomorrow night with 800 bales for government account at Nassau."

That was all. Not a word about his trial by fire. However, beyond a few shell-splinter gouges, there was no damage carpenters couldn't patch up with a few days of work and splashes of paint.

By ten o'clock the formalities were over, and John Maffitt went ashore to wend his way through the crowd on Market Street to Bailey's Hotel, where he lodged between runs. Tagging at his heels was a band of goggle-eyed urchins, firing questions by the dozen. Their one desire in life was to grow up and become a daredevil runner just like the captain.

John Maffitt had known Wilmington in happier days when its tempo had been attuned to the placid flow of the Cape Fear River. The war-racked hurlyburly of 1862 that had so changed the town made him melancholy. Many were the cotillions he had danced in the fine homes hereabouts, many the lovely eyes he had gazed into. For he had a charm and elegance that seemed adapted to finer things than blockade running.

The old town of Wilmington was no longer staid. Now it was the chief port of the Confederacy, and vultures of every breed had flown in to partake of the feast. On the streets, in the hotel lobbies, along the waterfront, one rubbed elbows with gamblers who'd never played a straight game in their lives; profiteers ready to swindle their mothers for a gold dollar or less; speculators far more interested in amassing quick fortunes than in the survival of the nation; con men selling shares in imaginary blockade runners to eager buyers; pickpockets, vagrants, rogues, desperadoes. On street corners "gentlemen" stood in knots, arrayed in gorgeous clothes, puffing long Havana segars and jingling gold pieces in their pockets.

How could it be otherwise? Cotton bought for six cents or less at Wilmington could be sold for sixty (in gold) at Liverpool and for one dollar at New York, if you could get it there. A millennium of sorts had descended on the town. Along came the riffraff and the

undesirables to take a hand in a desperate game of chance, blockade-breaking, where the stakes were high and the profits even
higher.

The California Gold Rush a dozen years before had wrought no
swifter changes than those witnessed at Wilmington, a town
which, up until the first blast of war, had grown and prospered in
an orderly fashion.

By 1862 Wilmington was a whore's paradise, what with bloc-
runner captains getting five thousand dollars a month, pilots drawing two thousand per round trip, ordinary seamen fetching one
hundred dollars in gold plus a fifty dollar bonus for a successful
roundabout from Wilmington to Nassau or Bermuda. In every
clime and age the men who man ships have been easy pickings, and
the crews of the runners were no exceptions. They lived high,
drank deep, and paid the price per night the trollops asked, be it
five dollars or fifty (Confederate money, of course). At the height
of Wilmington's revelry the lowest deckhand was a man of mark,
living like a potentate.

But Confederate naval officers, commanding government-leased
runners, didn't draw such wages. They were paid in gold at their
grade, for Congress had fixed a lieutenant's pay at twenty-five hundred a year. Had Maffitt's loyalty and services been for sale he
might have shed his uniform and hired out to one of the runner
corporations. As elusive as the Flying Dutchman, able to slip repeatedly through the blockade, he possessed a commodity that
would have commanded a high price.

It was an axiom along Wilmington's waterfront that after a runner got through twice with merchandise and out twice with cotton,
the Yankees were welcome to her. Her owners could retire. Great
fortunes were accumulated in a few months. The *Banshee*, a
famed example, after eight round trips to the blessed isles, Bermuda
and Nassau, paid back to her owners her cost and operating ex-
penses seven times over. Early venturers in this hazardous enterprise were content with profits of one or two hundred percent, allowing for a ship to be captured occasionally. But as the blockade
tightened and the risks increased and Confederate money depreci-
ated, the profits were compounded. An "investor" frequently realized fifteen hundred to two thousand percent in paper profits on
his original costs.

"It was not unusual," recorded John Maffitt, "for a steamer with the average capacity of eight hundred bales to net on her round trip about four hundred and twenty thousand dollars. These fabulous profits, coupled with the increasing demand, excited not only the cupidity, but characteristic enterprise of British merchants. In less than eight months after the inception of hostilities and closing of Confederate ports the shipyards of England and Scotland were engaged in constructing suitable steamers for blockade running. In a brief time the harbors of Bermuda and Nassau swarmed with sky-colored vessels eagerly seeking pilots and adventurous seamen to assist in transporting desirable cargoes into Dixie. Thus, as an institution, blockade running was established."

Current in wartime Wilmington was the classic story of a retired New Bedford whaling captain who hauled his rotting brig out of her sleep on the marshes and finagled her through the blockade. At Wilmington he traded his life savings for cotton. Running out to Nassau, he converted his cargo into gold. In less than three months he was back in Yankeeland with half a million dollars. He flew the Stars and Stripes the whole way.

Blockade-breaking became a road to riches. Great corporations, with fleets of runners, credit and capital unlimited, and no conscience, waxed fat and greedy. Their agents at Wilmington lived like lords in magnificent style in houses rented at enormous prices from town residents who retired to the country. These interlopers (with bales of Confederate money) commandeered every necessity of life, paid fabulous prices for quarters of lamb and fresh vegetables, and imbibed oceans of wine imported by their employers to keep them happy. They walked the streets as if they owned them. For those who could pay the piper's price there was Southdown mutton brought in ice from England, exotic patés from France, fruits from Italy and Spain, all washed down with Europe's rarest vintages—this amid a people reduced in the main to cornbread and poor substitutes for coffee, and a ragged soldiery footsore and hungry.

Nightly brawls between drunken crews of steamers in port and soldiers stationed to keep order kept the town on edge. Knife-play and pistol-flashing, robbery and murder, ran wild. The civil authorities gave up. *Inter arma silent leges!*

Freight and passenger rates on runners skyrocketed. Travelers were mulcted of three to five hundred dollars in gold, in advance, for one-way passage between Wilmington and Nassau or Bermuda. Twenty-five hundred dollars in gold was paid the owners of a runner named *Whisper* for freighting a small box of medicines from Bermuda. This was an all-time high.

Losses were staggering and Davy Jones prospered. Many valuable cargoes were thrown overboard by hotly pursued runners to lighten the ships and increase their speed. A Confederate official stationed at Wilmington stated that the sea approaches to the inlets were as thickly paved with valuable merchandise as hell with good intentions. But huge profits outstripped the erosion of the blockade until the Confederate jig was almost up.

2

Captaining a runner was not what John Maffitt had expected when he resigned from the United States Navy and cast his lot with the South. Severing old moorings was not easy, but in offering his sword he tied no strings to it. If this was the way the Confederacy wished him to serve her, so be it. After all, hauling nine hundred barrels of gunpowder through an avalanche of gunfire was not to be sneezed at. Nor should he forget other items brought in by his water-walking, death-defying cornucopia: twenty thousand ounces of quinine and heaven knows how many bottles of chloroform to ease the agonies of shattered boys. For the runners brought the plasma, as it were, for the gray armies bleeding on a dozen fronts.

Maffitt had hoped to command a sloop-of-war with a Confederate high-seas fleet, if and when the South—by magic, gold, or sheer hard work—created a navy. But improvising warships by a preponderantly agricultural people was a task to appall the imagination of even resourceful Stephen R. Mallory, holding down the naval lid at Richmond.

The slow squeeze of the blockade had begun like a creeping paralysis. Union blockaders off Wilmington, Charleston, Mobile, Galveston, and the Mississippi Passes were already nipping off even yawls and pilot boats carrying two or three bales of cotton, and manned by juveniles lured by prospects of profit. Between puffs of his clay pipe, Lincoln's imperturbable Secretary of the Navy, Gideon Welles, had vowed to cork up the South so securely its ships would have to fly or swim under water to reach the sea. Welles's dire prediction had given the South a good ha-ha. The vast stretch of the South Atlantic and Gulf coasts would of itself defeat old Gideon's scheme for sealing it off from the rest of the world. Certainly, he couldn't do it with the peanut navy of forty-two ships on hand when he took office. To the vocal ninety-nine percent of the South and a goodly segment of the North, Welles was talking through his ill-fitting wig. The best he could hope for was keeping a loose watch over the chief Southern ports, and even if these were shut off effectually, bold spirits would get in or out elsewhere along the ragged coast.

John Maffitt belonged to the one percent that did not indulge in an optimistic view of the blockade. For him its import was deadly enough, though he was to give the best he had to defeat it. If the Yankee stranglehold was made effective, the South would suffocate. The North had money enough to station armed ships and patrols in every mile of water if need be. Nor could the South match fighting dollars with the North. Cotton was a powerful weapon, but Northern industry carried a far bigger wallop.

The one way to destroy the blockade was to dilute it. Such was top-level thinking at Montgomery (and subsequently at Richmond) in the first year of war. Fast Southern cruisers raiding rich, vulnerable Northern shipping would oblige the Lincoln hierarchy to detach their best fighting ships to scotch the marauders. A score of these stingarees would force the North to convoy its merchantmen, and that would take first-class warships. This done, men with clear heads and iron nerves, like Maffitt, Wilkinson, and others, who had become experts at the deadly steeplechase with Welles's cordons, could infiltrate at will and reduce the blockade to a mere name. Then, Mallory's yet-unbuilt pets (the ironclad rams) could trundle out and demolish what was left.

Already Commander Raphael Semmes, Maffitt's longtime companion-in-arms, was handily demonstrating the wisdom of a *guerre de course* naval policy. With the makeshift *Sumter* he was burning Northern commerce in the Caribbean and scaring hundreds of others off the ocean. Federal warships were whipping after him like mad, only to discover they were chasing a will-o'-the-wisp. The Northern press and politicians were denouncing him as a pirate, because only pirates captured and burned ships at sea.

Could John Maffitt have peered into a crystal ball he might have seen "pirate" written beside his own name on Welles's list of the most-wanted "war-criminals." He did not yet know it, but he was ordained to command the *Florida*, sister ship of the yet unborn *Alabama*, and the *Florida* and her tenders were to rack up a score of fifty-five Yankee vessels captured or burned. Also unrevealed to him was Welles's promise of a necktie-party, once the honorable secretary got his hands on "Pirate Maffitt."

Yankee Admiral David Dixon Porter made a fine distinction between these two Southern "pirates." Semmes was a "bad pirate"; there wasn't a worth-while bone in his body, if we are to accept the good admiral's opinion; John Maffitt was "a pirate as pleasant while emptying a ship of her cargo and then scuttling her, as Claude Duval when robbing a man of his purse and then borrowing his watch from his pocket."

CHAPTER III

Chinese Wall off Wilmington

FATHOMS DEEP, IN THE WRECK of the blockade runner *Fanny and Jenny* on the shoals near Cape Fear, lies a gold-and-jewel-hilted sword, a gift for General Robert E. Lee from admirers in England. It was destined never to reach his hand. Its blade, buried under a pall of white sand and green waters, is symbolic of the South's struggle to circumvent the strangling coils of the North's relentless blockade.

No stretch of the imagination is required to see that had the blockade failed, the effort to crush the Confederacy would also have fallen short. By the same token, the power that made the blockade so deadly was steam. For without steam on water, there might have been no Appomattox on land. The Union blockade of the Southern coast was the biggest operation of its kind in naval history. Its magnitude far surpassed England's blockade of France in the Napoleonic struggle for mastery of Europe.

At four-thirty on the afternoon of April 19, 1861, President Lincoln ordered the building of a wall of warships around the seceded states. It is doubtful if Lincoln and his advisers realized the full scope of that decree. One wonders if the gentlemen gathered in the President's study remembered that in the War of 1812, England, with over seven hundred vessels at sea, was unable to put a tight lid on a single American port. Walling up the sea-exits of the insurgent South had a high-sounding ring, but it was prob-

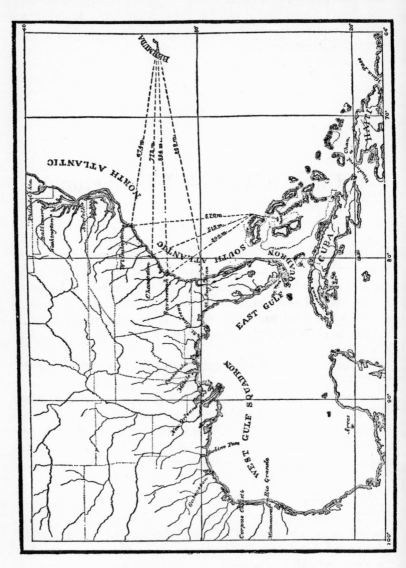

The blockaded coast of the Confederacy.

ably the least appreciated of all the North's endeavors to maintain the Union. Certainly the chief of state could hardly have foreseen the mountains of contraband that would slip through the loose-jointed picket of ships soon to be strung around the bottlenecks of the South. When Secretary Welles asked the New York shipping barons for suggestions for carrying out the proposed blockade, he was informed that thirty sailing vessels, armed with a gun or two apiece, could do the job. Actually, it took over six hundred ships, mostly steamers.

To understand the challenge of the blockade, one should glance at the map and trace the coastline from the Virginia Capes to the Rio Grande. This vast frontier of 3,549 miles had eight major ports, besides over two hundred anchorages and safe harbors where cargoes could be landed. Furthermore, it was nicked by countless bays, sounds, inlets, and river mouths which provided tempting shelters wherein light-draft ships could drop anchor and discharge freight. Blockading a nation endowed with so many coastal recesses was an undertaking whose scope seemed to have escaped the comprehension of the man in Northern streets; or rather, it was eclipsed by the more colorful, glamorous raising of armies and the clash of arms. Flag-waving, drumbeats, and bugle calls played little part in the blockade. Grit, human endurance, and steam made the blockade what it was, an operation that brought want and war to every Southern home.

In quarantining nine million people the North failed to reckon with the South's ingenuity, her passionate devotion to a cause, and the spirit of her people, determined to win at all costs.

In November, 1861, six months after Lincoln ordered the South boxed in by sea, the New York *Times* reminded its readers:

The South possesses a threefold coast. What with the sea islands formed in the alluvium of the shore by arms of the sea and the deltas at the mouths of her many rivers, there are countless passages which lie beyond the reach of our smallest war-vessels; and which are nevertheless penetrable by small commercial craft —the schooners and shallops of coastwise traffic. On the Atlantic side, a vessel of light draft can traverse nearly the entire coast from Norfolk to Cape Sable, without danger of molestation from the blockading fleet; and throughout that distance may select any outlet to the sea, which it finds momentarily released from the guardianship of a national ship of war.

More important in the public mind than the blockade were the well publicized naval victories at New Orleans and Mobile Bay, but these dim before the cumulative achievement of those lesser-sung squadrons that hung on like death. Admiral Porter maintained that the blockade was the greatest naval triumph of the war. No doubt, as a sailor, he was biased; nevertheless he stated a hard truth that has been neglected too long.

The North faced the war with only forty-two ships in commission, including twenty-three steamers. The rest were relics. Of naval guns there were 1,738 in the Yankee cupboard. Only three hundred of these were modern. Welles once recalled that on March 4, 1861, when he took office, he had only three dependable ships on the American East coast. By December, 1861, the forty-two had become 163. In December, 1864, Welles boasted to Congress that the navy had a fighting roster of 671 vessels and 4,610 guns afloat. By the same token, the Confederate Navy at its peak numbered about forty ships which one could call men-of-war.

The unaudited figures on traffic through the blockade were prodigious. The size of the runner fleet (ninety-nine percent privately owned) baffles imagination. The best authority on the subject estimated that the blockade was run over eight thousand times. But sauce for the runners was sauce for the blockaders also, who chased their toll of prizes up to 1,504 vessels captured, sunk, or stranded. The bones of over three hundred, caught by Union gunfire or crumpled on reefs and shoals, strewed the coast from Virginia to Texas. One thousand one hundred fifteen ships were brought into Union coastal bases with their cargoes, condemned and sold. Collectively, it was the biggest prize in the annals of navies—over thirty million dollars.

For the higher-ups on the blockade the monetary compensations for picking off runners ran into tall figures. Prize money awards were as old as the United States Navy. Commodore Stephen Decatur built his splendid home, which still stands in the nation's capital, with prize money paid for his captures in the War of 1812 and the trouncing he gave to the Barbary Pirates. In 1861, Congress, in a generous mood, agreed to split fifty-fifty the proceeds of prize

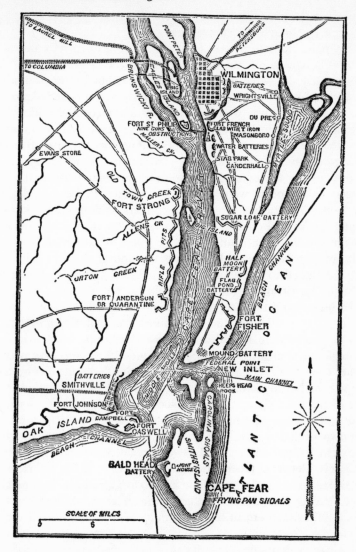

This wartime map shows the Cape Fear inlets to Wilmington. Through these portals poured the supplies and munitions that kept the Confederacy going. Indicated also is the massive bastion Fort Fisher, which guarded the New Inlet.

sales with the bluejackets and officers. The whole ship's company got a cut, although the government got its fifty percent first. The commander of the squadron that nipped off a prize took five percent, although he was usually asleep when the kill was made. Not infrequently, he woke up to find himself richer by ten thousand dollars, and once or twice, by twenty-five thousand. The balance of the prize money was whacked into twenty pieces, of which the captain of the ship that made the catch got three. After sifting it down to the ordinary seaman, the percentage was not royal. But the wide-gold-braids really cashed in. Hard-boiled David Porter raked in over ninety thousand dollars to take home from the war. The biggest chunk of all went to Admiral Samuel P. Lee, top-dog of the North Atlantic Squadron for three years. Wilmington, with the largest intake and outflow of contraband, was in his domain. His squadrons had more runners to pick from, or rather, to pick off. This was the North's gold coast. Officers moved heaven and earth to get assigned to it. Sailorman Lee enriched his bank account by $109,689 for sitting on the lid off Wilmington.

To understand the staging for the drama in which John Maffitt played a spectacular role the reader must glance at Wilmington on the map, and note her advantages for the South, as well as her strategic position in the shoot-to-kill game of hide and seek played in her front yard. As if in league with the South, nature herself had shaped the North Carolina coast for the town's dynamic role in the fate of the Confederacy. For the bloc-runner, it was an ideal setup. The town lay twenty-eight miles up the Cape Fear River, which has two outlets to the sea: the Eastern or New Inlet, and the Western Bar or main channel. Barely six miles separated these two channels. Between them was Smith's Island, a delta that tapered south ten miles to the high dune known as Cape Fear. Beyond the cape, Frying Pan Shoals whitened the breakers for another ten miles. Shipwise, it meant that forty miles of steaming separated the inlets.

This freak of nature necessitated a two-squadron blockade fleet. At the same time it made Wilmington more accessible to ships laden with contraband, in or out. From Smithville, a village on the river's west bank, equidistant from either bar, the offshore squadrons were plainly visible. They never quit. Outbound runners could drop down to Smithville, size up the hazards, and choose between the two gantlets. Inbounders, governed by wind and weather, had a like choice in making their final dash.

Protecting the New Inlet was massive Fort Fisher, which was to defy capture and keep open this last gateway between the South and the outer world almost until the flag fell. It was the Confederacy's most powerful bastion. Here blockaders, instead of lounging off the estuary, lay in a crescent just out of range of the fort's big guns. Keeping a similar vigil over the Western Bar was Fort Caswell. Fort Fisher was so important that Lee, in the final clutch of disaster, wired the fort's commandant, Colonel Lamb: "If Fort Fisher falls, I shall have to evacuate Richmond."

Inevitably, this town became the center of "our overseas commercial interests," as Secretary Mallory preferred to describe this heady business. Into this mart slithered four runners to one at any other port. What came and went through the Gulf ports was trifling compared with the intake at Wilmington. Through this channel came the materials that enabled Lee to make his long, last stand against Grant. The grayback, frying his meager slivers over a campfire at dawn, probably seldom realized he was eating "Nassau bacon" that had reached him by way of Wilmington, nearest port to the Virginia battle lines.

By 1862 this cat-and-mouse game was systematized, for the runners as well as for the blockaders. Time, weather, and stratagem dictated the rules of the game. Like packets, the sailings of the runners were made "on moons" or, to be more exact, on no moons. Nor was there fraternizing on the cordons. Here there was no swapping of coffee and tobacco as along the fronts in Virginia. The game was played for keeps, with never a breather.

As many as thirty blockaders made up the inshore squadrons off Wilmington. They lay in a crescent facing each entrance to the Cape Fear River. The center of the crescent off New Inlet was just out of range of Fort Fisher's big guns. Stationed at close intervals the blockaders patrolled by day, scanning the horizon for anything afloat. At night they anchored while patrol boats, crawling through the interstices, watched for gray ghosts sneaking through. During the night, according to Porter, a runner stood an eight-to-one chance of getting through; during the day, one in four. Broaching the nighttime blockade was not so much dreaded, particularly on thick nights, though the runner faced the double menace of shoals

and men-of-war. By 1864, the Gulf Stream swarmed with light, fast
Union cruisers, and the open sea offered a greater danger than inshore operations.

The advantage was with the runner. He could choose his time,
coming in or going out. The more blockaders clustered off the
inlets, the less the danger to the runner and the greater the chance
that the Federals would fire at each other. As the boys on the
swifties observed, the Federals were very apt to "miss the cow and
kill the calf." At night, if a blockader sighted a runner looking for
a loophole and flashed a signal, the runner would make a similar
one and in the confusion slide in or out.

New Inlet was the favorite doorway for Wilmington. Frequently a runner got in by slipping around the endmost vessel of
the inshore cordon, the noise of her paddles drowned by the roar
of the surf. With her light draft she needed little depth of water.
Literally hugging the shore, she could speed through the surf. Once
inside the blockade, she would show a light on her land side. Fort
Fisher, catching the signal, would answer with a dim blue light,
followed by others. These were the range-lights for the channel.
By lining them up the runner could take her bearings. A few moments would bring her under the guns of the fort.

Blinker lamps that could wink code messages to signal stations
at Fort Fisher for the New Inlet, or at Lockwood's Folly for the
Western Bar, were a boon to the inbound runners. These lamps
were screened on three sides. Over the fourth was a shutter window
that could be raised or lowered to click off the runner's position
and to seek guidance or covering from the fort's gunners.

2

Early in 1862 the Confederate cabinet decided to join the gold
rush and marshal its own fleet to compete with the private bloc-
breakers, who had turned a deaf ear to appeals for more munitions
and less frippery. To do this, six swift steamers were "borrowed"
from the Confederacy's fiscal agents, Fraser, Trenholm & Company,
who were already dipping into the rich and risky business of ex-
porting cotton.

First, the government had to repudiate its disastrous cotton embargo, which it had adopted in the hope that England and France,

needing the staple, would dispatch their war fleets to open up the sea-lanes to the cotton ports. The best minds of the South had warned against this disastrous policy. Diarist Mary Boykin Chesnut summed up the feeling of thousands when, with the first flash of war at Fort Sumter, and while the blockade was so much paper, she warned: "We must make cotton and send it to Europe as a bank to draw on. The very cotton we now have, if sent across the water, could be a gold mine to us."

Now—though really too late—the Confederacy would tap that vast, rich mine. Manning these "borrowed" vessels with navy personnel the government would rush cotton through the blockade to Nassau and Bermuda and exchange it for gold to buy more munitions and to build cruisers for striking out at Northern commerce.

"Because," John Maffitt explained, "of my knowledge of the Southern coast, I was ordered to command the first of these vessels, the *Cecile*, to run the blockade and bring in arms and ammunition for the Confederacy. She was reported to be uncommonly fast and could stow to advantage over seven hundred bales of cotton."

On January 11, 1862, the *Cecile* steamed down the Cape Fear River from Wilmington. On the bridge of the slim, trim speedster stood Lieutenant John Maffitt. He was off to frolic in the biggest game of cops and robbers in history.

CHAPTER IV

"I'll Shoot the First Man That
Touches Her"

PENSACOLA, FLORIDA, January 1, 1861. This naval outpost, over which the flags of France, Spain, and England had successively proclaimed dominion in the past, was now a powder keg with a lighted fuse sputtering relentlessly nearer. Tension gripped this Gulf city like a vise. Here the curtain was rising on a sullen tableau gazed on by a transfixed nation.

Across sun-drenched lands sparks were flying. War drums were beating. For thirty years the South had listened for them, and now, at last, their sound came rolling over the horizon. The pyre on which politicians and slave-baiters had piled hate and distrust for a generation was ready to burn.

Swiftly, the Cotton Kingdom was emerging from its cocoon. With a defiant blast at the North, the Deep South girded herself for her plunge into secession. Implacably, the "more perfect Union" was breaking up. Ten days before, on December 20, 1860, South Carolina had slipped her cable. With bonfires, bugles, bells, and cannon blasts, very much like an old-time Independence Day celebration, she had cut the constitutional knot. It didn't take long to raise the Palmetto Flag over Federal post-offices, forts, arsenals, custom houses, and the mint.

On New Year's Day, 1861, the spotlight played on Ponce de

Leon's Land of Flowers. Her soldiery was mobilizing, as if for a military spectacle. The Tallahassee Rifles strutted about like animated tin soldiers champing to be off to Pensacola, while the clock was ticking off the minutes to actual secession.

Yet from the bridge of the U.S.S. *Crusader*, riding at anchor off Fort Pickens in Pensacola Bay, one could see ships idle at their moorings, shoreboats coming and going, officers and men pursuing routine duties. Looking at this tranquil scene one would hardly have suspected the crisis that was in the offing. The eight-gun steamer *Crusader* was attached to the Home Squadron whose base was New York. She had run over to Pensacola from the Bahama Channel where she had been patrolling for slave-runners.

Pensacola was a highly strategic base. Here the United States had established a navy yard equipped with modern facilities for building, repairing, and docking war vessels. As a rendezvous for blockading squadrons, its wide harbor would be unexcelled. Eastward, seven miles up the bay, lay the city of Pensacola. Fortified by coastal batteries, the roadstead was considered impregnable unless implemented by powerful land attack.

On the western tip of Santa Rosa Island, straddling the bay where it enters the Gulf, the government had constructed Fort Pickens in 1838, a formidable pentagonal bastion named for a hard-riding partisan ranger of the Revolution. Its gun embrasures radiated to every point of the compass, every angle of approach by water and land. De-activated since the Mexican War, it could still be made defensible with modern cannon and a force of riflemen. On a war footing its complement was twelve hundred men.

Completing the circle of defense, army engineers had erected two sea batteries on the mainland, Forts Barrancas and McRee. Yet the builders had not foreseen attack by the people of Florida. These two forts were an easy prey for land forces because their guns only fired in one direction, seaward.

An enthusiastic military commentator had ventured the conviction that Pensacola Bay "could defy all the navies of the world combined till it filled the harbor's mouth with the carcasses of sunken ships."

Possession of Fort Pickens by the South, in the event of hostilities, was imperative. In enemy hands this fortification could be a knife pointed at the underbelly of the South, neutralizing the navy yard, denying the Confederacy use of the largest deep-water harbor on the Gulf Coast. It is not hard to understand why Fort Pickens and the Pensacola Navy Yard were prime targets on the take-over timetable of the Florida forces, if and when the State seceded. Bevies of secessionists were already prowling outside the navy yard gate, waving state flags and telling the marine guard to "Go back North!" Inside stood the commandant of the navy yard, Commodore James Armstrong, with half a century of service behind him and a corporal's guard of twenty-three marines. Of the civilian employees, mostly Southerners, nine-tenths were secretly pledged to support the budding Confederacy. The second in command was openly hostile to the North. Spies had ransacked the area. A military company at Pensacola, armed with muzzle-loading shotguns, was drilling feverishly, dedicated to lowering the United States flag flying over the yard. The imminent crackdown by Florida forces was no secret. South Carolina had seized Charleston's defenses, excepting Forts Moultrie and Sumter, the moment she seceded. If she could, Florida would do the same thing at Pensacola.

At four bells, ten o'clock, on this sparkling New Year's Day, Lieutenant John Maffitt stepped into his captain's gig to be rowed by ten bluejackets to the landing. Stepping ashore he strode off to offer greetings of the day to the commandant. It was an old naval custom. At mess time the Crusader's crew would splice the main brace with an extra noggin of rum. Shore leave would then be in order.

John Maffitt was a festive sea dog, to whom banter and merriment came naturally. An old hand at drowning care, his rum punches had acquired a certain fame in naval circles, as a shipmate's parody of a familiar song indicates:

> D'ye ken John Maffitt with his coat so blue?
> D'ye ken John Maffitt with his skill so true?
> D'ye ken John Maffitt gazing far far away
> Rum punch in his head at the break o' day?

Dusk was falling over the quiet bay waters when cutters began arriving at the Crusader's gangway. Maffitt was waiting to greet his guests with smiles and quips. But tonight there would be no ladies-God-bless-'em in the Crusader's wardroom, for at the first whiff of

trouble wives and sweethearts had scurried off to less tense surroundings. And now, up the gangway the men came, Northerners
and Southerners alike, all in blue, to cheer the magic moment when
John Maffitt performed the sacred rites. Presently, with jolly in-
cantations and the mock severity of an alchemist, he fell to work.
Into the big silver tureen on the wardroom table went dashes of
one thing and another, with tasters and sniffers standing by to give
expert advice, if need be. Lastly, in gurgled three bottles of old
Cuban rum stowed away for the occasion.

With the ladling out of the bumpers, the wardroom rang with
merriment. Yet not a word was said about the specter of war
hanging over these men who wore and loved the same navy blue.
From midshipmites they had plodded up the slow naval grades,
had fought the same seas, shared the same dangers. For most of
them, there had been no Annapolis. Now, their swords half out of
their scabbards, they were all set to make war on each other. Never
again would they gather in fellowship. Yet, whatever their feelings, tonight there would be one last burst of fun. Round went
the toast: "To the Flag!" Up came every glass, John Maffitt's
included. And downed they were with a right good will. It had
been his flag all his life. It would be his flag until . . . The
ship's bell struck eight, midnight. Time for good-byes and a last
bumper, "To John Maffitt, good fellow!"

Leaning on the rail he watched his visitors shove off from the
Crusader. The harbor was quiet. He could hear the cadenced splashing of the oars as they fetched the cutters homeward. Across the
bay, a quarter-mile from the *Crusader's* moorings, Fort Pickens
frowned. A single light showed on her parapet. Maffitt's thoughts
were spinning.

He had already charted the course he would follow when and
if the disruption of the States exploded. For the past two years,
while the abolitionists lashed the nation with hate and passion,
he had been at sea intercepting slave runners and pirates in the
Old Bahama Channel and adjacent West Indian waters. For half
a century the navy had carried on a running fight against the traffic
in black ivory.

Breaking off the ties of a generation of service in the United
States Navy was a cruel business for Southern-born officers. If the
Confederacy was to bloom in the garden of nations, well and

good; but if she perished under Northern fire, they would have wasted the work of a lifetime. Their profession was their fortune. The sea and ships had possessed John Maffitt since he sailed away at thirteen as midshipman on the sloop-of-war *St. Louis*. All his life, it seemed, he had known the salt spray, the winds in the rigging, and the pitch of the waves. He knew the waters of the western world like a book: their quirks, their dangers, their delights. Behind him, at forty-two, lay a panorama of splendid adventure.

But John Maffitt's allegiance to the South was fixed by background, not by birth. A son of Old Neptune, he was conceived in Ireland and born at sea on the way to America. Four early years spent in North Carolina had bound his heart and imagination to the Old North State. What North Carolina did in the present crisis would most likely determine what he would do. Yet he breathed not a word of this to his fellow officers—nor did many another, faced with the bitter problem of choosing between state and country. Few dared reveal their true leanings amidst all the accusations of treason which were being bandied about. Aboard ship, at the messes, on naval stations, secession was a taboo subject, at least for those Southerners whose hearts had already pointed out the road they must take.

Every naval officer who wore the blue had taken to heart the eloquent picture, drawn in the United States Senate by William F. Seward of New York, of an American warship entering a foreign port *after* the break-up of the Union:

The American man-of-war is a noble spectacle. I have seen it enter an ancient port of the Mediterranean. All the world wondered at it, and talked of it. Salvos of artillery, from forts and shipping in the harbor saluted its flag. Princes and princesses and merchants paid it homage, and all the people blessed it as the harbinger of hope for their own ultimate freedom. I imagine now the same noble vessel again entering the same haven. The flag of thirty-three stars and thirteen stripes has been hauled down, and in its place a signal is run up, which flaunts the device of a lone star or a palmetto tree. Men ask, "Who is the stranger who thus steals into our waters?" The answer contemptuously given is, "She comes from one of the obscure republics of North America. Let her pass on."

John Maffitt had read those words thoughtfully, but stronger
voices were calling. Sadly, he kept his own counsel, and watched
the nation dashing headlong toward Henry Clay's "dreadful preci-
pice."

2

On January 3, 1861, Secretary of the Navy Isaac Toucey flashed a
cipher telegram to Commodore James Armstrong, commanding
the Pensacola Navy Yard. Its import was ominous:

> Sir: Be vigilant to protect public property. The commanding
> officer at Fort Barrancas has been instructed to consult with you
> and you will consult with him.

Alarmed by secessionist threats, Armstrong had already taken a
hopeless view of any attempt to frustrate Florida's intent to capture Federal naval installations at Pensacola. Hostile hands had
already filched the navy codebook. On the brink of secession Floridian officials were monitoring and decoding every message that
filtered over the single wire to Pensacola. Mail from Washington
was sifted and censored or destroyed. Toucey's admonition to Armstrong was permitted to reach its destination on January 9, six
days after leaving Washington.

Yet, "Be on your guard!" was the motif of warnings rushed to
naval stations in the South by Connecticut Yankee Isaac Toucey,
who at this critical moment administered the naval portfolio in
President Buchanan's cabinet. Every message gave out the same
ominous refrain. Toucey's political enemies accused him of letting
his Southern sympathies come before loyalty and duty, and of
placing the nation's weak naval forces so as to aid the South in her
move toward secession. Toucey's successor, acid, bewigged Gideon
Welles, had long nursed a political grudge, which he paid off with
accusations of near-treason. The Official Records dispute these
calumnies against Toucey, testifying to his zeal and foresight in
alerting officers ashore and afloat on whose loyalty he could depend. Toucey met the threat at Pensacola head on. Officers of
Southern background were already suspect. Quietly, Toucey began
relieving them of active command. At the Navy Department the
burning question was: would Southern officers who commanded

naval vessels on the high seas sail them into Southern ports and hand them over to the seceding states? There is no single instance that this was ever done. Nor is there a shred of suspicion that John Maffitt ever contemplated such a betrayal of trust.

On January 5, Toucey flashed a cipher message to Pensacola ordering Maffitt to proceed immediately with the *Crusader* to the Tortugas to cooperate with the commanding officer at Fort Jefferson. The Official Records intimate that this missive was entrusted to an officer who tried to serve the South by delaying its delivery. Just how it got through to Maffitt is still unknown.

Under previous sailing orders the *Crusader* had already weighed anchor for Mobile. Maffitt's mission was to cash a prize money check, drawn, as was customary, on the Collector of the Port and payable to the officers and crew of the warship for their success in nabbing slave runners. Hardly had the vessel's mudhook touched bottom off Dog River, when she was enmeshed in the fervor and frenzy of war that was sweeping the city. Alabama's withdrawal from the Union (still six days off) was already a *fait accompli*, at least in Mobile. Here the spark flashed; here the bonfire began. War was coming, let it come! Mobile's youth were springing to arms, decked out in gay uniforms. Visiting reporter William H. Russell of the London *Times* described the people of Mobile as a "fierce Marseillaise, drilling, marching, drum beating."

From the balcony of Battle House, orators were shouting against the "Northern hordes." Their fiery eloquence was music to the ears of their excited listeners. The South must lock shields to meet the giant she had aroused, and Mobile's youth must be in the van. Eager-eyed, these beardless "defenders of the right" yearned for battles and glory.

From the *Crusader's* cutter, manned by brawny bluejackets, John Maffitt stepped onto the quay at the foot of Government Street and hurried along to the office of the Collector of the Port. He was unaware of the distrustful stares bent on his blue naval uniform. Once, in this hospitable seaport town, the navy blue had been respected and admired. Today it represented the North. Suspicion had already fastened on the *Crusader*. Rumor had raced ahead of her. The Federal government (so it was noised about) had hustled a gunboat to Mobile to crush the "insurrection," and now the *Crusader's* arrival confirmed it. Marines armed to the teeth were supposedly concealed below the *Crusader's* deck, ready to seize the city and jail secessionists. Presenting his check, Maffitt met prompt refusal. Whatever money the Collector of the Port had on hand would be handed over to Alabama, soon to secede. Maffitt tried to explain . . . it was the crew's prize money for capturing slave ships. That only made it worse. What right had the Federal government to interfere with slavery? It was a colossal piece of impertinence, tampering with the basic institution of the Southern way of life.

John Maffitt returned to his ship, yet hardly had he stepped on deck before the watch reported a barge coming alongside. Up the gangway, blood in their eyes, climbed a delegation of Mobile's Vigilance Committee. They glanced truculently at the Stars and Stripes flapping at the gunboat's gaff. Spokesman for the visitors was the city's mayor, John Forsyth, hotspur editor of Mobile's leading daily. What was the government's motive in dispatching the *Crusader* to Mobile at this critical moment? Wasn't Lieutenant Maffitt aware of Alabama's imminent exit from the Union? Maffitt sought to explain, but the visitors riposted with veiled threats. It was quite obvious that the idea of boarding and capturing a Federal man-of-war on the eve of Alabama's secession had an enticing flavor for certain gentlemen from Mobile. The *Crusader* would be a beautiful nest egg for Alabama's own navy.

John Maffitt stood his ground. The *Crusader* belonged to the government whose uniform he wore and whose flag he had sworn to uphold as long as he wore it.

In a quiet voice he replied, "My vessel belongs to the United States. I'll shoot the first man that touches her."

This was no bluff. His dark eyes reinforced his words.

"Aren't you a Southerner, Lieutenant?" inquired the spokesman.

"That has nothing to do with what you obviously threaten. If any vessel approaches this ship with hostile intent, I'll open my broadsides and sink her on the spot."

Duly impressed, the delegation decamped. The *Crusader's* guns offered formidable confirmation of Maffitt's words. Taking no chances, he cleared for action. Tompions were removed, gun ports opened, cutlasses and pikes passed out, steam gotten up, and the deckwatch doubled. Toward dusk a shore boat gingerly edged alongside with a package for Lieutenant Maffitt. It was cash for the prize money check. In twenty minutes the *Crusader* had up-anchored and was steaming down Mobile Bay. On she sped past Fort Morgan, a grim sentinel squatting at the mouth of the bay. Beyond John Maffitt's farthest vision was the afternoon when he would crash his helpless cruiser, *Florida*, through a cataract of Yankee gunfire over these same waters. Turning her head south by east the *Crusader* shaped her course over the gently heaving Gulf for Key West, en route, presumably, for her old cruising grounds off the north Cuban coast. Nor did the dark waters reveal an inkling of coming disaster. Overhead a million stars peered down on a peaceful scene.

At Key West the purposely delayed orders reached Maffitt. Isaac Toucey was sounding the tocsin far and wide. His instructions read:

> Proceed immediately to Garden Key and cooperate with the commanding officer to protect public property and prevent anyone from landing improperly.

Take-over of nearby Fort Jefferson was imminent. Floridian militia were poised to filch the enormous brick fortress the moment the state seceded. Garrisoned with a corporal's guard, without a pound of powder in her magazine to load her imaginary guns, this outpost was a setup for a man with a horse pistol and a bit of nerve.

But more awesome tidings hurtled down to the southernmost rampart of the United States. Like shocks of an earthquake, on January 9, 10, and 11, Mississippi, Alabama, and Florida declared themselves "sovereign, independent States," and dissolved the bonds of Union existing under "a compact of government entitled the Constitution of the United States."

At nine A.M., January 12, the blow fell at Pensacola. It was dress rehearsal for civil war. Crashing the Navy Yard gate, Florida and Alabama militia seized the magazine and demanded the station's surrender. That same afternoon a calamitous message reached the Secretary of the Navy at Washington: "I surrendered the Navy Yard and struck my flag at half past one o'clock P.M. this day. James Armstrong, Captain, U.S. Navy, *late* Commandant Navy Yard, Warrington, Florida." Yet not a word was said about old Quartermaster William Conway, who had refused to lower the flag when ordered to do so. His hands, gnarled by forty years of naval service, simply refused.

Only a miracle, or rather the cool courage of Lieutenant Adam J. Slemmer and a handful of seamen, saved Fort Pickens. When asked to surrender the bastion, Slemmer replied, "Come and get it!" Fort Pickens was to be a thorn in the Confederacy's flesh to the bitter end.

What now for John Maffitt? A later dispatch from the future Quartermaster General of the Union Armies, Captain M. C. Meigs, now commanding Fort Jefferson on Tortugas, offers this revealing sidelight: "To Captain Maffitt, of the U.S.S. *Crusader*, we are under obligation for convoying the vessels bringing the armament and ammunition which rendered this place safe from attack." Maffitt also brought gangs of bluejackets to mount and man the guns at Fort Jefferson.

Time was running out, but John Maffitt, man of honor, still served. He had taken little part in verbal joustings, though he resented the screams of the abolitionists against the South. For him, as for the great Expounder of the Constitution, the United States was one and indivisible. But now all the splendid beacons lit by the hands of the founding fathers were burning low. As darkness swept across the land, John Maffitt knew his destinies were inevitably wrapped up with those of North Carolina.

In his dilemma he opened his heart to an old shipmate, Lieutenant Tunis Augustus Craven. The two of them had sailed together since their reefer days. John Maffitt left no record of this last meeting, but Craven did. From Maffitt's cabin on the *Crusader* at Key West, Craven wrote a letter to Maffitt's daughters, whom he loved as if they were his own:

In the cabin of the *Crusader* I seize a moment of quiet to say God bless you. Your father has given me such agreeable accounts of his visit to you that I can almost fancy I have just seen you (Florie) and Mary.

In these days of gloom, my dear girls, it is always pleasant to remember the sweet, young and fresh hearts of Florie and Mary —long may you live in the enjoyment of every happiness—may the perils which encompass our country never come near or disturb you—may no dark clouds shadow your journey through life, but at each turn of the road, brighter and brighter be your days.

Impromptu do I write on this stray sheet of paper, but my heart's prayers may be wafted to you on the air which brings to me remembrance of other and cheerful days.

Be assured, dear girls, of the affectionate remembrance of your friend,

T. Augs. Craven, U.S.N.

This gallant sailor was to glorify his name by a life laid down at Mobile Bay in 1864. As the waters closed over the torpedoed *Tecumseh* he stood aside—"After you, pilot"—to let his pilot take the escape-ladder first as the ironclad turned turtle and sank.

Toward sunset two good friends cut their last ties. The Gulf waters were gleaming purple and gold as Craven's cutter shoved off. Maffitt stood on the bridge. With moist eyes he went to his cabin. It would be one of his keepsakes to the end, Craven's smile as he went down the gangway.

It remained only for John Maffitt to do what he felt honor bound to do: deliver his ship into the hands of the Federal government. The *Crusader* would have been invaluable to the Confederacy. He might have sailed her into any port of a seceded state and received great acclaim for his coup. Not so John Maffitt, not so scores of Southern naval officers. Yet, apparently, in the melee of distrust Washington suspected John Maffitt. A sharp query went to Pensacola: "Where is Lieutenant Maffitt?" It was a needless worry.

A cold February wind was whitecapping New York harbor the day the *Crusader* steamed in and nosed up the East River to the Greenpoint navy yard. On her bridge, wrapped in thought, stood Maffitt. Warping his ship into her mooring, with scrupulous exactitude he handed her over and settled his accounts, though he was never to be reimbursed for the money he had advanced—his own share of the prize money—to keep the ship in funds after leaving Mobile.

His good-byes to his old shipmates at the navy yard were soon said and, with a feeling of heartbreak, he rang down the curtain. Now he could slip his cable when and if the South made her appeal.

CHAPTER V

Upping Anchor

THE DEATH OF John Maffitt's wife in the winter of 1859 had broken his heart. Now duty summoned him to sea and a long absence from home. Renting his house on K Street in Washington, he placed his daughters, Florie Maffitt and Mary Read, in a boarding school in the capital, and his sons, Eugene Maffitt and Laurens Read, under the tutelage of a clergyman in Georgetown.

Hurrying now to Washington he found scores of army and navy officers waiting for the inevitable to happen. These men faced hard decisions. The future was uncertain. Few were the "treasonable" meetings of Southern-bred officers, imputed to them by Gideon Welles. They were reared in the tradition of States' Rights. Even Admiral Porter went astray when he said, "Officers with pleasant faces, but with treason in their hearts, assembled in conclave in the Department to devise plans for the overthrow of the government." Yes, they met in the corridors and chatted with obvious restraint, but hardly of treason.

Facing an unpredictable future, John Maffitt tried unsuccessfully to sell his house in Washington. Later, it would be confiscated and libeled by a passenger on a Northern merchantman burned by the *Florida* under Maffitt's command. The government and the apparently vindictive appellant would split the proceeds.

On the day Abraham Lincoln was inaugurated, Maffitt went to the Capitol to stand with the mute crowds who listened to the

39

Westerner's words of hope: "I hold that, in contemplation of universal law, and of the Constitution, the Union of these States is perpetual. We are not enemies, but friends."

But this was hardly the case. For all Lincoln's conciliatory words, "we" were enemies, and had been for thirty years. Even while he spoke, the Capitol windows and roof bristled with hawk-eyed riflemen, batteries stood ready to rake every avenue, soldiers ringed the inaugural platform with bayonets. Certainly there was no olive branch discernible in the new President's threat of re-welding, by force if necessary, a dissevered Union already bereft of seven states. The American experiment in democracy was rapidly disintegrating.

To the South, Lincoln's words had the tone of a stern father admonishing a wayward son. Picking up the gage, Jefferson Davis, President-elect of the newly-risen Confederate States of America, replied, "England will recognize us and a glorious future is before us. Grass will grow in Northern cities where pavements have been worn off by the tread of commerce. We will carry war where it is easy to advance, where food for the sword and torch await our armies in the densely populated cities."

Challenging words, but where were the Confederate armies to "carry the war into Africa"? Where was the navy to protect her coast and beat off Northern invaders?

Down in South Carolina, Virginia's "visiting fireman," truculent Roger Pryor, was spreading flame among excited crowds in Charleston. "Strike a blow!" he urged, promising that in one hour by Shrewsbury clock the Old Dominion would romp into the Confederacy's fold. A true prophet, Roger Pryor, though his timing was off.

On April 12, 1861, the nation's capital awoke to discover that the blow Roger Pryor had asked for had been struck. Confederate batteries ringing Charleston harbor had opened a shooting war. Twenty-four hours of battering by Beauregard's cannon brought Fort Sumter's flag fluttering down. After thirty years of verbal jousting, the North and South had come to gunfire.

The cannon that reduced Fort Sumter not only drove Virginia into the arms of the waiting Confederacy, but hurried North Carolina, Tennessee, and Arkansas along the same road, completing the eleven-state crescent of the Southern Republic. Hanging by an eyelash were the border states, Maryland, Kentucky, Missouri, and

Delaware. It would take bayonets, suspension of habeas corpus, and military dictatorship to keep this border bloc Unionized.

Admiral David Dixon Porter was easily the most colorful, and in many ways the greatest naval figure on the Union side. He was also the bitterest winner, generous in ladling out his post-war vitriol. He could never understand how men of Southern leanings, schooled in the traditions of the old navy, could so rapidly change creed and colors.

Target of the shellback's fiercest execrations was Raphael Semmes, whose depredations on Northern commerce the fiery sailor never forgot, nor forgave; yet, in assaying John Maffitt, Porter actually found something to praise in Maffitt's "heroism, skill and courage." He seems to have overlooked the fact that Maffitt and the *Florida* rang up a record of destruction almost as great as that of Semmes and the *Alabama*.

"This officer," wrote Porter of Maffitt, "it is true had gone from under the flag we venerate to fight against it; but we know that it was a sore trial for him to leave the service to which he was attached and that he believed he was doing his duty in following the fortunes of his State and had the courage to follow his convictions. He did not leave the United States Navy with any bitterness."

Porter was, of course, taking a backhand shot at Raphael Semmes, who had outwitted him in a long zigzag chase across the Caribbean. Of the exodus of Southern officers Semmes was to say, "Perhaps, they decided correctly—at all events a military, or a naval man, cannot go very far astray who abides by the point of honor."

Now, without undue haste, Maffitt sent his children south to safety with relatives and friends in North Carolina. In his Journal he reported the stern realities of the moment: "Southern families were daily departing, and resignations from the Army and Navy announced daily in the language of gall and bitterness."

Secession sympathizers in the nation's capital were legion. For days it was predicted that the Stars and Bars of the new Confederacy would soon fly over the Capitol. Certainly, it appeared that way. The defection and exodus of Southern officials and clerks had virtually paralyzed the government departments. In the chambers of the House and Senate, rows of vacant desks gaped at spectators. Southern legislators had flown to the new political feast being served up in Montgomery.

But for Southerners who had resigned from the armed services, Washington was no longer safe. The city became an armed camp, in the grip of martial law. Several of Maffitt's Southern friends who had expressed themselves indiscreetly vanished, having been secretly arrested and spirited off to Fort Warren, Boston. The Old Capitol Prison (just a block from the Capitol itself) was not yet "in business," but soon would be. Roads, bridges—every exit, in fact, was heavily picketed.

On April 28 John Maffitt discarded his commission in the United States Navy, following to a nicety the legal formality prescribed by regulations. He personally carried the single sheet of paper to the office of Gideon Welles, presiding naval deity, who had taken office heaping charges of treason and desertion on the heads of Southern naval officers who one by one doffed the navy blue and hurried home. Each day brought its quota of resignations. Among those who stepped out openly, without guile, were the Chief of the Bureau of Ordnance, the Commandant of the Washington Navy Yard, and the Superintendent of the Naval Observatory. Obviously, with only a small navy, Welles faced a critical situation.

Maffitt's resignation was accepted without comment. Welles, as he endorsed it, had little inkling that he would soon be dashing off feverish orders to chase and sink the "pirate Maffitt." It is likely that he noted the officer's excellent record of service, which his clerk had attached to the paper.

Getting South wasn't easy for army and navy resignees, or even for cadets, who shed their West Point uniforms for another shade of gray. These men were obliged to resort to disguise and subterfuge. They traveled by roundabout, expensive routes, arriving home with little but their will to serve and their swords.

Through a "reliable friend" (presumably an old shipmate in the know at the Navy Department) Maffitt learned he was to be proscribed, perhaps imprisoned, for the duration—or until he was exchanged or reaffirmed his oath of allegiance to the United States. Maffitt never identified this friend. But now his time had come to leave. Nor could he move suddenly without courting arrest. His unsold property must take care of itself. He hesitated to ask for a safe-conduct. It might be refused. Then what?

On May 2, he embarked southward, carrying only a small cabin trunk, his faded blue naval cloak, and the sword he would offer the Confederacy. In his pocket was exactly one hundred and eighteen dollars. There was no severance pay. Gone, too, was whatever pension might have eased his later years.

Getting a pass involved dangerous red tape. Already death-passes were being issued, prescribing death for the user "if hereafter found in arms against the government of the United States."

From a stableman whose loyalties melted at the sight of a ten-dollar bill, Maffitt hired a horse and buggy and joined the trek of refugees heading south over the Long Bridge in every conceivable sort of conveyance, even afoot. At the Virginia end he was halted by men with bayonets, who screened the procession as if their lives depended on it. Parleying with the youthful pickets got him nowhere. An officer was summoned to investigate. Maffitt explained that he was a naval officer who had resigned his commission and was going home. He was still clad in navy blue. He had had no time or money to buy other clothes.

"You have no pass, then?" inquired the officer.

John Maffitt made a clean breast of it: he had not even asked for one. Maybe it was the twinkle in his eyes that persuaded the officer to give him clearance. Who knows? Whatever the open-sesame, Maffitt never revealed it. He admitted only, "How 'twas done becomes me not to state even in a private journal, but this much I will say, the officer who befriended me did not imagine that hostilities would occur." Thus John Maffitt crossed his Rubicon.

That evening, below Alexandria, he boarded a dusty train that took him to Richmond, the first relay station on his journey to Montgomery, first capital of the newly risen Confederacy.

2

What manner of man was Maffitt? Many of his friends left their impressions of him, as did some of his enemies. Descriptions of him do not reveal the notorious Blackbeard that Northern newspapers would have us see—inspired, of course, by his success in burning Yankee ships and by his neatly-trimmed Imperial beard. He had no other piratical trimmings. Nor was he the burly bulldog of the sea. Here was a sailor who could take a hand at the tackles or dance a cotillion with equal skill.

His most engaging feature was his twinkling eyes, deep-set and dark. When his temper flared, or hot work rose ahead, his eyes fairly shot fire. His well-bronzed cheeks told of long cruises under tropic suns. To complete the picture, add a tuft of black chin-whiskers and a shock of bushy black hair shot with gray.

For the distaff side he possessed what Franklin had observed in John Paul Jones, "an indescribable charm of manner." Women loved him; many a scented *billet-doux* found its way to his cabin. His gallantries were faultless, while his conversation sparked an easy flow of *bon mots*. The twin delights of his life were beautiful ships and beautiful women.

John Maffitt could handle a ship like a toy. It was born in him. Legends of the great windjammer captains, who fought the naval war with France and the War of 1812, were still current when he came along as a midshipman. He drank deep of this heady wine, and sought to apply his early lessons to his own career, though sail was bowing out to steam as he was mounting to the quarter-deck.

Maffitt could be flint-hard. Woe to the man before the mast who provoked his wrath. He would put him in irons and on a ration of bread and water. Disobedience and insubordination were the cardinal sins in Maffitt's book, to be punished on the spot.

In dress he was the dandy. This was his chief concession to vanity. For ladies coming aboard he always donned his finery. He bought a new uniform in every port, yet he was to come home with only the one on his back, threadbare and faded.

Debonair and friendly, the happy-go-lucky reefer in his makeup was never quenched, not even by the hard grind of war and his dual role of blockade running and commerce raiding. General Robert E. Lee, whose mess Maffitt brightened for several weeks in Georgia, said, "John Maffitt is the most irrepressibly merry person I've ever met." It should be added that this is more legend than fact, yet it fits well. Personality was not a word too current in the Sixties, but this was what Maffitt had—in plenty.

Maffitt's cabin lockers were always well stocked. Champagne and brandy were indispensables. Hosting came as naturally to him as breathing the sea air.

By every measure he was the fastest chance-taker in the Confederate Navy, and even more feared than Raphael Semmes. He rode through the war with a flourish, gravitating toward the bold course as the needle to the pole. He demonstrated this often—twice at Mobile Bay against odds few other men would have dared face. To his audacity, even enemy Admiral Porter paid his respects.

A Virginian, one Richard Corbin, who ran the blockade as a passenger under Maffitt's command, saw him as "The perfection of coolness and self-possession. I became convinced that his reputation as a consummate navigator was deserved."

It cannot be said that, like Raphael Semmes, he indulged in daily religious devotions. If divine service was held on the *Florida*, as Confederate navy regulations prescribed, there is no record of it.

Poetry good and bad thrilled him; and Homeric lines rolled from his lips at the least provocation. He carried a tiny volume of *Childe Harold* throughout the war, only to lose it in England after the curtain fell. His last illness found him trying to repeat a jingle left over from his reefer days on the old *Constitution*:

> *With his frame a mere hulk*
> *And his reckoning on board,*
> *At length he drops down to mortality's road.*
> *With eternity's ocean before him in view*
> *Jack cheerfully pipes out,*
> *"My messmates, adieu!"*

CHAPTER VI

Glory! Hallelujah!

ON MAY 7, John Maffitt entered a new world where the war cry was: "Cotton is king." Even as his train rolled to a stop, cannon were saluting (ten guns for each state) the Johnny-come-latelies of the Confederacy: North Carolina, Tennessee, and Arkansas.

The very air of Montgomery proclaimed that the infant Southern Republic was feverishly arming herself to the teeth. The youth of the South had heard the bugle and were coming on the run. Out flashed a motley array of smoothbore ordnance, squirrel guns, and long rifles that had fought the white man's way into the wilderness.

The leaders of the Southern exodus were getting down to the business of staying in business. This meant a fight, and they knew it. The "wayward sisters" would never be allowed to leave in peace. Montgomery was a melee of drumming, drilling, and bugling. The people had risen en masse, for it was to be a rich man's war and a poor man's fight. Young fellows from the plantations and the offices, the cotton warehouses, the mountains, and the deltas, were marching and countermarching, clad in coarse gray tunics and butternut trousers with yellow piping. These were the vanguard, the sacrificial lambs, who had hurried off to battle at the first tap of the drum. The best blood in the land and the poorest throbbed in the ranks of these eager-faced young men whose bayonets bobbed up and down in the sunlight. They were the first gleaning, off to do or die for something that was as yet unjelled. Away they went as the trumpets sang "Listen to the Mocking Bird" and the bands drove the crowds wild with that "excellent quickstep, 'Dixie.' "

Until the raising of the Stars and Bars, Montgomery had been a sleepy upland village, basking in the beauty of Cherokee roses, crepe myrtle, and magnolias. She had awakened to find herself the Southern hub of the oncoming "irrepressible conflict." Overnight she became the mecca for droves of politicians, lobbymen, lawyers turned statesmen, faro dealers, tinhorns, pitchmen, brass-knuckle-men, fugitives from Northern law, and ladies of a profession not mentioned in polite conversation. With such easy pickings as political rodeos provide, courtesans had flocked in, and their business thrived. A New Orleans brothel swished into town to open house two blocks from the leading hotel. For two dollars (United States money) a gentleman could engage the services of a lady and return to boast of his prowess in other directions than affairs of state. The *carte-de-visite* of one "Cleo Belle of Mobile" may still be seen. The lady, apparently a go-getter, would mingle daily with the gentry in the lobby, distributing a card bearing her face, her name, and her address.

Built on seven hills, Montgomery shared her uncommon topographical feature with Rome and with Richmond, a city soon to inherit all the prestige and tawdriness that went with being capital of the cotton republic. From its green dominance, the State Capitol overlooked the provincial, picturesque town. A stately pile of Greco-Roman architecture, it stared boldly down Dexter Street. Beneath its white dome the promoters of the new republic were feverishly at work.

The city swarmed with "statesmen" and bureaucrats—political obstetricians who had assisted in the Confederacy's delivery and then climbed aboard the baby carriage to see where it was going. Fresh from his seat in the United States Senate, Wigfall of Texas posed this question for British newsmonger William H. Russell: "Is it not too bad these Yankees will not let us go our own way and keep their accursed Union to themselves? If they force us to it, we may be obliged to drive them beyond the Susquehanna." Had the august gentleman cupped his ears he might have heard a wind from the North sighing a single word, "Gettysburg."

Here gathered the political grandees of the South, proud of their new patrician empire: lean, lantern-jawed Jefferson Davis, who avowed to Russell, "As for our motives, we meet the eye of Heaven. . . . and we are driven to take up arms for the defense of our rights and liberties"; fiery Robert Toombs of Georgia, who once had boasted he would call the roll of his slaves on Bunker Hill; silver-tongued William Yancey, Alabama's pillar of words; burly, impassioned Howell Cobb; pale-faced Alexander Stephens; dark-visaged, resourceful Judah P. Benjamin—the whole coterie of those who had shaped this new ship of state.

In the spring of 1861 nine million people believed that they were divinely appointed to create a new republic. Three decades of powerhouse oratory had preached an independent South until the people were just as sure of their right to secede as they were of breathing. The Confederacy had sprung phoenixlike from the fragments of a dismembered Union, according to the starry-eyed solons who had conceived her out of political animosities and ambitions. Without spilling a drop of blood (not a man was killed at Fort Sumter) she had arisen and, by a simple declaration of will, undone the work of a century.

Into this topsy-turvy, flag-waving political paradise came John Maffitt. For twenty-five cents, United States money, he hired a hack driven by an antiquated black Jehu, who deposited him at the Exchange Hotel. The town's leading inn, it made some pretense as to comfort, but more to prestige. "Bull Run" Russell quipped caustically that it was packed with "nothing but noise, dirt, drinking, and wrangling." It had enjoyed the distinction of housing the executive headquarters of the Confederacy, which had already outgrown its cradle and was preparing to decamp to Richmond. For the politicians, its lobby was a forum. Every marble flag of the floor was a rostrum for some loose-mouthed fellow telling how to overrun Yankeedom in ninety days, commingling streams of words with tobacco juice, Southern Rights, Fort Sumter, Victory, and Black Republicans. Military "experts," hopeful of scavenging commissions, overran the place. Looking like founts of wisdom, long-haired newspaper pundits loaded with bourbon, paper, and pencil contributed to the babble. Like whelps nosing for scraps in a ship's galley, they wangled state secrets from government officials who didn't know enough to keep their mouths shut. Underneath it all, the ceaseless click of ivory balls echoed from the billiard parlor just off the lobby. Another door, always open, led to the ornate bar where gentlemen in broad-brimmed hats downed reservoirs of juleps and straight whiskies.

Refreshed by a good night's sleep, John Maffitt sallied forth into the sunlight to offer his services. A brisk walk along Commerce Street brought him to the Government building, a barnlike red-brick pile once dedicated to cotton auctions and commission houses. Floating above it was the new nation's seven-starred banner. Having walked down a whitewashed corridor past innumerable doors, Maffitt paused before an entrance marked simply, "The President." Here Jefferson Davis ran his one-man show. Fenced in by no protocol screen, he saw all comers, a habit brought from Washington. A single decoration adorned its walls: the crossed flags of Mississippi and the new Confederacy.

In three minutes John Maffitt stood face to face with the man who for decades had carried in his heart the dream of a Southern empire. He wasn't yet a target for barbs of cavil and jealousy. Today he was the beau ideal of a heaven-sent cause, the man with the clearest, coolest brain in the South.

"Welcome, Lieutenant Maffitt. Won't you sit down?"

Davis' greeting was courteous, unhurried. The emotional and physical strain of setting a new government on its feet had taken its toll. His frame was worn down almost to emaciation, yet he still bore the stamp of West Point. Maffitt noted the deep lines indenting his face, sharpening his features. The loss of an eye had etched his countenance with pain, but the deep, steady glow of his expression was undimmed.

"I have come, Mr. President, to offer my services to the Confederacy."

Davis smiled. Choosing his words meticulously, he explained— as if afraid of hurting the feelings of his visitor—that at the moment the South wasn't thinking in terms of a navy, only of a few ships, at best. Later, when the Confederacy was lost, Maffitt was to voice this caustic retrospection: "Unfortunately for the navy, Mr. Davis was not impressed with the necessity of building ships. All arrangements connected with the military status of the Confederacy appeared to move in a smooth and even groove, propelled, as it were, by the natural proclivities of the people; but when the question of the inauguration of a navy was propounded, the government instantly seemed at sea, without rudder, compass, or charts by which to steer upon the bewildering ocean of absolute necessity."

"Our friends at the North assure us there will be no war," said the President quietly.

"But, sir, why were naval officers invited to resign their commissions and hurry to Montgomery?" asked Maffitt.

"We sent telegrams to as many as we need for the present," said Davis. "We could use others in the army, if there is a war."

Davis hardly realized he was snatching the wind out of his visitor's sails. Maffitt winced. Was this the leader whose fighting words had resounded like buglecalls in every Southern heart?

"But, Mr. President," fenced Maffitt, "when I left Washington ten days ago, troops were pouring in by thousands, artillery rolling through the streets night and day. The North is at least getting ready for war. The South needs a navy, and the faster it can get it the better."

The Southern chieftain left no record of what occurred at this closed-door meeting, though events confirm Maffitt's memory of it. The name of Lieutenant Maffitt could not have been unfamiliar to Davis. Rabid Southern newspapers had taken bitter flings at him for his refusal to surrender the *Crusader* to the hotbloods at Mobile. The repercussions of this episode must have reached him. Davis may have taken the kindlier course of leaving unsaid what he thought, though in his *Rise and Fall of the Confederacy* he chided Southern-bred officers commanding United States vessels, who "under an idea more creditable to their sentiment than to their knowledge of the nature of constitutional Union, brought the vessels they commanded into ports of the United States government before tendering their resignations." It was a thankless slap at men who had made heart-rending decisions. Davis, indeed, expatiated on how a navy was lost to the Confederacy "by their view of what their honor and duty demanded. We were doubly bereft by losing our share of the navy we had contributed to build, and by having it all employed to assail us."

Yet, in this same volume of aftermath, Davis was to lay warm praise at the feet of this future sea-raider whose name was to become, like that of Raphael Semmes, a synonym for bold exploits.

The interview drew to an awkward close.

"I am a sailor, Mr. President," blurted Maffitt, rising. "I had hoped for sea service."

"I suggest you see Mr. Mallory, Secretary of the Navy," advised Davis. "He is making plans."

Up to this moment John Maffitt had felt that his naval experience was needed as acutely by the South as gunpowder. Only forty-two years old, fresh from command of a Federal warship, and deeply imbued with the righteousness of the Southern cause (though he felt the moral sentiment of the world sided with the North), he believed such qualifications would be instantly appreciated. He was not yet aware that ex-lieutenants of the old navy were as numerous in Montgomery as magnolias.

Yet he must have known that the act creating the Confederate Navy Department had authorized the appointment of only four captains, four commanders, thirty lieutenants, and as many "masters, midshipmen, sailmakers and other warrant and petty officers or seamen as not to exceed in the aggregate three thousand." Of the thirty lieutenancies, twenty-one had been distributed before he reached town. For the remaining nine, rabid claimants, with political backing, were besieging every bigwig in the Confederacy. He knew the provisional government had telegraphed a selected list of officers (among them his friend, Raphael Semmes), inviting them to help pick a navy out of thin air, but he did not know that over forty ex-lieutenants, resignees from the Union Navy, were shuffling along the streets watching the endless processions of boys in butternut and homespun gray. (Perhaps it should be made clear that the rank of lieutenant in the navy was invested with far more luster in those days than in this atom-age, when it has reached the dime-a-dozen grade.)

Disillusioned, John Maffitt smiled his way out. He had a stiff upper lip. Rebuffs only spurred him on. He strode down the corridor to the office of the man who probably knew his particular job better than any in the Southern sanhedrin, Stephen Russell Mallory, Secretary of the budding Navy Department. Mallory had the job of devising a naval policy for a nation that had no credit and no ships. He had no shipyards other than those at Norfolk and Pensacola; the former was burned when captured by Virginia forces, the latter neutralized by Fort Pickens. He had taken office with a naval force of one three-gun ship and a few beat-up revenue cutters, mounting a total of fifteen guns. Certainly not much with which to wage sea battles, even against the puny Federal naval assortment. The odds facing Mallory were overpowering. Besides, his chief of state was an army man whose interest was overwhelmingly pointed in that direction.

Mallory's appointment had barely squeaked by the Confederate Congress. The Fort Pickens episode had drawn him condemnation. Blame for Federal occupation of this key bastion was laid at his door. Florida's storming parties were about to seize the fort when a crucial telegram from Mallory (then one of Florida's senators at Washington) urged against the assault "because possession of the fort is not worth one drop of blood to us." The attack was called off.

Yet Mallory brought with him to the task of naval overseer two big ideas: an ironclad, or a dozen of them, to demolish the threatened blockade, and a number of fast cruisers to carry on a hit-and-run assault on Northern commerce.

John Maffitt felt some trepidation in approaching Mallory. Lingering resentment may have tinged his feelings. As chairman of the Senate Naval Affairs Committee, Mallory had in 1855 sponsored the Naval Retiring Board that summarily shelved many a naval officer. Its purpose was to weed out incompetent patriarchs who had enjoyed shore duty so long they had forgotten what a ship looked like. Demotions were handed out right and left. Retirement was forced on many experienced officers, now much needed by the North. Only by the skin of his teeth had John Maffitt staved off enforced retirement.

He found Mallory cordial but reticent. The stubby, chop-whiskered Secretary of the Navy was evidently harassed by eager commission-seekers, many of them with topflight political backers, who refused to take no for an answer. But he was more talkative than Davis. Commissions had already been bestowed on four higher-echelon officers: Rousseau, Randolph, Franklin, and Buchanan, former commandant of the Washington Navy Yard. Raphael Semmes was at New Orleans converting the packet *Habana* into a cruiser of sorts to try her luck on Federal shipping in the Gulf and nearby waters, if (Mallory stressed the word) she could elude the Federal blockaders thickening off the Mississippi Passes.

"We've renamed her *Sumter*," volunteered the rotund politician.

Did Lieutenant Maffitt have any suggestions? he inquired, as if to bring the interview to an end. He apparently expected a negative answer.

"I have, Mr. Secretary." There was no hesitation. "First, we should destroy the New York Navy Yard."

Mallory's blue eyes opened wide. Here was a man after his own heart bluntly suggesting a swoop on the chief citadel of the Federal navy. He had thought of such a fantastic enterprise himself. Or was it fantastic?

Without bombast, Maffitt put forward his idea. "With a fast steamer we could raid and burn it, at least put it out of business. Give me such a ship, one hundred and fifty men and plenty of Greek fire, and I'll do it. Right now is the time. I'd go in by night. I know the channel by heart."

He drew a crude chart from his pocket. Placing it before Mallory, he delineated his plan with such conviction that Mallory looked at him with obvious respect. But—"We are not prepared to undertake such a project," interposed the cabinet officer, who, in 1862, was to present precisely such a plan—too late.

"Nor is the North," argued Maffitt. "That's why the time is right. We could almost immobilize the port of New York, perhaps cut out a ship or two. The moral effect of such a raid would be immeasurable, here and abroad."

It certainly would, Mallory agreed silently. Aloud he said, "What else, Lieutenant?"

After giving Mallory a fast rundown of the U.S. Navy by ships and guns, he added, "We should import arms and ammunition from Europe as fast as we can. Mr. Lincoln's paper blockade won't always be as flimsy as it is now."

"I am urging that," Mallory assured him.

"I have one final suggestion, Mr. Secretary. The government should build fast gunboats to strike at Northern shipping. It would oblige Mr. Welles to send his best steamers to protect his commerce."

"We are considering that also," admitted Mallory, whose poker-face gave not the slightest intimation that Maffitt had unconsciously pulled out one of the aces up his own sleeve.

John Maffitt reached the street still "Late Lieutenant, United States Navy," a man without a country, or so he felt. Not a word had been asked about his experience, nor was there the barest hint of a commission in the new Confederate Navy.

His future naval career hinged on the events of the next few hours. Dispirited, he returned to his hotel to repack his belongings and take a train to North Carolina to rejoin his daughters. A knock on the door brought the turning point. He opened to find Senator Ben Hill of Georgia, presidential spokesman in the Confederate Congress, who explained that he had come at Mr. Davis' behest. A mistake had been made. He had come to rectify it. Would Lieutenant Maffitt call to see the Secretary of the Navy in the morning? Maffitt never learned exactly what had happened behind the scenes. After his rise to raiding fame, it was rumored that his blunt proposal to pounce on the New York Navy Yard made such an impact on Mallory that he dashed up to the Presidential sanctum to make amends for his discouraging reception of the brilliant Maffitt.

Perhaps it was ordained by fate that John Maffitt—now in a happier mood—would encounter that evening an old shipmate in the overflowing hotel lobby, one James Dunwoody Bulloch, an animated, side-whiskered package of energy and a good sailor to boot. Their friendship ran back to less rigorous days of charting for the Coastal Survey the rocks and reefs, shoals and depths, inlets and channels along the Atlantic and Gulf seaboard. Bulloch once boasted that he and Maffitt knew "their way into every harbor from Boston to the Mississippi." In 1857, when the Naval Retiring Board threatened to cut short Maffitt's naval career, Bulloch came forward to defend Maffitt's uncanny skill as a navigator and his superb seamanship.

That same day, within three hours after Maffitt's disappointing visit, Mallory had given Bulloch full power as secret naval emissary to Britain. His official grade on the Confederate Navy list was commander. To Bulloch was given the delicate task of constructing in foreign shipyards, preferably England's, cruisers to rove the seas and burn American shipping. It was a big order. Confederate credits at Liverpool were rising. A nest egg of gold snatched from Federal custom houses and mints and rushed through the rickety blockade had already reached the Liverpool counting house of Fraser, Trenholm & Company. A new internal loan would soon fleece Southern patriots of more yellow metal. Blockade runners were champing at the wharves to flood England with cotton the moment the government lifted its silly embargo.

The average American has never heard of this Georgian whose three-year-old nephew would one day become the inimitable "Teddy," twenty-fifth president of the United States. History has passed Bulloch up, but it would be revealing to digress a moment and look at him.

A product of the old service, he had forsaken the stagnant navy list for duty as captain of the mail steamer *Bienville*, plying between New Orleans and New York. When Louisiana seceded, she immediately seized Forts St. Philip and Jackson on the Mississippi forty miles below New Orleans. For her Board of War the forts posed a knotty question: could their gunfire prevent a hostile fleet from ascending the river and capturing the city? On an outbound voyage Bulloch had timed the passage of his ship from a position where the fort's guns could first be brought to bear until she reached a point at which the curve of the river interposed the protection of the shore. He found that, coming down-river, his vessel had been in the zones of fire only fifteen minutes. On his return trip up-river it required twenty-five minutes to clear the fire-zones, not long enough to guarantee the destruction of a hostile man-of-war. His size-up was to prove correct when Farragut stormed past the forts in 1862. Bulloch had transmitted his findings to Montgomery, appending to them an offer to serve the Confederacy if it had need of him. It brought an immediate summons from the embryo navy department.

A modern pronouncement by the State Department defined a diplomat as "an extraordinary man who executes American foreign policy abroad." Such a man was James Bulloch. He illustrated this definition to a nicety, provided "Confederate" is substituted for "American." No man ever sent abroad to represent this side of the Atlantic was more astute than he. A fashion plate, though not of the striped-pants variety, he was endowed with discretion and energy, traits that fitted him admirably for his undercover role of constructing a Confederate Navy in overseas shipyards and wriggling it, by legal means or otherwise, through Britain's neutral barricade. To Bulloch and his unstinting resourcefulness belongs the distinction of creating the famed Confederate raider *Alabama* and her sister ship, *Florida*, and of getting them to sea, masterful feats in themselves.

It cannot be proved that Bulloch revealed to Maffitt the precise nature of the mission just entrusted to him. He was too circumspect for that, too versed in concealing from his right hand what his left was doing. He was leaving for Europe the next day. Mallory had ordered him to return to his hotel and make such notes as he needed to impress the substance of his mission on his memory. He must carry no papers, no memoranda that might betray the nature of his assignment in case of capture. His orders were to proceed to England by way of Canada, a risky enterprise in itself. Speed and secrecy were essential. His mental dossier of instructions included wide discretionary powers.

It is conjecturable that Bulloch unfolded just enough to whet Maffitt's appetite. Neither Maffitt nor Bulloch ever told what happened between them that evening. In after-years, an unidentified naval officer said that he had seen them conversing deep into the night.

2

Promptly next morning John Maffitt presented himself in the scantily-furnished room where the naval secretary was performing the operation that would bring forth what, for want of a better term, was called the Confederate Navy. Mallory went directly to the point.

"Lieutenant Maffitt, the President has authorized me to give you this."

He held out a square of coarse paper to which Jefferson Davis had appended his signature. It was Maffitt's commission as Lieutenant, Confederate States Navy.

"I have already issued your orders," went on Mallory. "You will report to Commodore Tatnall, commanding the battlefleet at Savannah."

With a sharp salute John Maffitt hurried off. He could never have sat out the war anchored at a desk. He had not reached the age where quiet and repose were the things most desired in life. Forty-two and physically fit, he was ready for action and plenty of it. His friend, Raphael Semmes, ten years his senior, was about to take flight across the Gulf with the makeshift raider *Sumter*. Maffitt might have added that Isaac Hull was forty-eight when he captured the *Guerrière* in 1812.

On this same day, the Confederate Provincial Congress rushed through the legislative mill Secret Act, Number 117, empowering the Navy Department to dispatch an agent to Europe to purchase six steam-propelled cruisers to skim the seas and destroy Northern shipping, as well as armament for the cruisers and munitions to run the blockade. To implement the act, one million dollars was appropriated out of the Confederate Treasury, which at the moment was as bare as Mother Hubbard's cupboard. Yet this was no deterrent. The government was scooping in millions of bales of cotton, as good as gold, and even better in England, when and if the Confederacy abandoned her foolish embargo.

Vast projects were brewing in Washington also. From a tiny, scattered force, the navy of the North would expand to a fleet of over six hundred assorted ships. The Confederacy had to meet the threat by water, for there were 3,549 miles of Southern coastline to be defended, as well as important beachheads to be made safe.

But the North did have an Achilles heel in her canvas-winged commerce, and in her steamers that bade to do better what sail had done for so many centuries. American merchantmen were threatening to rule the waves commercially. These were the targets to shoot at from torch-bearing cruisers that could streak across the sea lanes like ghosts and leave Yankee ships burning in their wake.

CHAPTER VII

Midshipman Gallant

For the sake of the South, John Maffitt gladly sacrificed his dreams of honorable retirement. He had envisioned himself, duty done and dangers past, tranquilly watching the world go by until the time came for him to heave anchor and set sail into the sunset. Such had been his fancy before the Confederate galaxy blazed upon the horizon.

The sea had summoned him at thirteen. In 1832, with President Jackson's scrawling signature on his midshipman's warrant, he had sailed away on the sloop-of-war *St. Louis* to the Windward Islands and the Spanish Main, where once Sir Henry Morgan had plied a thriving, black-flagged business. On this cruise to the iridescent Caribbean he was initiated into the mysteries of the great deep.

In 1835, at fifteen, John Maffitt sprang up the gangway of the U.S.S. *Constitution*, "Old Ironsides," then at Boston preening herself for an overseas assignment in the Mediterranean. Service aboard the historic frigate rated high, and John Maffitt considered himself lucky indeed. Fresh from the hands of the shipwrights, refitted, re-timbered, and re-commissioned, she was ready to buffet the seas once again. From truck to keel, forecastle to quarter-deck, she was as perfect as when her "thunders shook the mighty deep." She presented a lovely vision to a sailor's eye. Her tapering main-topmast shot up dizzily over one hundred feet. Her quarter-deck had felt the tread of Hull, Bainbridge, and Preble, whose very names set young Maffitt's heart beating faster. It was enough to fire the imagination of a seastruck youth to whom the single gold-braided star on his enormous collar and his shiny anchor buttons were precious jewels.

As flagship of the Mediterranean squadron, the *Constitution* would fly the broad pennant of Commodore Jesse Elliot. Pomp and circumstance personified was "Old Bruin," hard as nails, and an excellent seaman. To him, midshipmen were "damned young whelps," and John Maffitt was to be one of them.

With his orders countersigned by the watch officer, Midshipman Maffitt hurried below to the port messroom. One bell had just gonged, and the meal pennant floated at the fore. En route he could hear the boisterous laughter of the boy-officers echoing up from the messroom. He paused to deposit his luggage in the steerage, the "Reefers' Den" where the youngsters were quartered and berthed. Here they could roar and cut capers to their hearts' content. Blow high, blow low, these midshipmites did not heed the weather, nor, indeed, anything in the heavens above or the waters below. They took their fun where they found it, and find it they did, even amid their rigid duties as apprentices on a sailing frigate.

"John Maffitt! By all the rosy gods!" exclaimed young George Preble, whose surname was a watchword in the navy. He was just uncorking a bottle as Maffitt entered.

"Ah, George!" smiled the new arrival. "Still tinkering with a corkscrew, I see."

The bottle followed handshakes round the table, and the new-comer's health was downed with proper spirit.

Came Saturday night and the reefers all were there. Under clouds of canvas the frigate was breasting the rollers of the Gulf Stream while Old Neptune claimed his tribute from the uninitiated, to the gibes of the oldsters. Time-honored was the custom—"dating from the ancient days of Admiral Benbow"—of concocting hot rum punch on Saturday nights aboard the frigate, and the reefers were old stagers at it. Into a vast tureen squatting on the table went the "mixings": sugar, butter, cloves, and "white eye" aplenty. Then, two gallons of smoking hot water, and they had it.

"Well, gentlemen"—he was a stripling from Kentucky—"fill up and we'll drink to a jolly cruise, a happy return, and speedy promotion."

They drank it down, smacking their lips. "Give us a song." The poet laureate of the steerage arose, and a guitar appeared.

"What shall it be? Love, murder, or choragic?"

It was Preble who spoke. "Let's take a pull at the sentimental halliards. Something to remind us of the land and the ladies we're leaving behind."

Out floated "Farewell, but whenever you welcome the hour." Quiet reigned in the Reefers' Den. The ship was rolling, and Moore's exquisite melody blended with the moaning of the wind as it came puffing from the northwest.

"Now, boys, gather round and prime your glasses."

The revelers filled up.

"My good fellows"—it was Preble again—"some of us are Oriental in our tastes and have sweethearts by the score, like John Maffitt. So I'll give you the good old Saturday night toast, 'Sweethearts and wives, if you have them!' "

Down it went, all hands round. Now standing, with the guitar twanging accompaniment, they swung into:

> All hands ahoy to the anchor,
> From friends and sweethearts we go.
> 'Vast grieving—why, damn it—it's folly, boys;
> Up with the anchor, ho! ho!

The ship gave a great lurch. Away to the lee scuppers went midshipmen, tureen, tumblers, hot punch, and all. Sails above them were crackling like bull whips as the frigate pitched and swayed. A Gulf Stream squall had struck, and she was going to ride it out like a thoroughbred.

Across the Atlantic the frigate surged. On the wings of a fair wind she flew past the Pillars of Hercules and onto the "millpond" Mediterranean, whose waters were as blue as when the galleys of Carthage, Rome, Greece, and Phoenicia swept over her. To port crouched Gibraltar; to starboard the land of the Moor. Wafted on by a brisk levanter she sped to Port Mahon, on the island of Minorca. This was the Elysium of budding naval heroes—the commodores, captains, and admirals whose names would one day adorn the storybooks of the Civil War. Here America had rendezvoused her Mediterranean squadron for half a century. From her base at Port Mahon she had fought her naval wars with Tripoli and the Barbary pirates.

Here, on nineteen dollars a month, reefers could really feast at Cachio's. This gastronomic magician, with his rotund figure, his white apron, and his ineffable larder, was a theme song for countless future big-name officers. For this glamorous naval caravansary on the Mediterranean, one of them penned a nostalgic memoir:

Port Mahon of the red-legged partridges and the monkey soup; the toothsome date-fish and the succulent salsiche sausage; Port Mahon, that was whitewashed all over every Saturday afternoon; Mahon, where even a midshipman could borrow money and yet be prevented from paying his debt with the "maintop bowline," which means not at all; Mahon, of the best nougat in the world and other confections dear to the sweet tooth of youth; Mahon of the Conchitas and Mercedeses

—and scores of *inamoratas* whose delicately-perfumed *billets-doux* inundated the Reefers' Den and whose kisses and hearts were toyed with like bright baubles by these happy-go-lucky youngsters. Port Mahon was at its zenith when John Maffitt sailed into its harbor as a midshipman on the *Constitution*.

But even more idyllic days awaited him as the frigate sailed off on a goodwill cruise that would also display the naval prowess of the rising American republic. In the flagship's wake the squadron fanned out like cygnets paddling after their mother. Naples, Malta, Alexandria, Tenedos, and Syria unreeled like magic-lantern slides.

Pashas, titled rulers, emperors, and sultans stalked up the gangway, trailed by retinues in plush and gold and red. The frigate loafed along from one port to another. Salvos from ancient forts welcomed the Stars and Stripes at her peak, while her own broadsides answered with thunderous salutes. As for the middies, they danced at the functions, imbibed oceans of wine, and ran off with the prettiest girls.

Such was the jolly side of life aboard a sailing man-of-war, where the raw stuff of future captains was hewed into shape. Its curriculum was as inflexible as the laws of the Medes and the Persians. Here the novices crammed the ABC's of an able seaman: to hand, to reef, and to steer. Seamanship and navigation were learned from the jack-tars; gunnery from the men who handled the guns; the duties of commanding a vessel of war from epauletted martinets who ruled with rods of iron. By first-hand experience they learned the sails and the ropes, knotting and splicing, how to chart a course and take the sun, the lore of the stars, the fickleness of the winds, and the vagaries of the currents. They dangled aloft with the crew in howling gales while the ship below tossed on the seething waters. All these ingredients went into the makeup of a Passed Midshipman, first rung up the naval ladder to the quarter-deck.

At last the *Constitution* glided into the calm Aegean. Threading her way through the isles of Greece, "where burning Sappho loved and sang," she anchored off Piraeus, seaport of Athens. In bold relief, the crumbling magnificence of the age of Pericles stood out against the northern sky. Drawn by the fame of *"Old Ironsides"* came the fairy princess of the Balkans, Queen Amalie of Greece, and King Otho. The ship was agog, the Reefers' Den beside itself. To Midshipman Maffitt fell the coveted assignment for the royal visit. As Commodore's aide, he would escort the royal pair aboard.

With twelve bronzed jack-tars manning the sweeps, the Commodore's barge hauled up to the Piraeus mole. In the stern-sheets sat Midshipman Maffitt in gold lace, high collar, and cocked hat, about as handsome as a youngster could be. The royal cortege clattered onto the quay in glittering state—the King, the Queen, and her ladies in waiting. With the modest assurance peculiar to midshipmen, he handed Her Majesty from her carriage onto the barge. Fifteen and full-blown, she was arrayed in the romantic costume of her country, her dark brown hair set off by a silk-tasseled red cap. John Maffitt didn't miss a single feature. Her jacket of crimson velvet revealed exquisitely rounded shoulders. Her tapering waist was girdled by a scarf as blue as the Mediterranean.

On the passage to the frigate the breeze caught the spray from the oars, and with unseemly discourtesy sprinkled the royal party in the stern-sheets, whereupon Midshipman Maffitt gallantly doffed his blue naval cloak and threw it around her Majesty. Their glance met, and she must have seen the merry lights dancing in his dark, dark eyes.

The ship was dressed, the yards manned, the marine guard presented arms. Salutes echoed up amid the ruins on the hills. The ship's band toyed with the Grecian national air. Drawn up smartly on the quarter-deck were Commodore Elliot and his officers, gold-laced and sworded. The Queen looked delicious, fresh and lovely as a morning in spring. Refreshments were served in the open air, but alas! the ice cream was salty. "Old Bruin" was full of apologies. With quiet dignity, the Queen put aside the salty mixture. The rascally boatman who brought it aboard had let the freezer fall into the sea, recovered it, and said nothing.

Dusk drifted over the harbor. Lights twinkled under the snowy awnings. The muskets of the marines were ranged around the capstan with sperm candles in their muzzles, making a unique chandelier. As if by magic, the quarter-deck, shorn of its guns, was transformed into a fairy ballroom, and overhead a million white lamps burned in the dark Grecian sky.

Dancing was the Queen's particular passion. The ship's band struck up an animated waltz, one the Queen fancied. Electrified, she gazed wistfully at the Commodore, who gazed embarrassedly back at the Queen. In her eyes he had read, "Do let's waltz." At least, that was how he described his helplessness.

"I am no waltzer, your Majesty," admitted Old Bruin with a tinge of regret. "But I have a number of young gallants aboard. My aide, Midshipman Maffitt, is quite adept at the business." He turned to the enthralled reefer, "Mr. Maffitt!"

With a nod and a smile (a rarity with Old Bruin), he beckoned to Maffitt. The young gentleman's eyes again met the Queen's. He bowed, then his arm encircled her waist and they were off with alacrity. Gracefully he whirled her around the deck with as much zest as if she were a señorita at a masked ball at Port Mahon. Soon a dozen couples were spinning about them, but the Queen seemed to prefer her first partner above all the others who tried to replace him. The dancing was protracted. The candles in their musket sconces glowed like topaz. The night grew chilly. John Maffitt fetched his naval cloak. Wrapped in its folds she danced on. It was observed that the Queen whispered things to him that only he could hear.

"Your name is not Meester Maffeet," she breathed. "To me you are Meedsheepman Gallant."

Eight bells had long struck before the royal party went ashore. The boats were manned, the yards and masts illuminated. Twenty-one guns broke the silence of the harbor. This time, with fast-beating heart, John Maffitt anticipated the spray. Enveloped in his naval cloak, the Queen stepped down the gangway. At the landing he bent and kissed her hand. She invited him to a grand ball at the palace the next night, and early in the morning invitations were handed up for the Commodore and Midshipman Maffitt. But Old Bruin said no. "What would be the feelings of the other young men if you should go and they be excluded?"

Yet John Maffitt would long remember that thrilling night. The silent folds of his naval cloak would hold a romantic zest to the end of his life. The Queen of Greece had worn it the night she dubbed him "Midshipman Gallant."

Next day the frigate sailed from Piraeus to stop at Cape Colonna, where the reefers wandered through ruins of the magnificent temples of Minerva and Jupiter Olympus. But the glory that was Greece did not tempt John Maffitt. His thoughts were speeding back to Athens.

In 1838 he was ordered home on the U.S.S. *Shark*. In mid-ocean he helped quell an incipient mutiny instigated by crewmen breaking out the spirit-room. At Baltimore he was summoned before the dread tribunal that assayed the fitness of aspirants for naval glory. Maffitt negotiated this ordeal with flying colors. The "Tiger" himself was one of the inquisitors—Commodore Isaac Hull, whose victory over the *Guerrière* was the naval showpiece of the War of 1812. Hull propounded a question inspired by his own (and the *Constitution's*) escape from an enemy squadron. His stern countenance radiated pleasure when John Maffitt, comprehending the bearing of the question, answered it to his satisfaction.

At nineteen, Maffitt was warranted Passed Midshipman, and was on his way up the ladder. Here was a youth as handsome as they come, with a great wave of black hair and such dark, merry eyes that even his enemies in the Sixties remembered and admired them.

Ordered to the sloop-of-war *Vandalia* in 1838, he sailed for Vera Cruz to police the French punitive foray and make sure it did not violate America's basic foreign policy, the Monroe Doctrine. After watching the French storm and capture the bastion of San Juan de Uloa, he went ashore to observe the effects of naval gunfire. Roaming through the city it irked him that "not a bright eye peered from one of the beautiful balconies around the Alameda to cheer me in my wanderings." Off Matamoras, while crossing the bar in a tropical storm, he almost lost his life, only to be cast up by the hurricane on a miserable island "they had the impudence to call Bagdad for one of the most luxurious and oriental cities of the past."

In 1839 he was promoted to lieutenant, just two years behind Raphael Semmes, who would pace him over the oceans in the fiery Sixties. Ordered to the Navy Yard at Pensacola, he was then assigned to the frigate *Macedonian* as acting master. At nearby Mobile, in 1840, he married Mary Florence Murrell, and in due time his beloved Florie arrived. She was baptized aboard the *Macedonian* by the frigate's chaplain. With the coming of a son, Eugene, it seemed as if his round of happiness was complete.

In 1842 he was assigned to the Coast Survey at Baltimore. Renting a house, he moved in his ménage and engaged a "long-known and faithful" Irishman to look after his interests during his absences at sea. It was then that tragedy struck his household. What happened is still clouded over. Like Sam Houston facing a similar predicament, John Maffitt never revealed it. Yet it would seem as if the anonymous Irishman was too faithful in his duties. The catastrophe seems to have involved Mary Florence Maffitt and this unidentified individual. Sixty-odd years later, his third wife shed the only light we have on this episode: "Upon this period of his life let silence fall. The broken threads of his life were gathered up and its warp and woof rewoven, but the scars remained."

Hydrography had long fascinated John Maffitt. Nature seemed to have set his sights for this work of charting waters. For fourteen years he mapped the Atlantic coast. Few have ever known the nation's seaboard as intimately as he. Up and down the coast, from Nantucket Shoals to the mouth of the Mississippi, he plotted the waters. It was exacting, dangerous work, in good weather and often in bad. Gradually he came to know the coastal waters by heart. His reconnaissances, still preserved, were incredible. A recapitulation of several sections of them reveal staggering totals: 100,006 soundings taken, 2,746 miles of soundings run, 7,347 angles observed. Feeling his way over the waters leading to Charleston harbor he discovered a new channel, still identified as "Maffitt's Channel." He little knew that many a blockade runner would at a later day find it a handy access to the beleaguered port.

In 1851 Coast Survey officers were billeted at Fort Johnson, near the ancient and delightful village of Smithville, North Carolina, at the mouth of the Cape Fear River. It was a happy assignment in the state he loved. Up-river was gay, cultivated Wilmington, where culture and hospitality had reigned since colonial days. During the summer the inland planters and their families migrated to Smithville for the cooling sea breezes. They opened their hearts and their homes to John Maffitt. Sunshine and halcyon days returned. He was the gay one, as of yore. There were cotillions and masked balls, reminiscent of Port Mahon, picnics on the beaches and strolls in the moonlight through exquisite gardens, stolen kisses and words of love.

In 1852 he married again—a lovely widow, Caroline Read. Of her own children, Laurens Read was to become Maffitt's "beloved son." He was to perish in 1862, with John Maffitt at the point of death nearby, when yellow jack, dread visitation of the tropics, stalked up the gangway of the C.S.S. *Florida*. At his second marriage Maffitt's best man was Lieutenant Tunis Augustus Craven, devoted friend and co-worker on the Coast Survey assignment, who later won fame and death at Mobile Bay.

In 1857, at thirty-eight, Lieutenant John Maffitt was arbitrarily detached from active duty by the Naval Retiring Board and placed on the indefinite furlough list. It was a preamble to enforced retirement. His professional fitness was questioned, and he was declared incapable of efficiently performing his duties ashore and afloat. Maffitt demanded a hearing. To buttress his plea came officers destined to gather laurels aplenty in the oncoming struggle.

The wrong was rectified. Restored to rank and grade, he was ordered to command the *Dolphin*, overhauling slave runners off Cuba. In 1859 he transferred to the U.S.S. *Crusader*, eight guns and fast, cruising the same waters on the same mission.

It was a portentous year for the nation, a sad one for John Maffitt. Hardly had he bought a home in Washington before he lost his devoted wife, Caroline Read Maffitt.

Coming events were casting somber shadows. The cold war between the North and South was about to explode. A new constellation, long foretold by political seers, was rising in the Southern skies. At Capitol Hill in Washington, angry sectional debates crackled like lightning before a storm. Tempers ran amuck. Yet Washington was never more gay or brilliant than in these tense days when the capital rang with cries for dissolution of the Union.

Spectators flocked to the galleries to see the fireworks and cheer on their respective champions. Here, more than anywhere else, it was evident that the "irrepressible conflict" was indeed irrepressible. In an atmosphere of eat-drink-and-be-merry-for-tomorrow-we-die, ladies and gentlemen crowded to parties, ate prodigious feasts, and drank enormously.

The hills around Harper's Ferry, Virginia, were aglow with autumn pastels when a hawk-eyed old man, arch-abolitionist John Brown, set forth to show the bondsman how to kill and be free. He saw himself as God's agent sent to avenge the evils of slavery and deliver four million from servility. John Brown's scheme convulsed the nation. Even as he dangled at the end of a rope, the North canonized him. It was the summons to the all-star cast in the mightiest of American tragedies.

On that May day in 1860 when the new Republican Party at Chicago nominated Abraham Lincoln for the Presidency, the *Crusader*, Lieutenant Maffitt commanding, was running down a nameless, flagless slaver in the Old Bahama Channel. In a week she had overhauled over sixty sail suspected of trafficking in black ivory. On this day a square-rigger whose stench proclaimed her trade swept over the glistening water. Giving chase, the *Crusader* cut her short with a shot that meant what it said. Crammed below the bark's smelly hatches were four hundred and fifty Negroes, prisoners of war sold by the king of Dahomey out of Africa. Taking the prize in tow, Maffitt steamed off to Key West to deliver her to the naval agent in these matters. From Washington flashed official commendation. His temporary possession of these unfortunates was the nearest John Maffitt ever came to owning a human being.

Aboard the *Crusader* a correspondent of the New York *Herald* wrote a description of the slaver's chase and capture that was widely read. From pulpits and editorial pages came plaudits for the naval officer whose vigilance had rescued the unfortunate Negroes from bondage. In part, the account ran:

> For a little while there was dead silence aboard both ships, though the increasing strong ammoniacal African odor placed beyond all doubt the fact that the bark had under her hatches a cargo of negroes.
> And now we began to hear a sort of suppressed moaning, which soon swelled into the unmistakable murmur of many hu-

man voices. As our boat reached the side of the bark, and the officer in charge sprang on the deck, with a tremendous shout the hatches were forced open from below, and out burst hundreds of self-liberated slaves.

As they caught sight of the Stars and Stripes floating so near—which no doubt seemed to these poor wretches like a bright rainbow of promise—they became perfectly frantic with joy. They climbed up all along the rail—they hung on the shrouds, they clustered like swarming bees in the rigging, while rose from the sea to the sky the wildest acclamations of delight. They danced and leaped, and waved their arms in the air, and screamed and yelled in a discordant but pathetic concert. There was one thing, however, even more touching than all this outcry of barbaric rejoicing. My attention was attracted to a group consisting of somewhat more than one hundred women, withdrawn apart from the shouting and noisy men. Entirely nude, but innocently unabashed, they sat or knelt in tearful and silent thankfulness.

The scene of confusion aboard the bark, when the negroes found themselves released, baffles all description. They had, of course, been kept on a very small allowance of food and water during their passage. The first use they made of their liberty was to satisfy their hunger and thirst, which they did by breaking into the bread barrels and water casks, and then running about eating, drinking, dancing and screaming all at once.

Brought aboard the Crusader the captain of the slaver faced Captain Maffitt.

"I have no papers, no flag, no name," said this Frenchman with the amusing philosophy and sangfroid of his race. "I am a slaver, sir, and now your prisoner."

"Is that all you have to say?" asked Maffitt.

"The risk was run for money and here it ends, in failure."

In number the negroes amount to about 450. They were prisoners of war purchased in a large town on the slave coast from the king of Dahomey.

Three years later, when the Florida lay at Brest, France, a London Times reporter, on a visit to Maffitt's cabin, recalled the capture of this slaver:

For this feat his health was drunk at a public dinner in Liverpool; and it is a curious fact for those who maintain that the civil war in America is founded upon the slave question, that the commander of this important Confederate cruiser [Florida] should be the very man who has distinguished himself actively against the slave trade. In 1859 Captain Maffitt commanded the U.S. Steamer *Crusader* and captured four slavers.

2

John Maffitt boasted no generations of colonial forebears. His story ran back to the Emerald Isle and a father, the Reverend John Newland Maffitt, a poetic youth who had fallen under the spell of John Wesley's teachings, and a mother who clung to the Church of England. In 1819 John Maffitt, Irish Methodist preacher, decided to seek his fortune in the New World. Vanguard of his family, he crossed the sea and settled in Connecticut. His wife, Anne, impetuously followed at once, though a baby was coming. In midwinter, in the North Atlantic, on Washington's birthday, 1819, John Maffitt appeared in a watery, stormy world. He jestingly, in later years, fixed his birthplace as Longitude 40 W, Latitude 50 N.

But the going was hard for a minister's wife with seven small children, and Anne Maffitt fell by the way. At the age of five, dark-eyed John was adopted by an uncle and emigrated to Fayetteville, North Carolina. Here the lad's heart took hold, never to let go. Here, too, the sea took hold. At thirteen, through the good offices of a friend, President Jackson warranted him midshipman in the United States Navy. The date was February 25, 1832.

Now, twenty-nine years later, in May 1861, John Maffitt was lieutenant in the Confederate States Navy. Well might he quote Lord Byron's ringing lines:

> And I have loved thee, Ocean! and my joy
> Of youthful sports was on thy breast to be
> Borne, like thy bubbles, onward; from a boy
> I wantoned with thy breakers, . . .
> And laid my hand upon thy mane,—as I do here.

CHAPTER VIII

Wanted: A Confederate Navy

THE "BATTLE FLEET" to which Secretary Mallory had assigned John Maffitt was an odd naval assortment over which floated the broad pennant of Commodore Josiah Tatnall. Ruddy cheeked and blue-eyed, this old Triton maneuvered his nondescript task force about the Savannah estuary with as much bravado as if it were a heavily-gunned armada.

To visiting British journalist William Russell, who commented on the nature of his squadron, the doughty commodore sadly observed, "I have no fleet. Long before the Southern Confederacy has a fleet that can cope with the Stars and Stripes my bones will be white in the grave."

Take a look at this microscopic naval force mushing over the waters below Savannah. Flagship was the *Savannah*, a paddle-wheeler that in happier days plied back and forth through the inland marshy channels between Savannah and Jacksonville. Her engines and boilers squatted on deck, fair target for everything. She mounted two guns. Commanding her was Lieutenant John Maffitt, to whom she was "an absurd abortion of a man-of-war." In her wake steamed a retinue of naval oddities: three old tugs and a decaying cattle boat. Ten guns and a bit of carpentry had converted them into men-of-war with high-sounding names: *Reso-lute, Samson, Huntress, Lady Davis*, for the President's wife, and

Savannah, for the charming city nearby. Tatnall's command covered the coastal waters between this city and Charleston.

The Commodore will hardly be remembered for his prowess as flag officer of this popgun fleet. In 1859 he was a distinguished naval figure commanding America's East India Squadron based on the China coast. In that year he had opened his guns to aid British warships that were being lashed mercilessly by Chinese batteries at the mouth of the Pei-ho River. Hauled before an investigating board to explain his violation of America's neutrality, the sea dog made his famous plea, "Blood is thicker than water," a phrase that has illumined his memory ever since. Upheld by his superiors, he was given a vote of thanks by the British Parliament.

Tatnall's squadron, if it did nothing else, gave the good folk of Savannah and its neighboring sea-islands a thrill of pride as it steamed through the mazes of the Georgia sounds, attacking and sinking imaginary Yankee fleets. In such pursuits John Maffitt was obliged to spend the summer of 1861.

In the months before the glitter of the Confederacy wore off and the Northern giant came into his own, the South was engaged in the deceptive game of discounting Yankee enterprise. This was to prove a will-o'-the-wisp like the rosy belief in the kingship of cotton and the suicidal policy of withholding it from export. The pint-sized Union Navy could never keep more than a loose watch on a few Southern ports. So thought the man on the street. The Federals had already taken a body blow when Virginia troops captured the Norfolk Navy Yard where seven first class ships were scuttled, including the fifty-gun *Merrimack* that was to rise from the waters for a single day of havoc and glory. Blockading 3,549 miles of Confederate seacoast with one vessel every hundred miles looked ridiculous. Admittedly the Southern seaboard was vulnerable in hundreds of places, but how could the North fence in every inlet, sound, and estuary? Meanwhile, blockade runners were sweeping in and out through the wide-meshed Yankee cordons with the regularity of clockwork.

Moreover, a goodly segment of the South was convinced that the fate of the new empire would be settled on the battlefield, not on invasion beaches, and certainly not on the high seas. Others, far fewer in number, thought otherwise. Notable among these was Secretary of the Navy Mallory, who fought a losing battle for four years to build a navy, only to see it destroyed piecemeal until its last four ships went up in flames with Richmond in April, 1865.

Far too prevalent was the conviction that England would dispatch her battle fleet to crack President Lincoln's flimsy blockade and open Southern ports for outgoing cotton. This was one of the war's cruel delusions. Then English and French ships would crowd Southern wharves, bringing the necessities and luxuries of life, as well as matériel of war. The Confederacy—so ran this deceptive thinking—need only fight a delaying action until England stepped in and finished off what was left of the North.

Millions of Southerners reading these lines in Britain's *Punch* believed and took heart:

> We'll break your blockade, Cousin Jonathan yet;
>   Yes, darn your old stockings, Cousin Jonathan, but we will,
> And cotton we'll have and to work we will set
>   Every Lancashire hand, every Manchester mill.

The British fleet was coming to the rescue!

Meanwhile, to guard against seaborne assault and deny entrance to strategic inland waterways, the Confederate high command erected embankments of mud, moss, and sand on prominent headlands, lonely islands, and exposed beaches. Armed with a few guns and greenhorn gunners, these makeshift bastions performed miracles. One of them, notably Fort Fisher, was powerful enough to stall off Northern amphibious attack until the Confederacy had reached her last gasps.

In August, 1861, when the smog of defeat at Manassas hovered over Washington, a Blockading Board of four high-level naval officers sweated out secret plans and blueprints for sledgehammer strikes at the Southern coastline. The Official Records refer to this meeting as a "conference for measures for effectually blockading the South Atlantic Coast." Obviously, if the Confederacy was to be strangled by the as-yet paper blockade proclaimed by President Lincoln on April 19, the Union Navy must seize several commodious harbors where naval stations could be established to service the blockading squadrons soon to be riding out the gales and rollers off the major Southern ports. Strategic areas and waters must be repossessed. Fortress Monroe and Hampton Roads, firmly gripped

by Union forces, were too far north to be used as supply bases for
these operations.

First to feel the impact of mounting Union sea power was Fort
Hatteras, guarding the inlet to North Carolina's inland sea, Pam-
lico Sound. This vital passageway was presumably Yankee-proof.
Two forts guarded its narrow stretch. Besides, nature herself had
sheltered it by a shield of gales and heavy seas for which Hatteras
waters were notorious. Yet, in September, 1861, this barrier fell before an amphibious assault, the North's first, which was to set the
pattern for recovering the coast and harbors of the South.

Next came Port Royal, on the South Carolina coast, midway
between Charleston and Savannah. Its name was well chosen, for
nature had endowed it with a magnificent harbor, one of the finest
on the Atlantic coast. Ten miles up the Broad River that flowed
into this harbor lay Beaufort, heart-city of this lush region, where
sea-island cotton had brought wealth to the planters for generations. Forty thousand slaves produced three million dollars' worth
of high-quality cotton yearly.

To protect this vital expanse of anchorage and the rich district
environing it, Confederate engineers had constructed two mud
forts commanding the narrow passageway into Port Royal Sound.
Laid out with keen engineering acumen, Fort Beauregard on Bay
Point and Fort Walker on Hilton Head faced each other across
the two-mile roadstead. Armed mostly with 24- and 32-pounders,
they were garrisoned at the last moment with a few hundred raw
troops so rationed powderwise that they had fired hardly a dozen
practice shots before being called on to face the formidable Yankee
naval array.

Later in October, 1861, a vast armada weighed anchor at Hampton Roads to labor seaward through the Chesapeake capes and veer
southward. Never before had an American naval officer commanded
so mighty a fleet, seventy ships in all, including seventeen men-of-
war and a motley assortment of transports laden with supplies and
fifteen thousand troops. Flag officer of this expedition was a naval
captain whose surname was invested with considerable renown,
Samuel Francis du Pont. Well might his heart have swollen with
pride as he raised the signal "Weigh anchor," to strike a blow that
would send the North into panegyrics of Glory! Glory! Halle-
lujah!

Hardly had this parade of Northern naval might got under way when it was hit by a tempest off Cape Hatteras. Du Pont's squadrons were scattered like chaff, eliciting from the South an inevitable comparison with the fate of the Spanish Armada three centuries before. For days it appeared that the Northern vessels would pile up in masses of wreckage on Hatteras' graveyard of ships. Thousands of devout Confederate souls and prophetic newspaper editors viewed this raging gale as an omen of divine displeasure for the North, and undeniable proof that the Almighty's smile shone on the South.

But the gales subsided, and du Pont's battered ships straggled into the rendezvous off Port Royal to anchor safely out of range of Confederate shore batteries. On November 7 du Pont's seventeen men-of-war swept into the narrow roadway leading to the sound. In the van rode the flagship *Wabash*, mounting forty-four Dahlgrens. Off in the sound, looking on from a discreet distance, was Commodore Tatnall's "battle-fleet." On the map accompanying the Official Records of this "battle" it is designated by several ship-shaped dabs labeled "Rebel Squadron." From his ringside seat Tatnall had the temerity to fire his peanut broadsides at the Union bruisers that mounted a total of two hundred and fifteen guns.

After dumping the big iron balls of her starboard broadside on Fort Beauregard, the *Wabash* made her first turn to the left to give Fort Walker a dose of the same bad medicine, not forgetting to send a salvo or two flying toward Tatnall's pitiable grouping up the sound. An eleven-inch shell, which fortunately did not explode, bashed through the *Savannah's* gun deck, gouging a hole big as a buoy. So unwelcome was this Yankee intruder that Tatnall turned humorously to his flag captain.

"Mr. Maffitt, under the accumulation of circumstances, discretion is the better part of valor. We had best retire, and, like Mr. Micawber, wait for something to turn up."

But the eyewitness reporter of the Savannah *Republican* cheered up his readers by tossing bouquets at the "true Southern sailors who awaited with courage in their hearts and resolve stamped upon every countenance the approach of a foe to whom from old association they took peculiar pride in showing themselves ready to stand by their cause like men *sans peur et sans reproche*."

Standing by was praiseworthy enough, but Tatnall decided promptly that with seventeen warships belching devastation this was no time to dally. Dipping his broad pennant three times to his former associate in the old navy, he withdrew to safety through Skull Creek and onto the Savannah roadstead.

For four hours du Pont's vessels heaped shells on Forts Beauregard and Walker. A volcano could hardly have done better. After five runs-past of the fleet, the raw graybacks called it a day and decamped en masse. When Northern landing forces charged over the parapets they found only dead and wounded. Du Pont's ships had suffered fourteen casualties. Eight were killed—not quite half a man per ship—six wounded. He had fired 2,209 projectiles.

To Washington sped the fleet's fastest dispatch boat bearing "the first American ensign raised upon the soil of South Carolina since their rebellion broke out." Joy ripped off the Northern roof. Congress blossomed with resolutions of thanks for everyone from du Pont down to the powder monkeys. National salutes were fired in the streets.

From Judge Charles Cowley, Judge Advocate of the fleet, came this commentary: "The Federal forces engaged were so much greater than that of the Confederates, in the number and weight of guns, that to have failed of success would have covered it with disgrace." It is not improbable that the lowliest lieutenant in du Pont's fleet could have executed the Port Royal massacre with as much dispatch as the commander himself. It was an elephant treading on an anthill.

"Neptune" Welles laid aside his pipe long enough to emit the dispatch that made du Pont a national hero: "You have inscribed your name on one of the proudest pages of our history; but you are to do still more for the country's salvation. Go on, my dear sir, in this glorious work."

But—as an aside—Welles apparently forgot these glowing praises a year and a half later when du Pont, intent on furthering "this glorious work," moved his ironclads up against the real thing at Charleston. This was no Port Royal setup. When he retrieved his monitors out of the assault that was supposed to reduce hated Fort Sumter to rubble and capture iniquitous Charleston, they resembled shot-up tincans, and one ironclad rested on the bottom. Confederate cannoneers had plugged her ninety times. Before she sank she looked like a huge sieve. In the smoke and flash of gunfire at Charleston, the glory du Pont had won at Port Royal found a watery grave along with the *Keokuk*.

Raging with disappointment, Gideon Welles unleashed his ire on du Pont. Bitter was the crossfire of recrimination. Du Pont was demoted. The Secretary of the Navy couldn't lose. He had to be right. He broke off the official knife in du Pont's heart, and that was what killed the "hero of Port Royal" as the Civil War sputtered to its close.

Three days after the fall of Port Royal, Lieutenant John Maffitt was given temporary duties as naval aide to General Robert E. Lee, then military adviser to President Davis. With the threat of Union seizure of beachheads, Richmond had rushed Lee south to unify and bolster the coast defenses. It was a last-minute affair. Beyond fortifying a few salient points, erecting crude river obstructions, and emplacing cannon that trickled down from Richmond, there was little Lee could do. Loss of Port Royal was a bitter pill for the South. Lee was not to acquire his luster on the coast of Georgia and South Carolina.

Of the several memoirs Maffitt left of camp life with General Lee at Coosawhatchie, South Carolina, one tells of a Christmas turkey, which the staff had provided only to hear Lee order it hustled off to a nearby hospital with the remark, "Bacon and cornbread are good enough for well men."

But John Maffitt brought a touch of much-needed levity to the military family of Lee, which was then weighed down by a train of seaboard disasters.

Out of Maffitt's brief sojourn on Lee's staff flowed a friendship, and a desultory correspondence that was lost, with the exception of one letter.

2

It would be well to pause for a moment and focus our spotlight on the Confederate Navy. The South was never able to float a unified navy worthy of the name, nor was she powerful enough to mount a concerted attack at any given point. The eve of a bitter war found her without the essentials of a navy or the means of building one. With a blast of ballyhoo the seceded states promptly seized a baker's dozen decrepit revenue cutters, armed with a total of fifteen guns. Such was the nucleus of the Confederate Navy, though Secretary Mallory claimed he had even less, "one ship with three guns," when he took office.

The South can hardly be said ever to have had a navy at all. Save for the homemade ironclads and foreign-built cruisers it was a rag, tag, and bobtail affair made up of gunboats, cattle barges, river double-enders, and outworn coasters that were commandeered by the government, given highfalutin names, and equipped with antiquated ordnance. The *Sumter*, on which Raphael Semmes began his meteoric raiding career, was a beat-up overnighter on the Havana-New Orleans run, *Habana*, slapdashed to war usage. Semmes called her a tea-kettle, but she rendered valiant service.

The South had an abundance of resources she couldn't use. Timber for building ships stood in her forests in great quantities, though, when cut and laid, it was found to be soft and green. Iron from which armor plating could be rolled lay undug in the Alleghenies. When it came to coal, there was an unmined abundance. But of rolling mills she was virtually barren. She didn't have a mill capable of turning out two-and-a-half-inch plates. Nor were there any ropewalks. Hemp for ropes had to be sown, grown, and reaped. Nor was there a builder of marine engines in the whole of the South.

To sum up, the South possessed no advantages comparable to those of industrialized New England, early converted to war production. She had no powder factories to match the du Pont mills, which stretched endlessly along the Brandywine, nor were there generations of seafaring men on whom she could draw to man a navy, even were she able to conjure one up out of the Southern air.

Dire necessity coerced her into purchasing in the open market— as it did the North at the beginning—such ships as were available, arming them with such guns as she could dig up, and hustling them out to contest threatened seizure of her strategic beachheads. Of such was the Mosquito Squadron, as Maffitt dubbed it, with which Commodore Tatnall made his token attempt to beat off du Pont's attack on Port Royal. Brushed off like insects, this flotilla ended its days making angry gestures off the Savannah estuary.

Yet, the South learned how to build. Her impromptu ironclads wrote gallant, though futile, chapters. Better on the whole than the North's, they were crushed in their cradles or just as they began toddling. Take the *Mississippi*, for example. She was one of two ironclad floating batteries building at New Orleans when Farragut blasted his way up the river in the spring of 1862. The *Louisiana* was her sister. Knowledge that these two behemoths were nearing completion hastened Farragut's plans. His victory-day was April 24. Two weeks more and the *Mississippi* would have been armed and commissioned. Unable to fight or run away, she was fired and set afloat by the men who built her. Farragut's guns snuffed out the stationary *Louisiana*.

Now to quote again the war's best naval authority, then-Captain D. D. Porter, commanding the Mortar Flotilla in the attack on New Orleans. Testified Porter apropos of the *Mississippi*:

> In New Orleans we found the most splendid specimen of a floating battery the world has ever seen (a seagoing affair), and had she been finished and succeeded in getting to sea the whole American navy would have been destroyed.

In his *Naval History of the War*, published in 1886, Porter went even further, admitting that had New Orleans been afforded two months more to finish these ironclads, "Our wooden fleet would have been driven North, and the entire Southern coast sealed off against us. The blockade would have been raised, and the independence of the South recognized by the powers of Europe." Truly an amazing admission for the outspoken, called-them-as-he-saw-them Porter.

James Bulloch expressed a truth faultlessly when he said, "There is a lustre inseparable from successful enterprise, and a splendour inherent to victory which no power of language and no play of fancy can impart to defeat." Northern victories were gilded with the glamour of success, and rightly so.

John Maffitt was a practical sailor. Seamanship and navigation were his profession, his stock in trade. This was all he knew. He had joined the exodus from the old navy to get aboard the nascent Confederate Navy, but how could he, or those who went with him, utilize their talents with paltry, poorly-armored river craft, imperfectly constructed gunboats? How could they compete with ships of modern construction and the finest naval ordnance afloat,

Dahlgren guns? From the start they recognized the hopelessness of their struggle and their inability to achieve personal renown. They lacked the tools. For that reason, barely half a dozen Confederate naval officers ever made the "dean's list" of the war's history. Maffitt was one of them.

The Confederate Navy was never a determining factor in the war. Success never lay within its grasp, yet its failure was not ignominious. Defeat was conclusive, crushing; but the men who manned that navy left a luster that will outlast the years. They left no brilliant victories for posterity to glamorize, only their heroism and the will to do or die.

In war the public hopes for, and at heart expects, brilliant operations, even if marked by defeat. That is why the *Alabama* and *Florida* caught the imagination of the South and of the world. They streaked across the seas like comets, sending shivers up the Northern spine, driving American bottoms helterskelter to foreign registry. When they vanished below the waters, a woeful cry echoed through the South.

CHAPTER IX

Mystery Ship on the Mersey

In june of 1861 the city of Liverpool in neutral England began to assume her vital role in the life-and-death struggle of the Confederacy. One would think that this traffic was undercover, but the bulk of it was carried on in broad daylight under the very eyes of those appointed to safeguard English neutrality. Nor was it long before the wharves and storehouses along the Mersey had become a vast secret arsenal for the grayback armies. This British city was the very heart of a risky, profitable contraband trade. From her docks, ships by the score laden with war matériel, slithered down the Mersey for direct runs into Southern ports, or to Bermuda and Nassau where their cargoes would be transshipped to long, low blockade runners.

With the coming of James Dunwoody Bulloch, Liverpool's ship-yards got into swim. The two most famous Confederate cruisers were built here, the *Alabama* and the *Florida*, destined to light up the ocean with burning American merchantmen. Here were forged and launched two goliath ironclads that were impounded by Britain's Foreign Secretary, Lord John Russell, in the nick of time to save Lincoln's blockade from their ravages.

At Liverpool, cotton was worth a king's, or rather a queen's, ransom. A pound of the staple fetched nigh sixty cents, two shillings and more. England's cotton mills would soon be gasping for the fluffy stuff that kept their spindles whirling. Already darken-

ing the horizon were shadows of the "cotton famine" that would
visit untold misery on half a million millworkers and their families. A royal welcome was accorded even a single bale.

A Southern wartime visitor reported seeing more Stars and Bars
fluttering in Liverpool than in Richmond. Thomas H. Dudley,
United States Consul at this port, was ever so right when, early
in the struggle, he complained to Secretary of State Seward, "The
people here—I mean at Liverpool—undoubtedly desire to see the
Southern Confederacy established. Their sympathies for the South
and dislike of the North are too open and apparent to be mistaken. Each victory gained by our troops over the rebels seems but
to deepen their sympathies for the one and to intensify their bad
feelings, if not hatred, toward the other."

At Liverpool the Confederacy brought into being its *alter ego*,
Fraser, Trenholm & Company, actually a puppet of a banking
house at Charleston. It functioned for the South much as did
the House of Morgan in America for Great Britain during World
War I. The Liverpool resident partner, Charles K. Prioleau, was
an American citizen, who metamorphosed overnight into a nat-
uralized British subject. Prioleau rendered valiant financial service. With a virtual monopoly on Confederate buying abroad, and
on the sale of government cotton, this firm—British to outward
aspects—fattened prodigiously. In a war where gold abroad meant
defeat or victory, Fraser, Trenholm & Company became members
in absentia of the Southern Cabinet. One of them, George A.
Trenholm, occupied the Treasury portfolio when the Confederacy
went up in the smoke of a thousand battles.

In all wars there are men who contribute to success or failure,
yet are not marked for fame. They must content themselves with
the knowledge of duty faithfully performed. To this group belonged the Confederate agents at Liverpool, Bermuda, Nassau,
Havana, and way stations. For them there were no brilliant feats
of arms, no desperate charges, no myrtle crowns. They worked
silently, stifling their martial ambitions. So averred James D. Bulloch, hardly realizing he was pinpointing himself.

Bulloch's mission to Britain was top-secret; yet hardly had he
sped off from Montgomery, by way of Canada to take ship to
Liverpool, than cipher telegrams began flashing northward to a
relay station in Virginia, where they were "pipe-lined" to Wash-

ington. Who sent them? No one knows. The Official Records are silent. Decoded, they revealed the cold facts of Bulloch's mission. Northern secret agents hurried to intercept Bulloch crossing the Ohio at Louisville, but somehow he slipped through their fingers. It was a costly failure. However, the State Department decided not to reveal what it knew, for the simple reason that Federal buyers were already in Britain for a purpose identical with that of Bulloch's: to obtain warships.

Running through the roster of those who served the Confederacy on foreign shores, Bulloch's name easily leads the procession. His fine hand all but created a Southern navy in English shipyards. Reaching Liverpool in June, 1861, he first presented himself at the Fraser, Trenholm counting house, where he was to do much business. Next, he ran up to London for a courtesy call on Confederate diplomatic commissioners William L. Yancey and Dudley Mann. Permanent commissioner James Mason had not yet arrived.

No one was to prove so adept as Bulloch in legally flouting Britain's Foreign Enlistment Act, which, among other restrictions, forbade construction of ships-of-war for either of the American combatants within her Majesty's domain. Before taking a step, Bulloch engaged an astute Liverpool barrister, one F. S. Hull, who was prudent and respected, but happy enough to accept a fee for piloting the Confederate cruisers-to-be through the labyrinth of the Foreign Enlistment Act. This hurdle was embarrassing, but not insurmountable. Fixing his legal microscope upon it, Barrister Hull detected mouseholes through which warships that did not look like warships might wriggle, provided one did not stretch the law's pliable tenets too far. Lawyer Hull came up with the conclusion that "any shipbuilder may build a ship in her Majesty's dominions, provided he does not equip her within her Majesty's dominions, and he has nothing to do with the acts of the purchasers done within her Majesty's dominions without his concurrence, nor without her Majesty's dominions even with his concurrence." It was a legal brainchild, but served Bulloch's purposes.

It should be borne in mind that constructing a warship that wasn't a warship, getting her to sea out of an English port, and equipping and arming her on the high seas was a delicate process. To protect her from seizure or forfeiture between her dockyard swaddling clothes and the day she sailed off to destroy American commerce, she must be shorn of every semblance of belligerency. Her guns must be obtained from one source, her shot and shell from another, her stores, clothing, and food elsewhere. She must sail off under British registry, manned by a British crew, flying a British flag, and seemingly as innocent of future "wrongdoing" as *September Morn*. The thousand and one essentials of a warship must then be brought together at a hideout somewhere on the high seas, safe from prowling Union gunboats, where they could be coalesced into a rover ready to take off on her mission of pillaging America's merchant marine. Arming a ship on the deep was beyond British jurisdiction, unless on the waters of a British colony, as was actually done in the case of the *Florida*.

Within four weeks after disembarking at Liverpool, James Bulloch had laid the keel of the first foreign-built Confederate cruiser. Indeed, by the time Southern gold began clinking into the coffers of Fraser, Trenholm & Company, this ship was partly in frame.

Well-briefed by Barrister Hull on the intricacies and pitfalls of British neutrality, Bulloch got busy. One bright June morning he casually dropped in at the Liverpool yards of Messrs. Wm. C. Miller & Sons, shipbuilders, ostensibly to discuss construction of a merchant ship for a firm in Palermo, Italy. The "firm" was really a private party named James Bulloch. When completed, the ship was to be delivered to him personally on the Mersey at Liverpool. Bulloch had acted with calculated precision. He had "cased" the Miller firm and discovered that its senior member, William C. Miller, was the highly respected Chief Surveyor of shipping for the Port of Liverpool. If embarrassing questions arose, surely Mr. Miller (whose office, when he was not at his shipyard, was in the Liverpool Customs House) could foil them handily.

He found the Millers affable enough. Because they were not engineers, Bulloch deemed it advisable to make a rapprochement with Fawcett, Preston & Company, engine builders, with whom he contracted for the entire ship. The contract for hull, masts, rigging, and general sea equipment was sublet to the Barkis-is-willing Millers.

Using a scale drawing of one of her Majesty's newest, fastest gunboats as a base, Bulloch and the Millers drew up specifications for the "merchant ship" he wanted. She was to be an unarmed, sturdy wooden steamer. Iron, to which English shipbuilders had already turned, was too brittle to bear the weight and recoil of heavy guns, though Bulloch did not mention such a possibility. Of seven-hundred-odd tons, 192 feet long, three-masted, bark-rigged, she was to cost approximately 45,000 pounds. Her engines were to deliver a nominal three hundred horsepower, though actually it was seven hundred. She must clip through the water under sail and steam at twelve knots, though at times she was to make far better. Her two funnels would be hinged, one lowering forward, the other aft, enabling her to camouflage her identity. Because of this unique feature she was sometimes reported as a steamer with one funnel, then with two, and at other times as a sailing vessel. In the high-stakes game she was to play, disguise was essential. The ship must be delivered in the spring of 1862 with a spare suit of sail and boatswain's stores for a twelve months' cruise.

Bulloch admitted the Millers had a "tolerably clear notion" that the vessel would, by a tortuous, undisclosed piece of prestidigitation, glide into the ranks of the Confederate Navy. Yet he vowed they never mentioned their suspicions. Certainly Bulloch did not enlighten the Millers, who at least pretended they were in the dark as to the ship's ultimate destination. Nor did he tell them he had ordered her armament elsewhere.

This ship was to mount eight guns: two rifled seven-inch pivots and six smoothbore broadside thirty-two pounders. Anticipating occasional bloody business at close quarters when boarding prizes, and to beat off possible Union boarders, Bulloch provided two hundred rifles of the latest British navy model and an equal number of cutlasses.

To forestall snoopers, American spies—who were legion—and British officials sniffing out neutrality violations, Bulloch suggested that the ship masquerade under the dockyard name Oreto, which he himself concocted. This appellation, with its Italian flavor, soon appeared above the slip in which her keel was being laid.

Even Admiral Porter admitted that the only complaint the North could level at nimble-footed Bulloch was "too great fidelity to the cause he had espoused, coupled with the ability he manifested in getting Confederate cruisers afloat. It was never charged he resorted to dishonorable means to attain his ends." That, from Admiral Porter, was laurel enough for any laborer in the Confederacy's vineyard.

On leaving the Miller shipyards, Bulloch hurried off to see Barrister Hull, whom he had employed to advise him how to infringe the Foreign Enlistments Act without appearing to do so. The two were jubilant. When the *Oreto* dropped down the Mersey she would be as much within her legal rights as a hundred cases of rifles, or as many tons of gunpowder, leaving for New York or any other Union port. Having tested his ability to infringe the Foreign Enlistment Act without seeming to violate it, Bulloch indulged in dreams of building a whole navy in British yards, provided the Southern hierarchy renounced its cotton embargo and permitted the white gold to flow across to Europe.

A few days later, after having made such a propitious start, Bulloch crossed the Mersey to call on England's leading shipbuilders, the Lairds, whose Birkenhead yards stretched for a quarter-mile along the waterfront. From these estimable gentlemen (one of them a member of Parliament) he ordered a finer, larger "merchant ship," she that would one day adorn and scourge the high seas as the famed Confederate raider, *Alabama*. The subterfuge routine that draped the *Oreto* in mystery was repeated.

By amazing coincidence the first remittance for the account of the Navy Department reached Fraser, Trenholm & Company on the day the South was demolishing McDowell's army in the first pitched battle of the war at Bull Run. England was enraptured by the news. She was already dazzled by the exploits of Raphael Semmes and his fingerling raider, *Sumter*, on Caribbean waters, where she was playing havoc with Federal shipping. It gave England a considerable thrill. Naval glory was dear to the hearts of her people, and Semmes had a Nelsonesque flair that won instant acclaim.

But James Bulloch little relished building ships for others to command. He had accepted this mission in the same spirit as had Raphael Semmes his first assignment to go North and buy munitions of war before the conflict broke loose at Fort Sumter. With his heart set on going afloat, Bulloch began nudging the Navy Department at Richmond for command of the first of his two "infants" to be ready for sea. Even before the *Trent* Affair in November, 1861, brought England and America to the brink of war, Bulloch was convinced that the former would indubitably cast her armed might into the fray with the South. One sensed it in the very air of Britain, on the streets, in the pubs, in the fine clubs Bulloch frequented, at the upper-class goings-on where he charmed all he met with his Southern born-to-the-manor manner and ready wit.

Yet he went further than seeking command. He proposed, first, swooping down on coastwise shipping between New York and Portland. After flecking this populous sealane with burning hulks he would sheer off for the west coast of Africa, picking off prizes as he went, and head for the China Seas, where the stately, defenseless white-winged clippers glided along in apparent security, pouring profits into the coffers of mercantile New York, whose enmity against the Confederacy ran bitter and deep.

Secretary Mallory was prompt in his reply: "So soon as either of the vessels under contract in England shall be completed and delivered to you, you will adopt such measures as you may deem best to arm and equip her as a war vessel, without infringing the laws of Great Britain or giving to that government just cause for offense; and having obtained a crew and all things necessary for an extended cruise, you will leave England in command and proceed against the enemy in whatever quarter of the ocean circumstances may then indicate as affording the greatest chances of success."

It gave Bulloch *carte blanche* to strike where he would. In this same letter Mallory informed Bulloch that the ship, on leaving England, should be re-christened, *ad interim*, *Manassas*, and later adorned with the mellifluous name *Florida*, in honor of the Secretary's home state.

So rosy were the prospects, and in such good train, the indefatigable Bulloch felt it advisable to make a personal report to his superiors at Richmond. Via Nassau and a blockade runner he could travel to the Confederate capital and return to Liverpool by February, 1862. By that time the *Oreto's* graceful hull would be ready for the high seas. Absenting himself from the scene of his operations for a few weeks might prove handy in throwing sniffers off his trail, though he hadn't yet broken cover.

Rumors that the South was fitting out ships in England to cruise against American commerce were already in the wind. For that reason Bulloch sought to cloak every move. Federal spies refused to be thrown off guard, and skulduggery ran rampant.

Being both practical and efficient, Bulloch decided to make his trip home really worthwhile. He would carry along a shipload of war munitions. At Greenock, Scotland, on the Clyde, he purchased a new steamer called *Fingal*. He took her as she stood "and was amused to find, in the inventory of cabin-stores, six dozen toddy glasses, with ladles to match." With an eye to business, he added, "Each glass had the capacity of about a half-pint, and they were hard and thick and heavy enough to serve for grapeshot in case of need."

The *Fingal's* cargo and her subsequent fate as the Confederate ironclad *Atlanta* invest her with some historical acclaim. Into her hold went four hundred barrels of gunpowder, ten thousand Enfield rifles, fifteen hundred rifled Brown Bessies, one million ball cartridges, revolvers, cutlasses, rifled cannon, shot and shell, and enough assorted mankillers to have turned the most bloodthirsty Suvarov green with envy. She enjoyed the distinction of being the first ship to run the blockade solely for the account of the Confederate government. Under the half-shut eyes of port officials she left Greenock and ran down the Irish Sea to Holyhead where, in a pea soup fog, Bulloch boarded her outside the harbor. He later avowed that no single ship ever carried into the Confederacy a cargo so entirely composed of war supplies.

But Gideon Welles's snoopers had stolen a march on Bulloch, scented out his floating arsenal, and alerted Washington. In turn, Welles ordered the South Atlantic Blockading Squadron to waylay a steamer named *Fingal* laden with a prodigious quantity of munitions and bound for a Southern port. She was even pinpointed as having "the bust of a man for a figurehead."

On November 12, after a thrill-packed, nip-and-tuck voyage across the Atlantic, the *Fingal* ghosted through the porous blockade and slid safely into the Savannah estuary. A fishing smack came alongside to greet the newcomer with the depressing tidings that three days earlier Port Royal had fallen under the Union's amphibious attack. On her way up to the city, the *Fingal* stranded on a mud bank. To haul her off came the flagship of Commodore Tatnall's "fleet," the *Savannah*. Once freed, the *Fingal* steamed up the roadstead, past Fort Pulaski, to anchor abreast of the city and receive a tumultuous welcome. On her bridge stood fashion-

plate James Bulloch. One of the first to come aboard to shake his
hand was Lieutenant John Maffitt, the very man he was seeking.

That evening in a quiet room, Bullock gave Maffitt a fast brief-
ing of his operations in Britain. Two cruisers were on the way. The
first, which he was slated to command, was literally fretting at her
hawsers. She should be ready for sea by the time he returned to
Britain. While in Richmond (where he dashed at once) Bulloch
would urge Secretary Mallory to give Maffitt command of the
second. It was a welcome prospect.

2

Meanwhile, back in England, diplomatic lightning was crackling
over the Oreto, at the finishing dock in the Miller shipyards. With
Bulloch three thousand miles away, the villain of the piece, American Consul Thomas H. Dudley, stepped on stage. To this man
history and officialdom has long denied the myrtle for his role in
the drama, "Confederacy over England." As a secret agent, Dudley
would make the average present-day hawkshaw look like a village
constable. Praise for keeping England out of the war has been
lavished on Minister Charles Francis Adams, who brightened up
(with a navy blue coat) the funereal garb affected by previous
American diplomats at Queen Victoria's court. Yet it was Dudley
who unearthed the evidence on which Adams based his protests
against Britain's unneutral dealings with secret agent James Bulloch. Finest of his achievements was ferreting out the two Laird-
built ironclads, forthcoming on Bulloch's agenda.

Between this man and Bulloch flared an undercover war that
reached into the very dregs of Liverpool's waterfront. Yet Bulloch
was unstinting in his "act of justice" commendation of his bitterest enemy in this touch-and-go battle. Dudley had his faults.
He was too eager to accept the words of tale-bearers as gospel
truth. If he erred, he did it on the right side.

In the massive array of documentary evidence (over seven hundred pages) bulwarking this nation's post-war Alabama Claims
against Great Britain for depredations by English-built vessels on
American commerce, the section devoted to the Oreto (later the
Florida) leads off with Dudley's first report of a mysterious screw-

gunboat, presumably building for the Italian government. To Minister Adams, Dudley dispatched his doubts: "Circumstances make me suspicious and cause me to believe she is intended for the South." Yet so well was the *Oreto's* secret kept, that the ship had reached the outfitting stage before Dudley suspected "her insidious designs." It was no time to hold back. Marching boldly into the Miller shipyard, he sized up the *Oreto* for just what she was—an embryonic warship. She swarmed with workmen rushing her to completion. Barging into the Miller office, Dudley bluntly demanded the name of the purchaser of the sleek new ship. To the conservative Millers his inquiry was preposterous. The names of their customers was hardly the business of an outsider, and particularly not of the consul of the Lincoln government, then decidedly loathsome to the ruling and upper castes. Dudley was given a prompt but courteous brush-off.

But Dudley was not to be packed off so easily. Hurrying to London, he poured out his sleuthwork to Minister Adams. Taking up his pen, Adams fired his first protest at Foreign Minister Russell, charging that at Liverpool an armed steamer was building, "evidently intended for hostile operations on the ocean and I entertain little doubt that her intention is that of carrying on war against the United States."

Next, Dudley briefed Secretary of State Seward at Washington. "They pretend she is being built for the Italian government, but the Italian consul here informs me he knows nothing about it. There is much secrecy about her. When she sails it will be to burn and destroy whatever she meets bearing the American flag."

But his lordship, John Russell, was not impressed by Adams' protestations that the *Oreto* was a Confederate cruiser with the wraps on. Consul Dudley was talking through his diplomatic cocked hat, if he had one. The royal commissioners of customs at Liverpool had duly inspected the *Oreto*. Her innocence of warlike intentions was only surpassed by the comeliness of her hull—and Britons admired beautiful ships.

But more to the point at this critical juncture, it seemed quite likely to Britain's triple-decked political hierarchy, including Lord Russell, that the Confederate upstart would win her fight for an independent place in the sun. So why worry?

3

The Confederate cruisers were the cavalry of the sea. Their role was bold, eye-filling, and inspiring, and legends still cluster around their exploits. These commerce destroyers, *Alabama*, *Florida*, and their six lesser-known sister raiders, did greater permanent damage to the North than the blockade ever inflicted on the South. Their torch all but drove the American flag from the sea. Indeed, they herded more than half the nation's shipping to foreign registry. And it never came back.

Glance briefly at the lot of a Confederate cruiser. It was a hard one. Once on the high seas she had no home port for outfit or retreat. In all the world there was no open-arm sanctuary where this seahawk could rest and repair after her fierce hit-and-run swoops on America's carrying trade.

The commander of a Confederate cruiser must combine recklessness and resource, tinctured with caution. Lesser men broke under the strain of the chase, the unending battle with the elements themselves. It was a killing pace for man and ship. Yet the service had its lure, and it produced the two most accomplished sea-raiders the world has ever known, Raphael Semmes and John Newland Maffitt.

Homeless, the Confederate cruiser was compelled to be self-supporting unless she could live on her prizes. This was uncertain, though feasible, as Raphael Semmes was at this moment proving with the *Sumter* and John Maffitt was to demonstrate with the *Florida*. Nowhere could these lone rangers re-supply their wastage of offense or defense. The Stars and Bars was tolerated, but never recognized as the flag of an independent nation. The shadow of internment hung over them in every neutral port they entered.

American consuls the world over were their sharp-eyed, tireless enemies. The moment a Confederate cruiser appeared out of the blue the alarm was relayed to every nearby Union warship, while the Consul himself began throwing up every diplomatic roadblock conceivable. Only by England and France were these gray wayfarers accorded fair and courteous treatment, and even this source of succor was to dry up. Yet in their distant colonies, the enforcement of neutral restrictions depended largely on the individual sympathy or hostility of the local governor, or the amount of influence the American consul could bring to bear. Partiality or excessive hospitality could lead to gunfire repercussions, though in every port where they called, Confederate sympathizers were seemingly legion.

Less powerful nations shrank from hurting the feelings of the Northern giant whose expanding naval might thundered across the distant waterways of the world. Fear of Union gunboats and pressure by American consuls produced a one-sided neutrality that denied Confederate raiders the staff of life while often, at literal gunpoint, gave aid and comfort to Northern warships. Even far-off China outlawed Southern commerce destroyers in her ports. No country was so restrictive or exacting as Great Britain, though her colonial officials, taking their cue from London's high-level partiality, often shut their eyes to Confederate violations of neutrality, or found other means to circumvent the proclamation of their gracious Queen. Delusive, indeed, were the belligerent rights accorded the Confederacy.

A Confederate raider could never replenish her magazine if her powder went foul, as did the *Alabama's*. Roving up and down the latitudes made for fast climatic changes which were deadly to the vigor of black powder. Nor could she, in neutral ports, recruit or reinforce her crew, if decimated by disease or desertion; nor could her armament be increased or changed. Even so, resourceful Semmes and Maffitt found ways to surmount these barriers.

Thwarted and pinioned the world over, the cruisers that sailed away from Britian hung up glowing records. Their bonfires reddened the seven seas. They penned up American ships in ports the world over while, at the same time, driving hundreds to foreign registry. Even the tiny *Sumter* cut deep into American trade. Apparently these rovers had charmed lives. The Union Navy seemed utterly incapable of running them down. No less than one hundred and fifty Federal warships hotfooted futilely after the *Alabama*, *Florida*, *Shenandoah*, and the armed tenders for which they set the pattern.

Had the Confederacy been able to muster a score of these torch-bearing raiders, the war's outcome might have been different, but this was another of the imponderable "ifs" of the struggle.

No Confederate raider was ever captured at sea. Only by a gross violation of Brazil's neutrality was the *Florida* (originally the

Oreto) taken. By night, the Federal *Wachusett* invaded Bahia's neutral harbor, rammed the *Florida*, seized her, and hustled her northward to Hampton Roads. Had this occurred in a port of an English possession, the Queen's Navy would have exacted swift retribution. Brazil had to swallow it: she had no navy. It was the old story of might making right. Even so, the United States ate huge chunks of crow pie.

The Confederate Navy was always a fledgling, and never really took wing. Its achievements are imbedded in the Official Records published by the government in 1893. It should be recalled that no fighting ship built within the confines of the Confederacy ever reached the high seas. The *Merrimack* never ventured outside the Virginia capes. She reached the end of her tether on the mudflats of the nearby James. To the cruisers hatched in England—and the converted *Sumter*—belonged the chief glory achieved by the Confederate Navy. Nor could defeat ever erase it.

CHAPTER X

The Falcon Takes Wing

THE *Oreto* was off on the first lap of her safari, and James Bulloch was never to see her again. Down the Mersey she streaked, her Union Jack snapping in the breeze. The day was March 22, 1862. No *ruse de guerre* masked her getaway. She sailed off in broad daylight as bevies of faithful British well-wishers lined the dockside to wave her bon voyage with Confederate flags.

Keeping a sharp lookout for Federal dogs of war, she arched her head southabout into the Irish Sea. Once clear of St. George's Channel, her long bowsprit veered south by west, not for Palermo, Italy, by way of Gibraltar (her mythical destination), but for Nassau in the Bahamas, forty-eight hours' steaming from the land whose flag she would eventually fly. Soon she was rising and dipping over the long, blue Atlantic rollers.

As guileless as the sunshine that gleamed on her newness, as bellicose as the gulls that screamed for scraps from her galley, as trim and eye-catching as anything afloat, her name belied her beauty.

Yet, she must contrive to play her bogus role of British merchantman. On her bridge stood Captain James Duguid, a silent, trustworthy Scotch master, as sturdy as the Grampian Hills. Bulloch had engaged him—no questions asked—to take her to a port in the Mediterranean, or to the West Indies. Not until moments before she weighed anchor did Bulloch instruct Captain Duguid to proceed direct to Nassau. But the American legation at London, and Consul Dudley at Liverpool, had taken the Palermo bait. Off dashed the *Ino*, a converted war clipper, to the Italian port as fast as the winds could carry her. Alerting telegrams clicked out to "any American ship" at Marseilles, Naples, Palermo, and other Mediterranean ports. The *Oreto* has gone to sea! Waylay her as she passes Gibraltar! It looked easy. The *Tuscarora* and *Kearsarge* were still hovering off the rocky fortress, blockading the wornout *Sumter*, which was about to fall apart. The *Oreto* would get a hot welcome, *if* she came that way.

Of the *Oreto's* crew, half of whom could only make their mark on the shipping articles, not one knew her actual destination. The ship was consigned to Henry Adderly & Company, the Nassau arm of the ubiquitous Fraser, Trenholm fiscal emporium. Not without a Confederate naval officer aboard did the *Oreto* say farewell to Britain. To that duty Bulloch entrusted Master John Low, who had recently transferred his British nationality to that of Georgia. Now, by a bit of sleight of hand, he was a warrant officer in the South's navy. Raphael Semmes was to find out—as had Bulloch— that Low was a "very trusty and prudent officer" and a splendid navigator. Low was the man in authority aboard the *Oreto*.

In his pocket was a letter from James Bulloch to "Captain" John Maffitt:

> Day after tomorrow I despatch for Nassau a gun-vessel built in England under contract with me for the Confederate Navy. In all sailing and steaming equipment she is very complete, but I have been forced to dispense with all outfit suited to her true character. It has been only with much difficulty, and only by the most cautious management, that she has escaped seizure or infinite detention here, and I send her as she is, the first regularly built war-vessel for your navy, to your care. Mr. Low goes in her to place her in the hands of any Confederate officer who may be in the West Indies on her arrival. I hope it may fall to your lot to command her, for I know of no officer whose tact and management could so well overcome the difficulties of equipping her, or who could make better use of her in cruising order.
>
> I have sent out four 7-inch rifled guns in the steam ship Bahama, with all necessary equipments.
>
> Another ship will be ready in about two months, and I will take

the sea in her myself by some means or other, although I perceive many difficulties looking in the future.

Write me as soon as you receive this, and give me full information of the state of affairs on the other side of the Atlantic, and if you get to sea in the cruiser I send out, appoint a rendezvous.

To Secretary Mallory, by the same emissary, Bulloch wrote:

Registered as an English ship, in the name of an Englishman, commanded by an Englishman, with a regular official number, and her tonnage marked upon the combings of the main hatch, under the direction of the Board of Trade, she seems perfectly secure against capture, or even interference, until an attempt is made to arm her, or to change the flag and this, it appears to me now, can only be effected at sea.

Bulloch said nothing of the diplomatic fireworks that crackled before the *Oreto* gathered up her petticoats and swept out of the Mersey. Consul Dudley was frantic. For weeks he had kept tabs on the ship 'round the clock. Daily he stirred the boiling diplomatic caldron with notes to Minister Adams at London about "conniving British officials" who refused to see the warlike complexion and intentions of the *Oreto*.

In turn, Adams shot protests to Lord Russell. Wrote Adams: "My Lord: It is no part of my intention to imply want of fidelity and good will in any quarter." Oh, no! Russell knew as well as did Adams that the *Oreto* had one purpose: to be armed as fast as the Almighty would permit and to set fire to as many American ships as she could run down.

But Lord Russell knew something further. The American Minister was asking John Bull to halt what the United States had already explored: building warships in the extensive yards of Great Britain. America's own precedent inveighed against her protestations. The right of a neutral to sell unarmed ships to a belligerent was established by international law. The pot was calling the kettle black. Adams would prevail a year later, but then only by threat of war; and his lordship would reluctantly cave in. But now Russell let Adams fulminate, and riposted with a masterpiece that temporarily took the sting out of Adams' challenges:

The charge that nearly all the assistance now obtained from abroad by the persons still in arms against the government of the United States, and which enables them to continue the struggle, comes from Great Britain and its dependencies, is somewhat vague. I believe the greater part of the arms and ammunitions sent from this country to America during the struggle has gone to the United States.

You have not yourself hitherto furnished me with evidence that any vessel has received a hostile or warlike equipment in British waters, which has been afterward used against the United States. If by cooperation with the policy of the United States is meant either taking part in the civil war still raging, or imposing restraints on the Queen's subjects unknown to international law, I cannot undertake that Her Majesty's government will adopt either of those courses. It would be an unheard of measure to prohibit merchants from sending ships to sea destined for southern ports.

In other words, James Bulloch could build all the merchant ships he could pay for. Russell was right. Bulloch had hewed to the line. During these diplomatic barrages Bulloch lay low. His inviolable rule was to take no part in petty squabbles with British officials. His task—while the United States and Britain bickered over the fine points of neutrality—was to get the *Oreto* to sea as fast as one-eye-shut Foreign Office inspectors would permit. The *Oreto* was his first-born, as dear to his heart as the *Enrica* (*Alabama*) soon would be. Bulloch had even bigger prospects—two ironclads already on the Laird drawing boards, and a finer, faster cruiser now in the Laird graving dock. Not once did this man ever show his hand or raise his voice officially. The Confederacy's ashes were twenty years cold before he unfolded the saga of his stupendous role in the Sixties as secret naval agent for the Confederate government.

Yet, reasoned Bulloch, it was easily possible that the Dudley-to-Adams-to-Russell tattoo on the Foreign Secretary's door might irritate his lordship to the point of seizing the vessel as a violator of the Foreign Enlistment Act, if only to get rid of the distasteful Yankee clamor on his threshold.

Even so, the *Oreto* did not make her adieu without a send-off by her accomplices, or at least a few libations poured for the success of her odyssey. The wardroom was packed the evening before she sailed, but the windows and ports were battened. Not a flicker of light showed outside. Decanters aglow with rare vintages gleamed on a long mahogany table. Round went the toast. "Success to the *Oreto!* May she be successful in defeating her enemies!" No one identified her enemies. No one intimated that she was a man-of-war in embryo, yet everyone knew that down below were specially built rooms that would soon be marked "Magazine," "Gunroom," and "Shellroom." Gunports she had, too, though closed, and other appurtenances of an armed cruiser. She lacked only her shooting irons.

At this very hour, out of West Hartlepool, on Scotland's North Sea coast, the freighter *Bahama* was churning seaward, laden with guns for the *Oreto* and the fare they would need to play her game of hide-and-seek and incineration. Her clearance for Hamburg was fake. Obviously, Bulloch had not let his right hand at Liverpool know what his left was doing on the coast of the "land o' the leal."

2

On April 28 the *Oreto's* mudhook rattled to the bottom of Cochrane's Anchorage, nine miles east of Nassau, where her position immediately became precarious. On the evening of May 4, Master John Low knocked on the door of a quiet room in the Royal Victoria Hotel and handed Lieutenant John Maffitt the letter from Bulloch requesting him to assume command of the *Oreto* at once and hustle her to sea before the colonial government became too greatly exercised as to her character and ultimate occupation. Thus began the saga of John Maffitt and the *Florida*, the ship whose name he was to make famous. Maffitt had arrived that same day on the Nassau, having run the blockade with eight hundred bales of cotton and a passenger list that included his own daughter, Florie.

Carefully, Maffitt perused Bulloch's letter. Then, as he confided to his Journal, "Fully appreciating the necessity for prompt action I immediately surrendered the blockade runner I commanded and informed Adderly & Company to whom the *Oreto* was consigned that, as a Southern officer, it was my duty to become custodian of the lone Confederate waif upon the waters until the pleasure of the Navy Department should be expressed."

To Mallory, Maffitt wrote, "I have personally assumed command of the *Manassas* (the *Oreto's* second name); and my whole soul will be devoted to giving *éclat* to our cause and annoyance to our enemies. My difficulties are great, my ambition greater."

From Mallory came what Maffitt called a "complacent order to equip, fit out, and proceed on a cruise of aggression, as though a navy yard and enlisting rendezvous were at my disposal, clearly indicating that the Navy Department had failed to properly consider the very many obstacles and difficulties that surrounded me at Nassau—the stringent Foreign Enlistment Act, with its penal enactments (not to mention Federal detective espionage), the want of officers, men and money—all these hampers to my proceedings were constantly springing up from ambush like the armed men of Roderic Dhu."

On the afternoon of May 6, Maffitt went aboard the *Oreto* for the first time. His emotions ran deep. Fine, shapely ships lay close to his heart, and the *Oreto* won him completely the moment his eye fell on her. Infinitely proud, he inspected her from stem to stern.

"James Bulloch had not exaggerated her beauty," he admitted, "and she caught my heart and eye the instant I saw her." After the cramped quarters of the *Cecile* and *Nassau*, with tiers of cotton bales usurping every spare inch of the deck fore and aft, permitting only a runway to his captain's cubicle, John Maffitt reveled in the spacious stern cabin where he was to spend so many watchful hours by day and restless ones by night. Men have loved their ships from time immemorial. So it was with John Maffitt and the *Oreto*. So it would be with Raphael Semmes and the *Alabama*.

Yet caution was essential. At Nassau Maffitt enjoyed a breath-taking rating as the man who could out-phantom the phantoms on the blockade. This ability had elevated him to the seventh heaven of admiration. Had he, a Confederate naval officer, been too outspoken, it might have been prima-facie evidence of the *Oreto's* mission in life. Yet he was determined "faithfully to guard the interests of the Confederacy in this its first constructed bantling of the billows."

His request for officers brought three inexperienced young gentlemen, one of whom had never seen the ocean until he crossed to Nassau to join Maffitt. Yet this newcomer, Midshipman Sinclair, was to prove both capable and resourceful. One arrival was a host unto himself, Lieutenant John M. Stribling, who had served on

the *Sumter* with Semmes and was en route to his home in South
Carolina to rejoin his bride. Hearing of Maffitt's dilemma, he
promptly volunteered his services, which were joyfully accepted. To
the rocklike character of the "chivalric Stribling," Raphael Semmes
had paid high tribute. Welcome, too, was John Maffitt's stepson,
Lieutenant J. Laurens Read, a fine-eyed youth eager for adventure.

Nassau, like most of her Majesty's possessions in the western
world, was Confederate to the core. Valiantly did American Consul Samuel Whiting seek to stem the tide, but he might as well
have asked the flying fish to stop frolicking on the iridescent waters
surrounding the islands.

Whiting wrote plaintively to Secretary of State Seward:

> Myself and wife have been socially isolated on account of our
> Union sentiments. Scarce a day passes here without our receiving
> some insult. "There goes Abe Lincoln's spy!" has been shouted
> as we drove along the public thoroughfares while a night prom-
> enade is attended with personal risk. Men in uniform of the
> West India regiment, and sailors clad in navy dress, pass my
> office, uttering anathemas upon my flag; and not long since
> while I was absent from my office, the master of a schooner con-
> signed to Adderly & Company, regardless of the protestations of
> my servant, went to my balcony and was unloosening my ensign
> halyards, for the purpose of hoisting the secession flag, when I
> arrived and prevented the indignity.

Scenting game afar, and intent on boxing up the *Oreto*, Federal
warships began pacing back and forth in the offing beyond the
marine league. "Some twelve Union men-of-war are waiting outside for me," postscripted Maffitt to the Navy Department, though
this complication did not seem to daunt him. To set the trap more
securely, the Union *Adirondack* steamed in and anchored while her
commander went ashore for a huddle with Consul Whiting. Signals and warning were arranged between them. The Consul's eaves-
droppers would keep tabs on the *Oreto*. Industriously, they drove
nails into what they believed might be the *Oreto's* coffin.

In reporting his visit to Secretary Welles, the outraged naval officer took a fling at the island's Confederate proclivities:

> Nassau is in sympathy with the rebels. As we passed to our
> anchorage Dixie was played for our benefit; when we walked on
> the streets we heard the term Yankee and occasionally a more

impudent blackguard would, as we passed, hurrah in our ears for Jeff Davis. The warehouses of the town, and very many private houses, are stored to the full with arms and munitions of war, notoriously intended for the South. In the daytime, at all hours, without pretense or concealment, boxes of arms and munitions, cannon and ammunition, marked in large capitals C. S. A. are dragged through the streets to be shipped on vessels going to Wilmington, Charleston and other Southern ports.

Commander Guert Gansevoort had stated the truth only mildly. Overnight, Nassau had spread-eagled into a vast entrepôt of prohibited get-rich-quick trade with the South. Until the first shell splattered over Fort Sumter on April 12, Nassau's population had extracted a sparse livelihood from sponges, green turtles, conch shells, coral knickknacks, and salvaging vessels stabbed to death on uncharted coral reefs. Nassau was not then the seagirt, air-conditioned arcadia of fashion it is now, or rather, as it is painted by the gentlemen of Madison Avenue. Maffitt expressed the contemporary feeling aptly: "A summer in Nassau is no paradise."

Yet hardly was the ink dry on President Lincoln's blockade proclamation before Nassau's Gold Rush set in. Beyond the dreams of Croesus were the rewards of those who succeeded at the hazardous business of breaching the undermanned, and as-yet unskilled, cordons roping off Southern ports from intercourse with the world. From England, France, and even Greece came bulky freighters crammed with everything conceivable to fight a war with. In Nassau's neutral harbor they discharged their cargoes into the holds of swift, low-slung, flat-chested blockade runners. Steaming distance to Charleston was 515 miles; to Wilmington, 570. Fast runners could make either port in about forty-eight hours.

Nassau's wharves groaned under chests of medicines, mounds of cannon, barrels of gunpowder, pyramiding cases of fine wines, stacks of coffin-shaped boxes filled with rifles—all bound for the Confederacy. It was the end of the rainbow for speculators, gamblers, pilots who got five thousand dollars per round trip into a Confederate port, sea captains of a dozen nationalities, British naval officers, soldiers of fortune, officers in blue and in gray brawling occasionally on the streets, prostitutes speaking every language under the sun—one and all lured by the hope of quick money. In the van marched Yankees, Connecticut and otherwise, hoping to turn a disloyal penny by feeding to the Confederacy what it hungered for. It didn't make sense, but it did make money.

Home base of the golden tide at Nassau was a delightful hostelry, the Royal Victoria Hotel. In its bar absorbing oceans of rum swizzles, on its thousand-foot piazza, in its packed lobby, in its vast dining room that boasted the most costly food in the world, one could observe the motleyest collection of individuals ever to come together this side of the Atlantic.

On the evening of May 6, 1862—so ran Consul Whiting's report to the State Department—a spectacular drama entitled "The Fall of Fort Sumter" was performed at the Queen's Theatre in Nassau. It was a smash hit. The climactic scene, depicting the shooting down of the Stars and Stripes, was cheered to the rafters.

This one-sided divertissement was the last straw of indignity for Whiting. He had sizzled ever since the *Oreto* dropped anchor two days earlier. Even while he still smarted under this affront, the sea-weary *Bahama* straggled into the harbor laden with the guns and other indispensables to set up the *Oreto* in the commerce-raiding business. Whiting promptly protested to his Excellency, C. J. Bayley, Royal Governor of the Bahamas, that the steamer *Oreto* "is being prepared and fitted out as a Confederate privateer, to prey on the commerce of the North."

The governor was impressed. At least, he gave that appearance. He ordered officers of the Royal Navy's *Bulldog* to seize the *Oreto* as a lawful prize for infringing the Queen's neutrality proclamation, but the Crown's attorney promptly released her. Two days later the ship was re-seized, and again reprieved. It was farcical, most likely an attempt to keep clear his own skirts and to silence the outcries of the American Consul.

Refusing to be squelched, Whiting raised his official gun again:

I solemnly appeal to your excellency, by the blood of my countrymen, daily wasted in the strife with the foul rebellion, not to grant immunity to those who seek, for base and selfish purposes, to prolong this fearful fratricidal war. If this vessel, the *Oreto*, is permitted to go forth upon her mad career of destruction, I cannot but believe that the colonial government will be held responsible in the eyes of the civilized world for a repetition of those piratical acts which have covered the names of the *Sumter* and her crew with merited obloquy for all future time.

Accompanying this blast was an affidavit Whiting had wheedled out of the *Oreto's* ex-Third Officer, Edward Jones, now confined in the Nassau jail for not fulfilling the articles he had signed.

Attested Jones, truthfully, "The ship *Oreto* is the model of an English gunboat, with magazines, shotlockers, ports and bolts for twenty guns. Everything is rigged and ready for mounting, with all the necessary articles for seamen, with three years' stores of provisions. In short she is a perfect man-of-war."

Maffitt decribed Jones as a "low, dirty Liverpool dockrat," but, even so, the fat was afire. The *Oreto* became a storm center. Recanting his first lame rebuttal that Crown officials had detected no intention on the part of the owners of the *Oreto* to arm her, Governor Bayley ordered the Crown's attorney to libel the ship and hail her before the Queen's Prize Court for possible seizure as a violator of the Foreign Enlistment Act. It looked like a genuine threat to the *Oreto's* future. It meant frustration and delay for Maffitt. Until now, he had hardly shown his hand. Nor did he attend the trial before the prize court. Officers of her Majesty's ship *Greyhound*, who had inspected the *Oreto*, testified what was quite manifest, that she was in all respects adaptable to war purposes, though unarmed and weaponless. The *Greyhound's* Captain Hinckley insisted, "The *Oreto*, as she now stands, in my professional opinion, with her crew, guns, arms and ammunition, could in twenty-four hours be equipped for battle."

Hinckley was right. Admiral Porter labeled the trial a farce. There was no pro-Confederate, or rather pro-*Oreto*, testimony. Yet had a cloud of witnesses corroborated the captain of the *Greyhound*, it could not have altered the outcome. The learned Justice Lees, taking refuge in the fact that the Liverpool authorities had permitted the vessel to sail, decided that "the evidence connecting the *Oreto* with the Confederate States of America as a vessel to be used in their service to cruise against the United States, was but slight." Most amazing was his conclusion, "Had there been a Confederate flag on board the *Oreto*, I should not consider it as very powerful evidence." Refusing to condemn her, he ordered her released. The packed courtroom cheered loudly.

Disgusted, Consul Whiting expostulated to Secretary Seward, "A person landing at Nassau, ignorant of the facts, would certainly think this was England's war."

John Maffitt had on August 1 briefed Secretary Mallory: "The case of the *Oreto* will be decided tomorrow, I hope. It is believed she will be liberated. In which event I shall depart for a certain place of rendezvous where a steamer will join me with armament and fittings. The difficulties are very great. Some twelve men-of-war are on the lookout. Seamen, firemen, and engineers are hard to obtain. The *Oreto* has never been in my possession for one moment."

It was noon, August 7. The falcon was free, the hood stripped from her eyes. At four o'clock John Maffitt went aboard the *Oreto*. As if to defy the decree of the "Sovereign Queen's Court of the Bahamas," the Union sloop of war *R. R. Cuyler* chose this hour to sail into the anchorage. With gunports open and guns run out, she pirouetted before the *Oreto* as if to ram her or blow her to splinters with a broadside. Maffitt and his men could only watch. Any moment they might be snuffed out like sitting ducks on a rail. Had not the British gunboat *Petrel* hustled over to investigate the warlike intrusion and order the *Cuyler* to leave the harbor, it is conceivable that blood would have splashed the *Oreto's* deck. Overzealous Union captains, who interpreted international law pretty much to suit themselves, were talking of ramming her no matter where they found her, even in a neutral British harbor.

Opening his sea orders Maffitt read:

You will cruise at discretion, the department being unwilling to circumscribe your movements in this regard by specific instructions. Should your judgment at any time hesitate in seeking the solution of any doubt on that point, it may be guided by the reflection that you are to do the enemy's commerce the greatest injury in the shortest time. The strictest regards for the rights of neutrals cannot be too sedulously observed, nor should an opportunity be lost of cultivating friendly relations with their naval and merchant service, and placing the true character of the contest in which we are engaged in its proper light.

3

Into this war-happy bazaar in the Bahamas in early June steamed the British liner *Melita*, twenty days out of Liverpool, to wind her way through the matting of blockade runners and freighters swapping cargoes—bales of cotton to be relayed to England, mountains of munitions to run the gantlet into the Confederacy.

Adorning the Melita's passenger list was the redoubtable sea-raider with the magnificent mustachios, Raphael Semmes, captain of the Sumter, who had captured not only eighteen Northern ships (most of which he burned), but world headlines as well.

Consul Whiting promptly notified Washington of the arrival of this distinguished "freebooter" whom Gideon Welles had vowed to hang from his own yardarm. "Among the Melita's passengers are Semmes, captain of the pirate Sumter, and his officers, who are now the lions at the Royal Victoria Hotel." Whiting guessed wrongly that Semmes had come to take command of the Oreto. So well had Maffitt veiled his intended role in this game of international hocus-pocus that no one had suspected he would preside over the Oreto's bridge, when and if she managed to free herself from the reels of red tape in which she was entangled.

The extensive Confederate "household" at the Royal Victoria promptly went into a dither. With two such "lions" as Semmes and Maffitt, there was a chorus of Oh-ing and Ah-ing from the ladies, hero-worship from scores of lesser naval and military lights in gray, and even from those in blue, who feasted their eyes on the audacious pair. Yes, they walked in glory—Semmes, who had strewn the Atlantic with charred Northern hulks; and Maffitt, master blockade runner, who could slip through the tentacles of the Union octopus as if they were cotton skeins.

In a room looking seaward from the Royal Victoria, Semmes and Maffitt, friends and messmates in the old navy, met again with a long handclasp. It was June 15, 1862—an exquisite day. But there were no formalities. It was "Raphael" and "John"—and mutual admiration. Homebound, Semmes said he planned to go to Richmond and seek a new command. He then informed Maffitt that Bulloch expected any day to get to sea with the second "merchantman" and would keep his rendezvous with Maffitt and the Florida off the Atlantic coast. Semmes transmitted to Maffitt the position and tentative date for this "conclave." Together they would rake American commerce.

As with Bulloch, who had offered to step out of the picture and let Semmes command the Alabama, John Maffitt proffered command of the Oreto to the luster-laden sea-raider. He was refused. It was Maffitt's turn. Semmes had had his. Besides, the Navy Department moved the pawns.

What did these companions-in-arms talk about? What else could they talk about? War, and how to bring it home to the North on the high seas. It was their first and only meeting during the war— their last this side of Valhalla. They were to have much in common. Their names would be bracketed by the Federals as the vilest pair of pirates ever to disgrace the waters of the world. Fervently would Northern ministers exhort their flocks to beseech the Almighty to rid civilization of the two "sea-beasts," personified in the captains of the *Alabama* and the *Florida.*

Now, as they sat quietly chatting over a bottle of champagne, a knock on the door brought another of the amazing coincidences in the career of John Maffitt. A letter was handed in for "Captain Raphael Semmes" in his care. Just arrived by blockade runner, it bore the imprint "C. S. N., Richmond, Virginia." Handing it to Semmes, Maffitt waited. It contained the orders that dispatched Semmes on the most destructive sea-mission of all time. James Bulloch was not, after all, to take command of the ship ready to take flight from the Laird yards at Liverpool. That assignment had been given to Semmes. The ironclad project, so precious to Secretary Mallory, was too vital to the Confederacy's existence. Bulloch must remain in England and get them to sea.

In his Journal Maffitt wrote, not without pride in having played even so small a part, "I handed Captain Semmes his orders to return to England and take command of the *Alabama.* . . ." But that's another story.

Yet, raconteur that he was, Semmes left a memoir of the enjoyable interlude at Nassau, between commands, and of his meeting with Maffitt, the man whom Admiral Porter crowned as the politest, most efficient of gentleman pirates:

Maffitt knew everybody, and everybody knew him, and he passed in and out of all the rooms, *sans cérémonie* at all hours. Being a jaunty, handsome fellow, young enough in appearance to pass for the elder brother of his son, a midshipman who was to go with me on the *Alabama,* he was a great favorite with the ladies. He was equally at home, with men or women, it being all the same to him, whether he was wanted to play a game of billiards, or take a hand at whist, or join in a duet with a young lady—except that he had the good taste always to prefer the lady. Social, gay, and convivial, he was much courted and flattered, and there was scarcely ever a dining or an evening party, at which he was not present.

But this was the mere outside glitter of the metal. Beneath all this *bagatelle* and *dolce far niente* Maffitt was a remarkable man. He was a perfect master of his profession, not only in its practical, but in its more scientific branches, and could handle his ship like a toy. Brave, cool, full of resource, he was equal to any and every emergency that could present itself in a sailor's life.

4

Maffitt was afloat, but his fledgling had no crew. To cope with this dilemma he had dredged up from the floating supply along the waterfront five firemen and fourteen deck hands. These were far from enough to work the ship, let alone to fight a battery. The Foreign Enlistment Act tabooed recruiting in her Majesty's colonies. The *Oreto's* normal complement was one hundred and thirty. Vanished with their gear and advance wages were the fourscore tars whom Bulloch had enticed to man the "British merchantman" from Liverpool across to Nassau. Maffitt decided to trust to recruiting a crew from disaffected volunteers on the prizes he captured.

Admiral Porter charged that the men Maffitt induced to enlist knew they were to embark on a "piracy cruise." Porter harped on the piracy theme: "But for English sailors to ship in an English port, on board a Confederate cruiser, to assist in burning or sinking American vessels, they considered to be merely exercise of belligerent rights." Had not England granted belligerent rights to the Confederacy?

The *Oreto's* clearance papers were filled out "Destination St. John's or any Confederate port . . . Captain, J. Laurens Read" (Maffitt's stepson).

That night the *Oreto* wriggled through the network of Federal cruisers watchdogging for her in the bright moonlight. Maffitt possessed an uncanny genius for scuttling through Union blockades. The *Adirondack* and *Cuyler* were both prowling outside the lower anchorage. Consul Whiting had chartered a tugboat to speed out and inform their captains the *Oreto* had been released by the Admiralty court. John Maffitt, arch blockade runner, had taken command of her. He would probably steal out that night. Whiting further urged them to keep a sharp lookout for a schooner named *Prince Alfred*, though he was unable to pinpoint her connection with the *Oreto*. Without a peer at this business of dematerializing in the very clutches of Union warships (save it be Raphael Semmes) Maffitt weighed anchor at midnight. Shadowed by the land, the *Oreto* sped southward for a desolate islet, Green Key, ninety miles from New Providence on the edge of the Great Bahama Bank, where she would anchor within the marine league, in British waters. In her wake plowed the *Prince Alfred*, her deck piled helter-skelter with the *Oreto's* guns, ammunition, armament, and supplies, hastily transshipped from the *Bahama*, which was already suspect, thanks to Consul Whiting's efficient private-eyes. This was no time to commit any overt violation of Nassau's neutrality. The *Oreto* had just escaped confiscation by grace of prejudiced officials, dazzled by anything in gray.

With Lieutenant John Stribling commanding, the *Prince Alfred* had proceeded to sea, as if for the purpose of running the blockade, only to veer southward. At daylight the *Oreto* fell in with the windjammer and took her in tow. That afternoon the *Prince Alfred* anchored alongside the *Oreto* off Green Key, a strip of coral whose white beach gleamed like pearl in the sunshine. Knowing the Bahamas like the pages of an oft-read book, Maffitt had mentally spotted this off-the-beaten-track hideaway where he could complete the arming of his defenseless, and almost crewless, ship. The odds were good against enemy cruisers intruding, provided she did not take too long. Eight fathoms below the blue waters, fascinating coral gardens gleamed like imprisoned rainbows, but Maffitt had not come to feast his eyes on submarine landscapes.

An ominous, undated entry in Maffitt's Journal reads:

About the 20th of July yellow fever in its worst form became an epidemic in Nassau. The first victim was my young friend, Lieutenant Brown of the Fourth West India Regiment; as high-toned a little gentleman as ever lived. Other friends fell victims to this dread disease. As a nurse my services were constantly required at the hotel. The cases were generally fatal.

CHAPTER XI

"I Haven't Time to Die"

CONVERTING THE Oreto from the arts of peace to the business of war; transshipping and mounting guns and their carriages weighing several thousand pounds each; teetering netloads of shell, shot, and gunpowder from the Prince Alfred's to the Oreto's decks; stowing barrels of salt pork and beef, boxes and bales, boatswain's stores—these were giant tasks. Stripped to the buff, officers and men fell to, straining every muscle, under a tropical sun that blistered and burned. Feelingly, Maffitt recorded, "An August sun in the tropics is no small matter to work in." He himself took a haul at the stay tackles hoisting the heavy guns. It was the most exhausting task of his life.

But the sea was calm. Hardly a ripple ruffled the surface. In the same space of time it took the Almighty to create the heavens, the earth, and all therein, six days, John Maffitt and his paltry crew completed the ponderous drudgery that readied the Oreto for overseas flight. On the seventh day, they rested from sheer prostration. Her bunkers were replenished with the best smokeless Cardiff coal. The chaotic disarray that littered her decks had vanished into appointed niches. Maffitt had a passion for a clean, sweet ship. The coating of grime that had soiled her in her Majesty's custody was peeled off, scrubbed, and holystoned. The prize crew had committed many acts of robbery and left the vessel in a sad plight, dirty and disreputable. Her taut rigging now gleamed; her brass-work shone; her yards were squared; and Maffitt's pride in her knew no bounds.

Even so, it seemed as if the gods themselves were conspiring against his ship. On the evening of the second day of toil the wardroom steward sickened. In eight hours, he had, as Maffitt told it, "slipped his mortal cable." Maffitt attributed the man's death to the severity of labor in excessive heat after indulging too freely in the allurements of Nassau, though the yellow appearance of the corpse gave him misgivings. The dread symptoms were unmistakable. He knew them of old. A boat's crew carried the body ashore that same night and dug a grave on the lone rocky islet. Lieutenant Stribling read the burial service, a sad duty that foreshadowed a similar one over Stribling himself within a month. But John Maffitt kept his suspicions to himself.

The guns had been mounted first: two seven-inch rifled pivots and a six-gun battery of six-inchers. The ship must be able to defend herself. The Yankee bloodhounds he had eluded at Nassau were, he knew, combing the Bahamas. One snooping warship could cut short the *Oreto's* career in a twinkle with a single broadside. The *Oreto* rested at the moment on British waters, to be sure, but who cared at this distance from Nassau? The *Oreto* would be at the bottom and her crew most likely with her. Maffitt himself traced out the pivot guns' circles on the scorching deck. Yet hardly was the battery in place before he heard a cry of despair from Lieutenant Stribling.

"What's the matter now?" asked Maffitt.

"Captain, we're ruined," moaned the young officer. "In the hurry and secrecy of loading the schooner, the rammers, sponges, sights, locks, and quoins were left on the *Bahama* at Nassau. The battery, sir, is useless. We couldn't shoot if we had to."

At any rate, the pivot guns were complete. Still, there was no way to fire them. Casting off from the *Prince Alfred* (which stood away for Nassau), the *Oreto* ran down into the Queen's Channel, struck the Union Jack, and with loyal but thinnish cheers flung the Confederate banner to the breeze. Maffitt then bestowed on the ship her new "official cognomen, *Florida*." He had planned ceremonials worthy of the occasion and mission, with salutes, his officers immaculate in new uniforms, his crew in the natty white and blue ducks Bulloch had provided, and the impressive formalities of commissioning the Confederacy's first foreign-built warship. In the event, he boiled it down to reading his commission and a few inspiring words to his handful crew.

"But Alas! poor *Florida!*" he bemoaned to his Journal. "Beautiful in model, warlike in guns, the absence of important essentials despoiled the reality, and left her afloat the mere typical representation of what a gallant cruiser should be."

This first day—August 17—of the *Florida's* openly proclaimed nationality was cloudless as a diamond. In soft, invigorating tradewinds the Southern ensign streamed out as if proud of investing this knight-errant of the sea with the emblem of the Confederate empire. By the time the shadows of night enveloped the waters, Maffitt had ingeniously brought forth on the *Florida* what he called "some tangible form of naval efficiency," even with a crew of five firemen and fourteen deckhands.

After setting the watch and fixing a southward course toward Cuba, he wearily sought his cabin, only to be aroused from uneasy dreams at daylight. Two of his crew were ill. He found them shivering, sweaty, and glassy-eyed. Black vomit flecked their lips. With no physician aboard, that duty devolved on him. The fact of being afloat "I knew would excite extraordinary expectation and to fail, under any circumstances, involved professional extinction."

In the early light he began pacing the quarter-deck, overwhelmed with despondency. His gloomy reveries were interrupted by the delirious cries of the sick men. He found them raving with fever, branded with the noisome symptoms of the yellow pestilence. "Thus were we assailed by an element of impotence more terrible to encounter than all that was endured in our past physical struggle." Admitting a "fondness for doctoring my crew," he went at it like a skilled nurse, applying, with implicit faith, the routine prescribed in the old navy. He bathed each patient's feet and back in steaming hot water, gave him a strong aperient, applied mustard plaster to his stomach, and finished off the treatment with a hot draught and swaddles of blankets to bring out the sweat. Lastly, he quarantined the sufferers under an awning on the quarter-deck.

Maffitt knew he no longer commanded his ship, for yellow jack, fearsome scourge of the tropics, was striding the quarter-deck as if determined to make a floating charnel house of the beautiful, newly-commissioned ship. In July, yellow fever had appeared at

Nassau and carried off three of his friends. He did not then know that the deadly *Aedes aegypti* was flitting about the forecastle and the cabins of his own ship. In his day, the guilt of spreading the fever was not yet fastened on the mosquito, whose sting was laden with the virus that had brought wholesale dissolution to rich and poor alike in the tropics, had decimated the ranks of the Conquistadores, had reduced many a galleon to a morgue on the waters. The Spanish had given it a grisly, repellent name, *vomito*.

All his life Maffitt had faced emergencies. This was another, more terrible than any he had met. He knew but one way to face it: head up. John Maffitt was no mean foeman, never one to cringe or draw back under fire. But now he was ringed and baited by an adversary he didn't know how to cope with. To Lieutenant Stribling alone, his Gibraltar-like right bower, did he impart the melancholy prospect. They determined to conceal, if possible, the appearance of the epidemic, in the delusive belief that these cases might prove sporadic. The trade winds freshened, and Maffitt indulged the hope that they might disinfect the *Florida* and relieve her of the disease. But "Alas! there was no balm in Gilead, at least, not for the *Florida*." By sundown half his crew and two officers were added to the sick list. No longer could the character of the affliction be concealed.

Let John Maffitt speak his own feelings:

> An epidemic on shore invariably produces a general panic. The well can obtain safety in flight, or, at least, free themselves from its constant, terrible presence. But at sea! imprisoned without the possibility of escape within the narrow confines of the vessel, there is no relief from the howls of the delirious, the death-heralding black vomit, the pinched and yellow countenances of those who have ceased to struggle and are reluctantly manipulated by their surviving shipmates as the hammock-shroud and ponderous shot are arranged for the final plunge into that ocean of rest, the seaman's uncoffined grave.

Reluctantly, Maffitt abandoned all idea of cruising for prizes. A harbor of refuge became an utter necessity. Nor could he turn back to Nassau. By now, his crew was reduced to one fireman and four deck hands; and it seemed as if one and all were slated to die. Macabre thoughts invaded his mind, harrowing tales of ships depopulated by the ferocious pestilence and left to float where they would until the waters mercifully sucked them under. Against his will, memory exhumed the ghastly story of the *Satanic*, which he first heard as a midshipman—how she had drifted into a Caribbean port with her crew of two hundred strewn in yellowed death on her deck where the vomito had left them. The Jolly Roger flew gaily at her peak, but her rails were lined with vultures.

It was August 19, and the *Florida*, off the islet of Anguilla, was absolutely helpless. The pastel shores of the Pearl of the Antilles glistened just over the southern horizon. He decided to run into Cárdenas. It was a familiar port and he had friends there. How he could evade the Union fighters only Providence knew, but somehow he eluded them and came to rest in the Cuban port at midnight, "our force having been meantime reduced by the epidemic to one fireman and two seamen!"

Forthwith, he dispatched Lieutenant Stribling to Havana to obtain medical aid and nurses, if possible, "for there were none to aid me, none to relieve me from this constant exhausting demand by the sick and dying." Stribling was at the same time to lay Maffitt's desperate plight before Governor-general Serrano, old friend and sympathizer with the South. Maffitt next petitioned the governor of Cárdenas for the services of a physician. Couching his reply in courteous but equivocal Spanish, that official asserted he had no physician to spare. Yellow fever was raging ashore also. In the same breath he reminded Maffitt of the Spanish Queen's proclamation of neutrality, enjoining him against increasing his armament or recruiting seamen, and ordering him to heave anchor and get out of the harbor within twenty-four hours. But John Maffitt had reached that bourne where the mandates of international law and the abnegations of petty officials had lost their power and meaning. He would let fate do her worst and battle with his misfortunes courageously to the bitter end. He refused to budge an inch. Meanwhile, "the sun rose and set upon the beautiful *Florida*. At her peak the Confederate flag waved in solemn dignity and no external spectator, who gazed upon her outside symmetrical appearance could for a moment fancy that burning fevers and fatal vomitos were devouring the life throbs of her scanty crew. There is a limit beyond which human ability is incapable of passing. The overwhelming duties and responsibilities that had been forced upon me had reduced me physically to that terminus of endurance."

Now he must wait and hope and nurse and watch men die. News that the *Florida* had broken cover at Cárdenas brought Union men-of-war at forced draft. Outside the port they congregated like vultures waiting for the kill. Maffitt could see them cruising back and forth beyond the marine league. God help the *Florida*! John Maffitt was not a forthright praying man, but in his cabin he fell to his knees and laid his case squarely before the Almighty. He had nowhere else to turn.

On the afternoon of August 22, Maffitt had a chill that he fancied resulted from getting wet in a thunder squall. After it passed, he began pacing the deck in gloomy reverie, interrupted now and then by the delirious cries of the sick. Presently, he went to his bunk. Needling pains were shooting up his back and loins. He had a disposition to vomit. "The painful conviction was forced upon me that I was boarded by this horrible tropical epidemic." Under the incessant bludgeoning of fate his iron constitution had caved in, leaving him a ready target for the scourge.

Knowing that fever invariably affected his brain, he summoned Acting Master Wyman and Midshipman Bryan to his cabin. To them he dictated minute directions for the care of the sick, as well as orders for the *Florida*.

"But why, Captain?" asked young Bryan, who would himself on the morrow be laid low by the yellow peril.

"Because I have every symptom of yellow fever. Broken down as I am, I doubt if I'll survive it."

Fever was already flushing Maffitt's cheeks, parching his veins. He took a warm mustard bath and went to his bunk. Maffitt's tragically picturesque description of his plight has hardly a parallel in American naval annals.

The demon of Hades tarried not long in his approach but came, and quickly, with a throbbing pulsation of the brain, accompanied with a dizzy blindness and shooting pains that produced excruciating agony, as if my bones had been converted into red hot tubes of iron, and the marrow in them boiling with fervent heat. My tongue and throat were blistered as if molten lead had been poured down into my stomach. Unquenchable thirst that nothing could alleviate was accompanied by the most violent nausea. There was no moisture in my eyes. The fountains were seared and parched, as if red hot irons had branded the well-spring of tears. Every pore of my body seemed to be hermetically sealed with a burning fever from the furnace of my heart. This was succeeded by icy chills rushing through my blood, as if swelled like a tidal wave, bursting through the meshes of my tortured brain.

At first the delirium of suffering ebbed and flowed, leaving brief periods of consciousness which, with singular determination, were employed in directing the management of my case. At last a dreary blank enveloped my mind, the vital spark flickered in its unstable tabernacle, as the battle of life was fought in painful, agonizing sufferings. Thus, in the struggle between life and death, a week elapsed.

It was dusk when Maffitt's mind became blank. Not until that moment had he lost his self-possession. While he journeyed through the dizzy montage of delirium, Death reaped his harvest— one engineer, three crewmen, and young Laurens Read, Maffitt's much-loved stepson, who had sat at his captain's bedside day and night until he himself was stricken.

Meanwhile, Lieutenant Stribling had returned from Havana accompanied by a kindly Georgia physician, a warm-hearted Irishman, Doctor Barrett, who, on hearing of the *Florida's* hapless plight, had vacated his post in the government hospital at Havana to demonstrate his devotion to the South in this hour of need. With Stribling came also fourteen deck hands.

On August 29, John Maffitt returned from the world of unreality. The cabin was flooded with sunshine. Not a word had passed his lips for three days. Black vomit was heralding his dissolution. He opened his eyes to find three sombre figures, "who to my dreaming fancy appeared like weird phantoms of the nether world," hovering over him. They were Doctor Barrett, Doctor Gilliard, a Spanish gunboat surgeon, and a third medical savant whom a friend in Cárdenas had sent aboard as a consultant. Doctor Barrett was holding his watch.

"Gentlemen," he observed sepulchrally, glancing at his timepiece, "it is now twenty minutes after nine o'clock. I am convinced, from careful investigation, that the Captain cannot survive beyond the meridian."

Just back from the world of fevered shadows and shapes was John Maffitt, but an irresistible impulse brought these words to his lips: "You're a liar, sir. I have too much to do. I haven't time to die."

The doctors smiled. One tried to be hopeful—"Captain, I think you may get well"—though the reverend medicos did not revoke their gloomy prognostications. But at that moment Maffitt's convalescence began. Maffitt's indomitable will to live had fended off the grim reaper, though he would later write in his Journal, "By the interposition of Divine Providence the messenger of death was arrested."

Next afternoon he asked to see his officers. Into the cabin they filed, three of them peaked and drawn, having paid toll at the halfway house. One was absent, his stepson, Lieutenant Laurens Read.

"Where is my beloved Laurens?" he asked weakly.

No one said anything, but their saddened countenances gave Maffitt his answer. Seized with the vomito two days before, the youth had succumbed within twenty-four hours. Already his body was resting in the Cárdenas cemetery. "This blow," says Maffitt, "came like the raven wings of fate, darkening my very soul and nearly producing a relapse."

For this young officer, Maffitt composed a sorrowful memoir: "John Laurens Read was a noble youth, a native of Charleston, South Carolina, and sixteen years of age. Well-born (Henry Laurens of Revolutionary fame being his great-grandsire), he was the possessor of all those noble characteristics of the purest blood of the most patriotic days of the country, and was much beloved by his brother officers."

Next morning a boatman handed up a telegram from Marshal Serrano, the governor-general, requesting that Maffitt steam over to Havana, where the *Florida* would be more secure under the guns of the Morro. Cárdenas was undefended and completely invested by Federal cruisers. Rumors had reached Havana that the Federals were planning a cutting out party to give the *Florida* her *coup de grâce* at her anchorage. Weak, decadent Spain might protest the violation of her neutrality, but Queen Isabella could like it or not, as she pleased. There wasn't much she could do about it. But the Federal Consul, getting wind of the move, protested against the *Florida's* sailing, as he had against giving succor to "pirate Maffitt." Weak voiced and unable to stand, Maffitt pledged not to take prizes on his way to Havana—this with the *Florida* and her crew completely helpless. When Marshal Serrano heard it, he wired, "Let her sail. The word of a Southern gentleman must be taken."

From his sickbed, Maffitt gave orders. The *Florida* would sail that night in the wake of the Spanish mail steamer. The fates were propitious. The sky was overcast when the *Florida* weighed anchor and left the harbor, "our reminiscences of the terrible sojourn being clouded with memories of our dead who slept beneath its sod." Mistaking the coaster for the *Florida*, the Federals bayed off after her with shot and shell. Running within the tabooed marine limit, Maffitt could see the flash of their guns, hear them barking across the waters as his Nemeses fanned out after the "wrong fox." Dousing all lights and keeping as close as he dared to shore, the *Florida* fled along the coast unmolested.

Next morning she anchored in Havana harbor, and was immediately ringed by small boats packed with visitors. Overjoyed Southerners by the score, residents of Havana, clamored at the gangway, their enthusiasm over the spanking-new Confederate cruiser outweighing their dread of yellow fever. Yet, the *Florida* tarried but a day. The governor-general was cordial, but surveillance was strict. The port officials didn't allow the purchase of even a single piece of timber long enough to be shaped into rammers and spongers. Refitment and reinforcement of her crew were outlawed. To be properly officered, equipped, and manned, the *Florida* must run for a Confederate port, if she could. Resolutely, Maffitt decided on Mobile. The ship's doom was sealed if he delayed. He would be forced to vacate the harbor the moment the fever had abated, or be interned. Unable to walk a step, he had himself lifted to a chair on deck in the sunshine. All day the rickety telegraph line out of Havana clicked frantic appeals from American Consul Shufeldt to ports on the island, imploring any Union warships in sight to hurry to Havana. By evening the wolf pack began thickening off the Morro, ready to sink the *Florida*.

With his crew incapable of manning her battery, or even casting loose a gun (guns which couldn't be fired, anyway), Maffitt had one recourse. He was determined she should not fall into enemy hands. He would blow her up first. If that was not feasible, he would run her aground on a reef and set her afire. Summoning Lieutenant Stribling, he ordered a fuse set to the magazine long enough, if capture loomed, to be lighted as the last man abandoned the ship. This done, he waited for night, which came down clear and moonless. Slipping his cable, he steered boldly past the Morro. Dark objects on the water revealed the Federal deathwatch waiting, guns poised, to blow the *Florida* to eternity. Doing the unexpected had paid off for Maffitt often. He was doing it again. The Official Records are singularly silent on just what happened that night aboard the Federal warships. A court of inquiry produced little more.

As she shaped her course northward across the Gulf, the Tortugas slid by off to starboard. On this broad highway Federal huntsmen swarmed like sharks. One wonders what the Federal ships were doing. Why didn't they sight the *Florida?* That was what Secretary Welles wanted to know. One could hardly blame him. The *Florida* was caged, only to vanish through the bars. But where? Old Gideon blued the air with hot cusses, threats of demotion, and hints of treason—just as when the *Sumter* had given the *Brooklyn* the slip off the Mississippi Passes. For months diplomatic and naval bigwigs had been having hysterics over the *Oreto*, now transformed into the *Florida*. It was beyond Welles's comprehension. Three times in a row she had slipped through their fingers. The jabbings of the Northern press were relentless.

CHAPTER XII

Death in the Afternoon

MARK WELL the day, September 4, 1862. Off the narrow entrance to Mobile Bay three Union blockaders were lazying about in the afternoon zephyrs that hardly riffled the gleaming sheet of the Gulf. Overhead stretched a canopy of pearl-blue. The day was radiant as spring water. Byron's "day on which Paradise was created," was not more fair. The masthead lookouts had thirty-mile visibility.

On watch off the Mobile Bay station were the new ten-gun sloop *Oneida*, whose eleven-inch iron cones possessed volcanic fury, the gunboat *Winona*, and the gun-schooner *Rachel Seaman*. A fourth member of the pack, *Cayuga*, was policing the western channel. Flagship was the *Oneida* and walking her quarter-deck was Commander George H. Preble, whose friendship with John Maffitt ran back to their reefer days aboard the *Constitution*. They had climbed the promotion rungs together until they reached the parting of the ways in 1861.

At the head of the sweeping bay lay Mobile, prime cotton port of the Deep South since the fall of New Orleans. The runway into this sheltered harbor was a hotspot over which the Western Gulf Blockading Squadron kept hawk-eyed vigil. It was their boast that not even a rowboat could squeak in or out unless she swam under water, but, even so, light-draft blockade runners made sport of the supposedly vigilant Federal seamen with face-reddening regularity. Havana was less than six hundred miles away; Matamoras even nearer.

Confederate wardens of the three-mile-wide roadstead that debouched into Mobile Bay were pentagon-shaped Fort Morgan, with a seven-hundred-man garrison, and the rather smaller Fort Gaines. These formidable bastions stood face to face, east and west, across the main channel that ran close under Fort Morgan's guns. Inside the bay, northwestward, rose Fort Powell, menacing inlets from Mississippi Sound and protecting the fairway to the city itself, thirty miles up. At the same time, these spitting dragons admonished Union blockaders to keep their distance. Occasionally they reached out a helping shot to panting inbound runners with Federal ships barking at their heels. The several channels leading up to Mobile were tortuous and shoal-ridden. Only experienced pilots could navigate them.

At 2 P.M. this September day the *Oneida* and *Winona* were slowly describing huge ellipses, one behind the other, clockwise, ten miles off the corridor to Mobile Bay. The lookouts had spotted two small steamers, apparently blockade runners, jockeying back and forth between the forts, perhaps waiting for dark to dart into the Gulf. Commander Preble was in his cabin addressing his weekly report to Flag-officer Farragut at Pensacola. It was a clean sheet. Nothing had wriggled in or out. The port of Mobile was lockboxed.

Suddenly, the *Oneida*'s lookout cried down "Sail ho! Off the starboard quarter!" A strange steamer, at first mistaken for the U.S.S. *Susquehanna*, hull-down southwestward, was standing directly and rapidly for the *Oneida*. Streamers of black smoke gushed from her twin funnels. A high press of steam feathered from her pipes. Commander Preble went on deck and scrutinized the newcomer with his glasses. Her English gunboat build and rig, her English ensign and pennant, advertised her nationality unmistakably—certainly to the satisfaction of Commander Preble, who inspected her as minutely as his telescope would permit. Wary of tampering with British ships since the *Trent* Affair had nearly involved the nation in war with John Bull, Preble was excessively cautious lest he, like Captain Wilkes, stir up another hornets' nest. The very boldness of the stranger's approach was disarming.

Intelligence of the *Florida*'s vanishing act at Nassau had reached the squadron base at Pensacola and been relayed to the cruisers, though her change of name to *Florida* and her arrival at Havana had not been passed along. The *Florida's* whereabouts at this moment was anybody's guess. Certainly there was no reason to expect her off Mobile. English warships had an annoying habit of dribbling along the coast to check the efficacy of the blockade, that is, to see if it was made of paper as Lord Russell had gleefully pronounced. Occasionally they entered blockaded ports, though not without first obtaining the sanction of the commanding blockade officers. Preble expected the supposed English gunboat now approaching to round to presently, hail him, and go through the customary formalities of requesting a pass-on.

But Preble took a chance, or, rather, he hesitated, and it was this that robbed him and his men of a possible fat bundle of prize money, and of the honor of capturing or sinking the vessel which was to destroy almost six million dollars in American shipping. He decided to let her close quarters to hailing distance before finding out what her business was. To be on the safe side, Preble sent his men to stations and signaled the *Winona* to chase at discretion.

Little did he imagine that the intrepid oncomer was the *Florida*, romping along at fourteen knots, as straight as a gun could shoot, for the entrance of Mobile Bay and the protecting umbrella of Fort Morgan's cannon.

2

For John Maffitt the three-day cruise up the Gulf from Havana was reinvigorating. The gods were on his side at last. Yellow fever was abating. Five men were still on cots under the quarter-deck awnings, but with Doctor Barrett's constant care they were convalescing fast. Since leaving Havana the *Florida* had sighted only two ships, Unioners, no doubt on the prowl for her. The *Florida* took to her pretty heels as fast as her fine new engines would let her, hugging the shore as close as she dared.

At 3 P.M. the *Florida* raised the dismantled lighthouse on Sand Island off the entrance to Mobile Bay. Between her and sanctuary lay fifteen miles of water and three Union blockaders. The Official Records vary on the exact time of the *Florida's* appearance on the scene, but the die for drama and death was cast the moment her smoke smudged the horizon.

As fate would have it, on this same day, at about the same hour, three thousand miles across the Atlantic, the *Florida's* sister ship, *Alabama,* was opening her historic cruise with a crackdown on America's whaling fleet off the Azores.

John Maffitt's sea legs were as yet unable to navigate him about the deck, though the clean, bracing Gulf air had begun its restorative wonders. To his daughter Florie he was to write, "They brought me on deck to take the ship in, though unfit for any place but a sickbed. I am still very weak and look like a poor ghost. To write this requires pillows and mental determination absolutely at war with my physical ability, but, my darling, I am determined to write home."

Yet Maffitt's mind was as clear as the day itself. Seated by the quarter rail he reconnoitred long and thoughtfully. His appraisal revealed three Union warcraft waiting to deny him entrance. He knew instinctively that they had sighted him. Lowering his glasses, he turned to Lieutenant Stribling.

"Take a look, sir, and tell what you think of our prospects."

The officer squinted hard. Stribling minced no words. "Our ship's a cripple, sir. We couldn't fight even one of them. We can't avoid passing close to them. That means certain destruction. We can't fire a gun. I suggest we haul off until dark and then try to double and get inshore of them."

Maffitt shook his head. "Our draft wouldn't permit it. We'd wind up on the shoals nosing about in the dark for the channel."

"Very possibly, sir, but," warned Stribling, "if we run in now, they'll sink us in two minutes."

But gambler Maffitt had already determined to take what Admiral Porter called his last, one-in-a-million, chance. It was either this or run the ship ashore and burn her. She was useless as she was. Capture was abhorrent to him. He had made up his mind to crash his way through the whole Western Gulf Blockading Squadron, if need be, with the odds and the cards stacked against him. There was a Nelsonesque note to his maneuver, plus a touch of suicide. One possibility of escape—but only one—favored him. The *Florida* was the exact duplicate of an English gunboat. He would impersonate an Englishman as long as he could.

He summoned the rest of his officers about him. "We'll take her in now," he said quietly. "The hazard is great, I'll admit. But it can't be avoided. Hoist English colors at once. We'll fool them as long as we can, and then run as fast as we can. Maybe they'll remember the *Trent* business and think twice before firing into what they think is a British ship. Four minutes' leeway will save us. Send every man below except the officers. Have the sick men carried to the berth deck. Now, Mr. Stribling, I'd be obliged if you'd get a piece of rope and secure me to the rail."

Next, Maffitt summoned Quartermaster Billups and Boatswain Sharkey, who stood at the wheel, tough young sea dogs ready to stand there till hell froze over or they were blasted to bits on the deck.

"Billups, Sharkey, I want you to steer for the biggest ship. Straight at her. She looks like one of the new sloops, probably a sister of the *Tuscarora*. That means ten guns, two of them eleven-inch."

"Aye, aye, sir. Straight at her like an arrow," responded young Billups with a tinge of Texas in his voice.

John Stribling returned with a piece of rope and a mild protest, "But, sir, if the ship goes down . . ."

"Then I'll go with her," jested Maffitt as the youngster bound him to the rail. Had Maffitt possessed second sight and been able to peer into the future he might have seen another sailor, blue-clad, lashed as he was to his ship, crashing into Mobile Bay.

Now to finesse herself as close as possible to the blockaders before drawing their fire. If she reached them unscathed, which meant unsunk, the *Florida* would put her trust in fortune and a clean pair of heels to give them the slip. Donning her seven-league boots, under a full head of steam, the vessel lunged boldly for the *Oneida*, closing distance fast.

The captain of the *Winona*, at the later naval inquiry, said he ranged his ship up alongside the *Florida* and hailed her "at 30 to 40 yards," receiving the reply, "Her Britannic Majesty's Steamer *Spitfire* or *Vixen*, I forget which." Thereupon, he signaled the *Oneida* a mile away that the newcomer was a friend. Of this by-play Maffitt had no knowledge or later recollection. Nor did any man on the *Florida*.

Maffitt's *ruse de guerre* was as old as naval warfare, yet it flatly deceived an able, efficient officer, who had thirty years of service to his credit. Blithely, speedily, the *Florida* bore up to less than a mile from her chief waylayer. Taken in also were the *Winona* and *Rachel Seaman*. They were hanging off to port, confident the *Oneida* would halt the "nervy Englishman." So they simply waited.

Down in the *Florida's* engine room her fever-weakened firemen forgot their recent woes and poured coal into their fireboxes. Life itself for ship and men depended on them now—and on their engines that purred like contented tigers.

Without warning, the *Oneida* suddenly veered as if to cut across the *Florida's* bow. Sheering to port, Maffitt's helmsman aimed his ship's prow directly at the *Oneida*. Barely two hundred yards separated the two ships. At this moment Commander Preble made the crucial mistake of his naval career. He reversed his engines to avoid being rammed by the "British ship." And thus he—or was it fate?—tossed Maffitt the momentary advantage he had hoped for and which he promptly seized, as a drowning man would a bunch of seaweed. Actually, Maffitt was trying desperately to pass the *Oneida* before she opened her batteries. He knew the *Florida* could outrun her. Preble was still tricked, or rather, hypnotized (there is no better word) by the English make-up. She looked too British to be anything but British. And a beauty, too, he noted. He hailed her himself, "Heave to! What ship are you?"

No answer. There was none to give now. It would have made little difference if she had. The transgressor of these tabooed waters was both closed-mouthed and audacious! Maffitt said he never heard the summons trumpeted by "the senior officer, who later proved to be my old friend and shipmate Captain Preble." He himself was gazing, entranced, into eternity, that is, into the maws of the *Oneida's* eleven-inchers, wondering, and waiting. He could see the gunners at stations. Suddenly, one of the *Oneida's* bow guns spat a spurt of flame and smoke. A shot went spinning over the *Florida's* forefoot. Still no reply. On she sped, faster if anything. A second shot, but nothing from the intruder save a welter of black smoke from her funnels.

The ships were abeam, hardly a pistol-shot apart, when the *Oneida* poured her broadside into her stark naked target. At point-blank range she couldn't miss, and didn't. The Confederate vessel staggered as the hot blast swept over her, smashing her boats, cutting away her hammock nettings and much of her rigging, tearing at her woodwork like invisible iron claws. Splinters and spars crashed on deck. In a moment she was despoiled of her symmetrical beauty. Fast and certain dissolution loomed on the shiny Gulf waters. Hope of escape vanished from Maffitt's thinking in the flash of the Oneida's guns. "Had their guns been depressed, the career of the Florida would have ended then and there," said Maffitt.

Coolly, he called to his executive officer, "Mr. Stribling, show them who we are. Haul down the English colors and hoist our own."

Young Sharkey, helmsman, sprang to carry out the order, but a piece of shrapnel sliced off a forefinger the moment he touched the halliards. Another bent to the task. Then the halliards were shot away, only to be promptly re-roved and "the Dixie flag floated in their faces." In a saddening flash, George Preble realized how well he had been duped. Now to recoup his blunder, and sink her as fast as gunfire could do it.

The Oneida's consorts were moving in like wolves ganging up on their wounded quarry. The Winona off the port beam and the Rachel Seaman off the port bow began snapping at her with every gun they could bring to bear. Having passed the Oneida, Maffitt starboarded his helm to bring the three Union ships into line and thus escape the fire of one of them. Yet, as the Florida forged ahead of the Oneida, eleven-inch shells were plunging into her with thuds that made her shiver from stem to stern. They were hulling her repeatedly. One monster bashed through the starboard side three inches above the water line, grazing the port boiler, decapitating James Duncan, captain of the maintop, and wounding nine others. It burst a moment after it went out the port side. Had it exploded a second sooner, it would have killed every man on the ship; and had the sea been running, she would have foundered in minutes. The hole was big as a cotton bale. Luck was riding at Maffitt's right hand so far.

A shell from the Winona crashed through the pantry, playing havoc with the plates, cups, and saucers. James Bulloch had taken such pride in the Confederate crockery adorned with the Stars and Bars. Another shell exploded beside the port gangway. As if the concentrated cannon of three ships was not enough, the Oneida's marines opened up with their muskets.

It wasn't a fight, but a clobbering—death in the afternoon for the shapely vessel on which James Bulloch had lavished so much tender care. She was being torn to pieces. The cannonading became rapid and precise. The wreckage of her shot-up beauty strewed her decks and ribboned out on the waters in her wake. Head high, she plunged on, absorbing shot and shell like a vast sponge. But she couldn't take it much longer. It looked like a one-way street to the bottom of the Gulf, and soon. But, as Maffitt later told it, "The loud explosions, roar of shot and shell, crashing spars and rigging, mingled with the moans of our sick and wounded, only increased our determination to enter our destined harbor."

An officer of the *Oneida* was to recall, after the war, that amid the fiery storm breaking over the *Florida*, he and his companions saw a man, sometimes standing, at others sitting, by the quarter rail, as cool and self-possessed as if there had been no enemy within miles of him. This officer admitted, "Those who longed for his discomfiture could not but admire the steady bearing of the brave man who sat alone on the deck."

The *Florida* was ranging ahead, but not fast enough. Maffitt ordered men aloft to loosen sail. They came on deck at a run and ran up the ratlines, but the moment they appeared on the yards, the gunboats showered them with shrapnel. One man's foot was sliced off clean as a knife could do it. He was to die three days later. The *Oneida's* marines began potshotting them like birds in a tree. Down came five bleeding men with musket balls in them. Even so, they set the sails, though not properly. Not much help would the wind give the *Florida*. The wounded were laid out on the berth deck beside the yellow fever convalescents.

"We made no effort at resistance," said Maffitt, "for though armed, we were not at all equipped to fire. Properly manned and equipped, the excitement of battle would have relieved the terrible strain upon our fortitude, which nevertheless sustained us through the withering assaults of a foe determined upon our capture or destruction."

Sustaining the fierce onslaught with calmness born of desperation, the *Florida* slowly cleared the grouping circle of her foes. As prospects began to brighten for the *Florida*, her foes redoubled their efforts, firing faster, feeding their furnaces with rosin and other combustibles to increase their heads of steam. Clouds of acrid smoke spread over the waters. A light south wind swept across the Gulf, as if nature herself was spreading a pall to shut out the death throes of a brave ship and crew. Fort Morgan was coming nearer, but not yet near enough. At fourteen knots Maffitt was pulling away from the *Oneida*. It was well that Bulloch had built speed into the ship. It was this that could save her; this and poor shooting. Not once did she slacken her gait. By a slight starboard turn, about four points, Maffitt again brought the *Winona* and *Rachel Seaman* into line, thus escaping the fire of one of them, and obliging the *Oneida* to yaw in order to bring her guns to bear on the fleet-footed *Florida*. Thus, claimed Admiral Farragut, three more minutes were lost that were never recaptured.

There seems to have been a dearth of efficiency aboard the *Oneida*, caught off base as it were. In his report, Boatswain James Herold said he took the hauling down of the *Florida's* English flag as a "token of her surrender," while Midshipman Wood vowed the *Florida* passed the *Oneida* so fast, the latter was obliged in fifteen minutes to increase her eleven-inch gun elevation from four hundred to fifteen hundred yards. Gunner William Parker said the *Oneida* fired twenty-one eleven-inch shells into the *Florida* plus an assortment of other calibers.

Thus was the *Florida* battered for two hours. Shelled, volleyed, and blasted by an enemy with really nothing to distract his aim, she fired back not a popgun. How she withstood this pelting *feu d'enfer* (as James Bulloch called it) was something the South was to marvel at. It was a long, terrible gantlet, but the old adage of a long lane that has no turning held for the *Florida*. Drawing on every navigation trick in his bag, John Maffitt was slowly converting the massacre into a stern chase. Only a lucky shot could sink him now, though they were still splashing and spraying her, trying desperately to deliver the knockout blow. But these closing gestures were futile, and the deadly drama hurried to its climax. The incredible was coming to pass. Fate had apparently carved out for the *Florida* a more extended career than a grave on the coral banks at the bottom of the Gulf, and this baptism of fire christened her—but what a christening!—as a Confederate torchbearer on the ocean of public events. Shot and shell were falling short now.

The afternoon was closing. It was nearing six-thirty. On the west rim of the Gulf, the sun was dipping into a lake of gold. About this time John Maffitt witnessed the most beautiful sight of his life: three sullen Federal warships, outsmarted, outrun, baffled and balked out of easy prey, their guns smoking dumbly, hauling off from the bar lest they draw the fire of Fort Morgan, whose gunners had watched the *Florida's* thrilling run-through, with lanyards taut for the moment the Federals came within range.

At this moment John Maffitt loosened the rope about him and rose unsteadily to his feet. Turning, he faced the little group of his officers, who had stood at stations throughout it all. Then, he raised his hand in salute.

"Gentlemen," he said with a smile, "if there's anything left of the wardroom, I suggest you splice the main brace."

Careening over to the wheel, he put out his hand to Quartermaster Billups, who had never once left his post.

"Billups, I congratulate you. Take her in slowly. We'll anchor off Melrose, above Fort Morgan."

At half speed, the *Florida* limped into the channel-way like a wounded fawn, her banner bright in the last rays of the sun. She was weary, beat up, riddled—but safe. Over fourteen hundred wounds scarred her hull and upper works. (They counted them later.) Fort Morgan's garrison lined the parapets to greet her as she came in. Cheers rolled out over the waters, and then, cannon fire. One, two, three, four . . . and on . . . twenty-one guns saluting the brave ship, crew and captain, who had written a record of chase and escape unparalleled in naval annals.

The South rang with praise, and, unbelievably, so did the North. From hard-hitting, outspoken Yankee Admiral David Dixon Porter came the accolade:

> During the whole war there was not a more exciting adventure than this escape of the *Florida* into Mobile Bay. The gallant manner in which it was conducted excited a great admiration even among the men who were responsible for permitting it. We do not suppose there was ever a case where a man, under all the attending circumstances, displayed more energy or more bravery.

England, too, took up the refrain. The eyes of Britain had followed this ship from the moment she slipped out to sea. News of her breath-taking break-through at Mobile brought a wave of admiration, while London's *Punch* enshrined Gideon Welles in a limerick:

> There was an old fogy named Welles,
> Quite worthy of cap and of bells,
> For he thot that a pirate
> Who steamed at a great rate,
> Would wait to be riddled with shells!

A Mobile newspaper editor promptly conferred on Maffitt a nickname that clung to him for the rest of his days—Old Salamander. He never liked it, but it fitted like a glove. Who else besides the mythical salamander could romp through fire as he had, and live to tell the tale? And his men liked it. In the forecastle they would tell and re-tell the story of Old Salamander's boldly sitting out the inferno on the *Florida's* deck that September afternoon.

Maffitt's brief report of his passage into Mobile Bay was a model of objectivity. He finished it off with a Shakespearian flourish: "Every man acted well his part."

CHAPTER XIII

Backfire at Washington

As NIGHT FELL over the embattled waters off Mobile Bay, Commander Preble sat in his cabin on the *Oneida* composing his report to Flag Officer Farragut at Pensacola. Starting with "I regret having to inform you that a two-masted screw-steamer having every appearance of an English man-of-war, ran the blockade this afternoon . . . " Preble sought to attribute the *Florida's* escape to "her superior speed and the unparalleled audacity of her commander." To admit such a thing was a mistake. Neglecting to identify the mysterious gate-crasher as the *Florida*, Preble also failed to state that she had not fired a single shot in reply to his broadsides. Closing his report "with great mortification," he sped it on to Farragut, who bluntly replied, "I am very much pained to hear of the passage into Mobile Bay of the gunboat No. 290." Even Farragut erred in thinking she was the *Alabama*.

By express ship Farragut shunted the news to Washington with the comment, "The passing of the blockade was owing to two things: first, not firing at her in time when she was so close they could not miss her; second, bad firing."

The news reached the Navy Department at Washington on September 19. Had somebody stuck a pin into Uncle Gideon, he could not have leaped out of his chair faster. Hopping mad, he trotted over to President Lincoln's office, his bewhiskered face ablaze with indignation.

"Well, what's up now?" inquired the genial Lincoln, who saw at once that something was obviously up. Tossing the telltale message from Farragut onto Lincoln's desk, Welles blurted it out. The "pirate Maffitt" and his ship had dashed into Mobile Bay. It may have been the 290 or the *Oreto*. He surmised it was the latter (Richmond was gleefully to confirm it a day or so later). Lincoln was more cheerful today. The blood was still wet along Antietam Creek, where McClellan had just rolled back Lee's gray tide; but the crucial days were over. Lee was re-crossing the Potomac into Virginia.

"What do you want to do about it?" asked the President.

Welles laid Preble's head on the block, "Dismiss him from the service."

"Dismiss him then," agreed Lincoln. "If that is your opinion, it is mine. I will do it."

In his diary Welles spluttered:

Preble, by sheer pusillanimous neglect, feebleness and indecision, let the pirate steamer *Oreto* run the blockade. She came right up and passed him flying English colors. Instead of checking her advance or sinking her, he fired all around, made a noise, and is said to have hurt none of her English crew. There must be a stop put to the timid, hesitating and, I fear, sometimes traitorous course of some of our officers. Tenderness, remonstrance, reproof do no good. Preble is not a traitor, but loyal. I am sorry for Preble, but shall be more sorry for my country if it is not done. Its effect upon the Navy will be more salutary than were he and fifty like him to fall in battle.

Hurrying back from Lincoln's office, the Secretary took up his pen and scratched off Preble's ouster from the navy. Welles was adept at sticking knives into those who displeased him. He addressed the missive to "George H. Preble, *Late* Commander, U.S. Navy." After a short preamble he wrote, "Upon submitting your letter to the President I received from him prompt directions to announce to you your dismissal from the service. You will from this date cease to be regarded as an officer of the Navy of the United States." To rub salt in the wound, Welles directed that Preble's name be stricken from the navy rolls and that the record of his "disgrace" be entered upon the log book and read to the assembled crews of every ship in the navy. Newspapers were howling for Preble's scalp. Welles dished it up with gusto.

Welles had good reason to be exasperated with the luckless Preble. American diplomats at London had failed dismally. James Bulloch had made a laughing stock of them. The *Oreto* had slipped down the Mersey, wriggled her way out of the prize court at Nassau, and run the blockade into Mobile. On top of this series of misadventures the 290 (*Alabama*) had, thanks to a leak in the British Foreign Office, escaped from Liverpool by a gnat's-eye margin. Since then, nothing had been seen or heard of her. Welles little reckoned that she had already broken cover in the Azores. But he was sure that the *Oreto* (*Florida*) was at last run to earth. He knew where she was. To Farragut he dispatched orders to seal off Mobile Bay, if he had to anchor ships end to end across the bar outside. The *Florida* must be immobilized for the duration. To Admiral Wilkes (upped to flag rank since the unfortunate *Trent* Affair) he dashed off a directive: Find the "pirate *Alabama*" at all costs. Don't capture her, sink her.

Five months after his dismissal, political manipulation restored Preble to rank. President Lincoln himself, yielding to political importunities, sent Preble back to duty, where he would a second time suffer humiliation at the hands of the *Florida*.

Yet, the Preble *cause célèbre* was to echo through the corridors of the Navy Department long after the North and South had ceased warring. In 1872 "Pirate Maffitt" (no longer a pirate) appeared before a Court of Inquiry at Washington to help clear the name and fame of the man whom he had humbled at Mobile Bay.

To his old-time friend Maffitt paid this tribute, "As an enemy Preble was consistent and honorable; as a friend, faithful and true; even through all the vicissitudes of untoward events that erected barriers between old naval associates, who in bygone days had buffeted together in happy unity the storms of Old Neptune and hardships of the sea."

CHAPTER XIV

Like a Ghost in the Night

MOBILE GAVE John Maffitt a hero's welcome.

For two weeks the *Florida* flew the yellow flag of quarantine, yet young and old alike boarded whatever would float them alongside and stared at the ship that had braved the gantlet of fire in broad daylight without being able to return a shot. The more venturesome tripped up the gangway to deliver their flowers and smiles to the ship's commander.

To his daughter Florie, Maffitt wrote, "A steamer has just come alongside with a crowd of ladies to visit me. Bless their souls! What would the soldiers and sailors of the South be worth without their brave, tender and cheering approbation. My cabin is like a flower garden, and as for jellies, cakes, and delicacies, the young ladies seem to exert great industry and gentle courtesy."

Down from Richmond, from the pen of Secretary Mallory, came official plaudits:

> The escape of your defenseless vessel from an overwhelming force with liberty to choose its own ground and mode of attack, was due to the handsome manner in which she was handled, and I do not remember that the union of thorough professional skill, coolness and daring have ever been better exhibited in a naval dash of a single ship.

Southern poets rhapsodized over the valorous *Florida*, her crew and her commander, who, if we accept his own words, looked like a scarecrow at the time. The South loved bold exploits executed in the grand manner, and Maffitt had achieved just that.

A surge of naval pride was soon to sweep the South. The *Alabama* would suddenly materialize out of the North Atlantic to begin her rampage down the New England coast, throwing flame with such abandon that Northern shipowners would implore the Navy Department to do something, anything. Behind her, she left a trail of terror. Now, if the *Florida* could get to sea . . . A third cruiser, the *Georgia*, was about to leave the lair. There was no telling how many rovers James Bulloch might hatch in his secure British nest. The Confederacy had taken illimitable pride in the ironclad *Merrimack*, whose luck ran out in two days. Her suicide on the James River flats had struck a hard blow at Southern sentiment. But now they had two ships. John Maffitt began dreaming that he would, after all, keep his rendezvous with Raphael Semmes. Together they would make swoops that would stagnate Yankee foreign trade. Adulation was meat and drink to him, but what Maffitt wanted most of all was to get to sea again.

Meanwhile, disappointment gnawed at him. He had expected promotion, which did not arrive, at least, not when he hoped for it. Philosophically, he accepted his own dictum, "The Richmond people flatter, but do not always act with justice."

The yellow pestilence was to hurl a Parthian shot at the *Florida*. On September 12 the "chivalric John Stribling," who had stood at Maffitt's side as the *Florida* ran her race of fire, furled his sails and slowly struck his flag. Two days after the *Florida* ran into Mobile Bay the dread vomito seized him. Medical skill and affectionate care were futile. Orders were issued in whispers so that nothing might disturb the last moments of the dying officer. For twenty-four hours Maffitt sat holding his hand. "Lightly the rough seaman trod the quarterdeck, and the harsh coils of rope were flemished in their places as noiselessly as falls the snowflakes upon the bosom of our mother earth." With honors—three volleys and a shroud of Stars and Bars—they buried him on the peaceful heights of Montrose overlooking the bay. John Maffitt read the simple burial service with deep emotion. Something of Maffitt went into the grave with this splendid young sailor, of whom he said: "Embalmed was he in our hearts, and every throbbing reminiscence of Confederate existence, re-writes there the epitaph that had no carving on his grave."

Meanwhile the *Florida* tarried at Mobile, where shipwrights and carpenters swarmed over her, repairing, refitting, and painting. Chafing with impatience, Maffitt watched her battle scars vanish. At the same slow pace, nature restored his sturdy body to rights. But frustration mounted daily. It was one thing to requisition new material and ordnance, and quite another to procure it from the hard-pressed ordnance department. Yet, just when patience was running low, it would arrive. Best of all came two new rifled pivot-guns, firing 110-pound shells.

The *Florida's* new crew arrived in driblets, garnered from every state in the Confederacy. By December the one hundred hammocks on her berth deck were filled with green, but willing, Jacks. Of these, four-fifths were Southern bred and born. The remainder, of a dozen nationalities, were volunteers from merchantmen impounded in Gulf ports. Maffitt admitted that many the Navy Department rated as seamen would, in the old service, "merely pass as very ordinary seamen." He knew he could whip them into first-class shape, because molding men for the hard usage of the sea came naturally to him. He had a way of binding men's hearts to his own, though he ruled with a rod of iron inherited from the old navy.

The *Florida's* officer complement, partly replenished by Maffitt's own choosing, numbered thirteen, including two surgeons. His first choice fell to Lieutenant Charles William Read, the "gallant Pelham" of the Confederate Navy, a Mississippian who had graduated from Annapolis just before the outbreak of war. The day Read arrived, Maffitt wrote in his Journal: "Mr. Read is quiet and slow, and not much of a military officer of the deck, but I think him reliable and sure, though slow." One day, not too far distant, Maffitt would revise this to: "Daring beyond the point of martial prudence." But watch this man. At the battle of New Orleans he had already distinguished himself. When the heroic Huger fell mortally wounded on the deck of the *McRae*, Read had assumed command, fought the ship until she was riddled by Farragut's guns, destroyed her, and escaped ashore.

Executive Officer of the *Florida*, to replace the missing Stribling, was Lieutenant S. W. Averett, whose "frank, manly manner pleases me much." But Maffitt was to find him ill suited to the rough and tumble business of commerce raiding, that broke or made men fast.

Late in October Maffitt's sea-orders came from Richmond. Named for his own state, Mallory took infinite pride in the raider and her coming career. Fifty thousand dollars in gold to fill her sea chest accompanied the orders. But Mallory laid down a hard, fast rule: Avoid a fight. Tilting with enemy warships is not the *Florida's* business. Fight if forced to it, but don't risk losing your ship. You are armed for defense, not for combat. Your weapon is the torch. Cruise at discretion. You are on your own. Live on the enemy if you can. Burn, sink, and destroy enemy merchantmen wherever you find them, save in neutral waters. The North would gladly sacrifice fifty vessels to rid the ocean of the *Florida* and *Alabama*. Hit the enemy in his pocketbook. Destroy enough Northern shipping and the wealthy merchant princes of New York and Boston will soon cry "Peace! Peace!" And the politicians at Washington would be quick to comply. Lastly, Mallory arranged a secret code for communicating with the Navy Department.

On January 1, 1863, a rejuvenated *Florida* chafed at her moorings. Her long, black new pivots shone like patent leather in the sunshine. Her well-drilled crew was restive. They would grow stale with more waiting. It was time to get out and get going. More to the point, Maffitt had to get his ship out intact, not crippled and shot to pieces. As a finishing touch, the *Florida* was daubed over with a mixture of whitewash and lampblack. Maffitt disapproved, but Admiral Franklin Buchanan, Mobile's naval commandant, prescribed it because "a vessel of that color cannot be well seen at night." It marred her beauty, but Maffitt submitted, knowing it would wash off in a hurry.

For weeks Northern newspapers had boasted of the *Florida's* being pinioned in Mobile Bay like a "straitjacketed prisoner"— hermetically stopped up, averred others, picking out the words of Welles's orders. Running out meant suicide. The trap was triggered. From Washington came a stern pronouncement: Heads would fall if the "pirate *Florida*" made a getaway.

On January 11 the *Florida* steamed casually down to the anchorage, just inside the bay off Fort Morgan. Going ashore, Maffitt mounted the parapet and reconnoitered the Federal policemen outside the bar. Clustering off the channel he counted—as he wrote his daughter Florie—"thirteen so plainly in sight that I knew I could not pass without having sixty guns fired at me, and we would no doubt be lost."

Riding in line, the Union ships were almost stepping on each other's toes. The squadron included the speedy *Cuyler*, the flagship *Susquehanna*, and Maffitt's old friend, *Oneida*, burning to avenge the humiliation he had heaped upon her. The fourteen-knot *Cuyler* was assigned the task of overhauling the *Florida* if (seemingly beyond imagining) she evaded the reception committee awaiting her outside. Night and day they clung to their stations. The outlook was hardly promising. Even the editor of Mobile's leading paper had doubts. Wouldn't it be better to leave the *Florida* where she was, thus immobilizing a sizable flotilla of enemy warships to keep her buttoned up?

Blockading the entrance to Mobile Bay was comparatively simple. How could it be otherwise, with a dozen ships on watch? Farragut was adamant against a repetition of the Preble performance. The channel ran seaward for four miles beyond Fort Morgan, just far enough for Union ships to take stations, and anchor if they chose; close to the bar, yet out of range of Confederate batteries. Getting out meant running a double-line gantlet.

To anyone but Maffitt—and no doubt Semmes—extricating his ship from this trap would have resembled the proverbial journey through a needle's eye. Yet, never once did he doubt his ability to corkscrew his ship safely into the Gulf. He asked one chance, just one, to ride the wings of a northeast gale. But the weatherman seemed loath to comply. Twice by night, the *Florida* darted into the channel on false starts only to steam fretting back to her moorings. On the first trial, Maffitt sighted eleven ships waiting implacably to destroy him. His nerve-racked crew caught sight of at least twenty-five "phantom ships."

On January 15 signs of a norther were unmistakable. The wind was rising to gale fury, blowing offshore in spiteful gusts, and singing through the rigging. It was music to Maffitt. The sea was rolling. The gale he yearned for was coming. There was no moon and the night was bitter cold. The dark surface of the Gulf was lashed into foam and spume flying half-mast high.

From Mobile came last minute instructions from Admiral Buchanan:

> Have the *Florida* prepared in all respects for a fight, hammock nettings taken down, men at quarters. Exercise caution and judgment and escape the blockaders, if possible, without using your guns, as they would alarm the whole squadron at anchor and those cruising off the coast.

This was unnecessary. Maffitt knew his business.

At dusk the crew was alerted, but piped down and ordered to stretch out in their hammocks, clothes on, pea jackets handy. A double watch was set, steam upped and hissing at the safety valve. At midnight Maffitt summoned his officers to his cabin. As he stroked his chin whiskers, his gaze roved from one to another. If anything could abate the vigilance of enemy lookouts, it was the stinging blast now slashing down from the north.

"We're going out tonight," he announced. "This is what we've waited for. I want an officer stationed every twenty feet along the deck aft to the wheel. I'll be standing there by the quartermaster, if you need me."

At 2:20 A.M. the crew was quietly summoned to quarters. The *Florida* was heading out to sea, come hell or high water. The order was: "All hands up anchor!" The steam throttle was opened; gun crews took stations. The *Florida* bounded off, heading for the bar as if joyful at being released. Trumpet in hand, tense, alert, his eyes searching the murk, Maffitt stood beside the helmsman. About his shoulders was a faded naval cloak. He wore it only on occasions. Aloft, jack-tars clung to ropes waiting to loose sails at a moment's notice. Nimbly the *Florida* sped past Fort Morgan. Now she was in the channel, on her own, sprinting for life and the open Gulf.

Suddenly, the lookout announced, "Sail right ahead, sir!" The *Florida* was literally on top of a black towering object. "Starboard your helm!" ordered Maffitt. Again the lookout piped, "Sail right ahead, sir!" "Port your helm!" said Maffitt sharply. Thus she worked her way, in and out, until five had been sighted and passed. Now there were two, one lying on each beam: the *Cuyler* and the flagship *Susquehanna*, with hardly three hundred feet to spare on each side. Maffitt drew a deep breath. Not yet was he discovered. He was abreast of the two ships when a bright coal-dust flash shot out of the *Florida's* funnels. It was the give-away. The engine room had run out of smokeless coke and was feeding coal to the boilers. At least, thought Maffitt, he had surprised his wardens. Even so, the odds were overwhelming, eleven to one. Coston lights flared on the *Susquehanna*. Out in the darkness bloomed a carnival of blue, red, and white lights signaling madly to the squadron. Maffitt could hear drums beating to quarters, the rattle of chains, the general commotion as cables were slipped, and the confusion of a surprise. There was to be "racing and chasing" that night.

Maffitt's commands crackled like whips as he ordered men aloft to throw on every rag of sail the vessel carried. The gale seemed to grip the canvas with mighty sinews, as if to lift her out of the water and speed her on. Off she flew like a frightened deer over the rugged rollers. Under steam and sail, she was making fourteen knots and riding the seas like a pilot boat.

Fanning out behind her came half a dozen Federals. Guns began barking. Shells whistled through the dark. Was the *Florida* to be clawed to pieces a second time? One would have supposed— wrote Admiral Porter—that every man would have been at his post, the vessels with steam up, chains ready to slip. They had sighted the *Florida* for two days, inside the bay, apparently waiting for just such a night to make her dash for freedom. At sunset the flagship had signaled her consorts, "*Florida* expected out. Keep full steam up." At least, there should have been an ace in the hole, that is, one vessel (the *Cuyler*, fastest of the pack) stationed eight to ten miles off, just in case the *Florida's* breakaway was successful.

But, unbelievably, the *Cuyler* took half an hour to get moving. Her commander later admitted he had gone to bed. It subsequently developed that the ship had a rule requiring the watch officer to rouse the commander, but to wait his appearance before slipping the cable.

On through the night went the chase. Applying whip and spur, all that steam and canvas could give, the Federals sped after the saucy Confederate—"the rebel craft whose escape from thraldom was sorely dreaded at the North in visions of burning vessels and commercial disasters." Just before day, when all hands on the *Florida* were breathing easier, dead ahead, close at hand, out of the haze loomed the *Brooklyn*, faster, bigger, with a broadside that could have blasted Maffitt & Company to the bottom. For minutes the *Florida* held her breath under the *Brooklyn's* guns. Sheering ever so slightly so as not to excite suspicion, she left the *Brooklyn* behind, unseeing, unwitting. Twice now had the *Brooklyn* muffed momentous opportunity. Raphael Semmes had outsmarted her in June, 1861, when he ran out of the Mississippi Passes on the *Sumter*. Her log still told the tragic story.

As the day wore on, a pinpoint on the horizon enlarged into a warship, the *Cuyler*, boiling up from behind to retrieve her lost laurels. She came within three miles of the *Florida*. From stormy morn to stormy eve, she hung on, gaining perceptibly as the afternoon waned. It was Captain Emmons' bid for the fame and the reward of capturing or sinking the *Florida*. Glory loomed just ahead. Realizing the *Florida's* sails were "a white and fleecy guiding mark for his persistent enemy," Maffitt resorted to ruse, the old hare-and-hound freeze-play. All hands were hustled aloft to shorten sail. This is how Maffitt described it: "The canvas was secured in long, neat bunts to the yards and the engines stopped. Between high, toppling seas, clear daylight was necessary to enable them to distinguish our low hull. In eager pursuit our fellow traveler swiftly passed us, and we jubilantly bade the enemy goodnight and steered northward." Shorn of her plumage, the *Florida* had turned end-on to the *Cuyler* and frozen in her tracks. It was a trick he had mastered running the blockade into Wilmington. The *Cuyler*, meantime, kept up her relentless chase way down into the Gulf of Yucatan. She was running in the wrong direction.

Dolefully, the captain of the *Cuyler* unburdened his feelings in his report: "From fancying myself near promotion in the morning (when we sighted the *Florida*), I gradually dwindled down to a court of inquiry at dark when I lost sight of the enemy." Right he was. The inevitable court of inquiry picked him and his fellow captains to pieces. From a rabid press came scorching attack. Congress spent a day flaying the naval secretary and the navy in general. In turn, Gideon threatened to scalp eleven captains, including the commodore of the squadron, who was snoozing when Maffitt broke loose.

Admiral Porter shot his barbs impartially: "And so the *Florida* was allowed to go on her way without molestation, and Maffitt was enabled to commence that career on the high seas which has made his name one of the notable ones of the war. He lighted the seas wherever he passed along, and committed such havoc among American merchantmen, that, if possible, he was even more dreaded than Semmes. His being permitted to escape into Mobile Bay, and then out again, was the greatest example of blundering committed throughout the war."

The *Florida* was free, untrammeled, off to great adventure. As he gazed up at the stars, Maffitt remembered an all-but-forgotten prayer, an echo of Chaplain Lambert's words on the *Constitution* long ago: "Oh, Lord! who hast delivered us from the fury of the storm, send us fair winds and take the helm if we go wrong."

Now to vacate the Gulf before his pursuers closed off its two exits. Veering, he shaped his course for the happy hunting grounds off the Cuban coast. It was the broad highway for Yankee merchantmen trading in the West Indies. Also for Union warships.

Maffitt hadn't slept for thirty-six hours. Giving his orders for the night, he went to his bunk. The Gulf was boisterous, the *Florida* rolling and tumbling. But tonight he would sleep like a child.

Well might the New York *Herald* exclaim, "Another scourge of the deep is let loose," while the Richmond *Dispatch* threw its hat in the air with congratulations for Yankee shipowners on "the bright prospect that lies ahead for their merchantmen."

CHAPTER XV

Debut of Fire

On the afternoon of January 19, 1863, the brand-new brig, *Estelle* of Boston, was rounding the western tip of Cuba into Florida Strait. Off to starboard the coast gleamed like a faraway emerald. It was the last leg of her shakedown cruise. Two days out of Santa Cruz, homebound, she was spanking along in a freshening wind.

The *Estelle*, like her name, was a pretty thing with fresh, white sails. No amount of deception could have disguised her Yankee build and cut. She advertised it handsomely across the waters. Her figurehead was a neatly-carved girl on whose cheeks the bloom of youth was still paint-fresh.

In his cabin Master John Brown was figuring things up. The war had skyrocketed cargo rates. The *Estelle* wouldn't do so badly on her maiden voyage—and he was half-owner. He was as proud of her as of his two teen-age daughters back in Boston. And that reminded him of the things he had picked up for the homefolks at Santa Cruz: tortoise-shell combs for the young ladies and a mantilla for their mother. Down-easters didn't go in much for fripperies of dress, but they'd look sort of Spanish, and right smart too, wearing these things.

Millions of bees had pooled their labors to gather the *Estelle's* cargo. Stowed in her hold was honey, tons of it, drawn from countless millions of tropical flowers. Union armies were eating it prodigiously. Stacked below, there were also barrels of molasses for the rum factories of New England.

If Captain Brown was haunted by premonitions of danger from Confederate "pirates," he gave no evidence of it this serene, blessed afternoon. The *Alabama* was on the loose, he knew, but she had vanished, ducked off to the Far East, the newspapers said, after playing hob with shipping on the Atlantic coast. As for the *Florida*: she was jailed at Mobile Bay. Besides, Union warships kept a sharp watch on these waters for blockade runners in and out of Havana. The *Estelle* had spoken two of them since leaving Santa Cruz.

Key West, rendezvous of the Federal West Indian Squadron, was just around the bend. Tortugas was not far off to port. There was really no reason for Skipper Brown to be apprehensive.

At six bells the *Estelle's* lookout called down a sail. Coming on deck, the Boston mariner sighted a steamer about five miles off running toward his ship. She was a man-of-war. Her guns were plainly visible in his glasses. Presently, the stranger broke out the Stars and Stripes. At about a mile, to the skipper's amazement, the "Union" warship suddenly fired her bow gun and a shot whistled across the *Estelle's* bow to splash no great distance from the brig. It was a summons to haul up. Captain Brown obeyed with alacrity, though he was inclined to be wrathy. Couldn't they see his flag? Perhaps they had mistaken him for a blockade runner. Anyway, if it had to be, so be it.

The newcomer closed fast. At several hundred yards she lay to. While the Down-easter stared and waited for something to happen he saw a cutter drop down from the warship's davits. Then, six brawnies pulling at the sweeps as the cutter slid over the choppy waters to come alongside the *Estelle*. Still, the captain had no qualms. In the cutter's stern sheets sat a young officer clad in gray. Nimbly, he scrambled up the ship's ladder. The Down-easter met him as he stepped on deck.

"Well, what do you want?" blazed out Brown.

"You are a prize of the Confederate States Steamer *Florida*, Lieutenant Maffitt commanding. I am Lieutenant Hoole, sir."

The deck seemed to drop from under Brown's feet. His eyes widened, his face paled. Astounded, his tongue refused to speak. Seconds dragged by before he found his voice.

"My God!" he gasped. "I thought you were at Mobile."

"We were," said Hoole bluntly. "Fetch your papers and come with us."

At that moment the mariner's gaze was transfixed by something that seemed beyond belief. The warship had lowered the Stars and Stripes and hoisted the flag that had haunted the slumbers of many a Northern merchant skipper. It was the Stars and Bars.

2

Quietly, John Maffitt leaned on the quarter rail watching his boarders work on their first prize. She was his raiding guinea pig. It was a businesslike operation and, so far, pleased him considerably. The *Estelle* was a beauty. Seven hundred tons, he reckoned. Beautiful ships and beautiful women had a way with his heart. He couldn't resist admiring them—and often saying so. He waited until his boarding party was halfway back to the *Florida* before going below. Soon he heard them coming up the gangway.

Following his captor, Skipper Brown was ushered aft into the spacious stern cabin where an officer, garbed in impeccable gray, rose to greet him with a smile. On his host's sleeves gleamed the double stripes of Lieutenant.

"I am Lieutenant Maffitt, Sir." He was graciously polite. "And you?"

"Captain John Brown, master of the *Estelle* of Boston."

A dismaying thought ran through the Bostonian's mind with his first glance at his captor. The bunch of black whiskers adorning his chin fleetingly reminded the Yankee master of tales he had heard of Blackbeard, who once did business on these waters. Dumbly, he handed over his papers. Motioning his guest to a chair, Maffitt scrutinized the *Estelle*'s credentials.

"Honey and molasses," commented Maffitt. "Good business, even in war time, I reckon."

"Spanish property, Sir." The Yankee spoke up boldly. Lie it was, but his New England conscience felt no pangs.

"Hardly, Captain," countered Maffitt. "There's nothing here that protects your ship or your cargo. Your manifest says the cargo was bought and paid for by Boston merchants. The ship belongs to you, under American registry. What's the value of the two?"

"About one hundred thousand dollars, I'd guess." Then, suddenly, sensing the drift of Maffitt's words he stammered, "You mean you'll burn my ship?"

"You've guessed it, Captain." Maffitt pronounced the *Estelle's* doom without the flicker of an eyelash. His eyes went cold as old ashes. Hard words they were, but ocean-scorching was a hard business. The *Estelle* carried no neutral cargo. Nor was she on Spanish waters. Cuba was ten miles or more off. "We'll have to burn your ship, Captain. Those are my orders. You are our first prize."

The New Englander shot a baleful glance at his captor. It was stark tragedy for John Brown, who wasn't too ardent a Unionist. Nor did he share New England's more violent abolition sentiments. He said so frankly. He may have nursed a hope that such a confession would win a reprieve for his beautiful *Estelle*.

"I'm sorry, Captain," went on Maffitt, "but this unnatural war falls hardest on those who disapproved it. I had hoped your ship was owned by an abolitionist. Go back to your ship. You and your men can pack up your personal belongings. Bring your flag, chronometer, and charts to my cabin. You'll be taken aboard my ship as prisoners of war and paroled at Havana."

Honest tears ran down Brown's weather-beaten cheeks as he left the cabin. Wasting no time, Maffitt gave the orders. First, she was stripped of her sails and spare rigging. The *Florida* might need them. A few cases of honey and barrels of molasses would sweeten the ship's messes. The *Estelle's* larder was nothing to smack one's lips over, but a firkin of New England butter brought smiles to the *Florida's* wardroom steward. Next came the *Estelle's* flag. Marked "Number One—*Estelle* of Boston," it would grace the ship's wardroom, with others to come.

Like a lady unafraid, the *Estelle* waited to die. There was a certain grace in her manner of waiting. The afternoon waned. The wind died to a whisper, the sea was quiet. From the quarter-deck Maffitt watched his boarders perform their incendiary rites over the fine, taut brig. Lining the rail were the officers and crew of the *Florida* nervously shifting from one foot to the other, waiting for "it" to happen. To the uninitiated lads of the berth deck the scene was a nightmare. Deliberately burning a beautiful ship! They were gazing on a spectacle whose actuality they had little envisioned.

Melancholy as a burial party, and thinking hard thoughts, stood the master and crew of the *Estelle*. Hanging would be too good for these Confederate pirates! If this was war, God damn it and those who made it this way!

But it was war, and destruction of enemy property on the high seas was as much part of it as bullets on a battlefield, or a bayonet in a man's guts, or burning barns and corn-cribs. For John Maffitt it was a gratifying sight. He had struck his first blow at the North. On with the business! Northern newspapers and politicians were already raging at Semmes and the *Alabama*. They would now turn their wrath on Maffitt and the *Florida*, preying on unarmed merchantmen. Let them rage!

Maffitt could see his torchmen climbing out of the hatches, clambering down the hull of the doomed *Estelle*. Into an afternoon fragrant with Cuba's offshore breeze, a column of smoke curled from the brig's forecastle. Then aft, another, until it was rising in thick, black clouds that shrouded masts and rigging. Pitiless business, but it had to be. It called for spartan nerves, and an executioner's resolve.

Suddenly, the *Estelle* erupted in two bursts of flame fore and aft. Flames of all sizes and shapes, yellows and reds, ran up the masts, out on the spars, wriggled along the freshly-tarred rigging, darting through the intricate spiderweb of cordage, and leaped hungrily at the sails.

Deep down in the *Estelle's* heart, an inferno was raging. Like a blast furnace, fanned by the indraughts, fire gushed out of the hatches in roaring currents, as if chanting the *Estelle's* requiem. The savory smell of stewing molasses and honey drifted across the water to the *Florida*. Presently, her masts, flaming like skyscraping sticks of kindling, began to totter, struggling to hold on to the last. Then, with a crash, they toppled into the sea.

Now to get under way, or rather out of the way. This was no place to loiter.

Smoke of the burning ship could be seen thirty miles or more, and Tortugas was just about that distance northward. Federal huntsmen might be lounging there or come snooping along the Cuban coast. Darkness fell out of the sky. Giving orders to stand in for Bahia Honda, Maffitt went to his cabin. There was no gloating. The deed could speak for itself. Dimming her lights, the gray wolf moved on.

The *Estelle* still glowed faintly in the distance, her blackened hulk ready to dive down through the dark waters to keep an unexpected tryst with Spanish galleons, pirate ships, and the countless wrecks whose bones adorned the coral gardens at the bottom of Florida Strait.

It was a day to remember—and to celebrate. In the wardroom out came a bottle whose contents bubbled joyfully, as if to share the general elation. The *Florida's* officers raised their glasses. "To the *Estelle!* May there be more like her!"

CHAPTER XVI

Bonfires on the Sea

HAVANA WAS AGOG. The *Florida* had re-appeared. Not the pest-ridden death-ship of four months ago, but a stylish Confederate man-of-war whose gun-muzzled deck amply justified the conclusion that she might be a tough customer in a fight.

The *Confederados* were popular with the *Habaneros*. The coffee houses bubbled excitedly while patriotic hysterics seized the sizable Confederate colony whose flags fluttered out, profuse as tropical flowers. Hardly was the ship awake this morning of January 21 before boatloads were clamoring at the gangway. Even more ambitious was the welcome accorded by a noisy group on a barge that circumnavigated the *Florida* with a band blaring out *Dixie, Bonnie Blue Flag,* and other melodies dear to Southern hearts.

Electrifying was the news brought by the *Florida*. She had out-witted the gang-up off Mobile and had already captured and burned her first prize on Havana's doorstep. But more wonderful tidings awaited Maffitt at Havana. The *Alabama* had slid into the Gulf, sunk the Union *Hatteras* off Galveston, and vanished. Not for months would Maffitt know that the gale that helped him foil the Union watchdogs off Mobile Bay had conspired against the *Alabama*, slowing her down as she sped out of the Gulf after the Galveston foray. The two commerce raiders had passed within two hundred miles of each other. It was the nearest they would ever come to meeting. The *Alabama's* victory had dazzled Cuban imagination. And now here was the *Florida* with a blazing example of the Roman holiday she intended to make of Yankee shipping. To the ardently Confederate populace, it appeared as if the South was taking over the seas. One swallow made a summer for the effervescent Latin temperament. The Yankee would be swept from the ocean! Of a sudden, "Pirata" Maffitt was exalted to the seventh heaven.

By noon a veritable cornucopia of flowers, fruits, and dainties had been handed oversides to spill on deck. The cruiser's mess boys and stewards went into ecstasies. There were cases marked Bordeaux and Cette; boxes of coronas and panetelas for the *capitán* and the wardroom. Jack's eyes bulged at the nifty packages of Cuba's fine weed to fill his pipe as he lounged on the forecastle in the evenings, spinning never-ending yarns.

Spain was neutral after a fashion (only because she was afraid not to be), but her last New World colonial jewel was hardly so. Havana had become a haven for blockade-runners, and assumed a substantial role in the destiny of the Confederacy. America's fratricidal war was making Cuba's sugar-rich oligarchy even richer. Spaniards, Cubans, Yankees, Confederates, cheek by jowl, were cashing in on surreptitious trade with the South. Cotton, of course, was the medium of trade. It came by runners in five-hundred-bale lots, or more, but an even bigger stream crossed the narrow strait on schooners and yawls that sneaked past the blockaders with five or ten bales each hidden in their holds. Breathlessly, Union cruisers dashed hither and yon trying to stifle this small-time traffic that added up to big business. Tracking these will-o'-the-wisps into their nearby lairs, Federal gunboats did not scruple to make sport of Cuban territorial waters.

But Maffitt had put in to Havana for a purpose other than showing off his ship. The *Florida* needed coal. Her boilers had a wolfish appetite, and had devoured fuel ravenously on her flight across the Gulf. Neutral restrictions permitted her to come in, re-fuel, and get out within twenty-four hours. A further imperative need was to divest herself of her prisoners, parole the captain and crew of the *Estelle*, and hand them over to the American Consul.

Before going ashore, Maffitt gave hard and fast orders—no liberty for Jack, no frolicking. It was too early in the game. Jack would have his playtime, but not yet. Maffitt knew the enticements of the city: grogshops, dance halls, the arms of friendly señoritas. He had seen West Indian rum play havoc with many a warship's crew. He had no time to send a trio of quartermasters rummaging Havana's dives to corral delinquents. He well remembered the obnoxious duty that had often fallen to him thirty years ago as a midshipman on the *Constitution*, when he had to comb the rum-dens and brothels of Port Mahon for over-timers. Nor had he forgotten how they lined up the "steal-aways" on deck and applied the cat. There was only one way to run a warship: with a strong arm and unrelaxing discipline. He intended to do just that, and it might as well begin here.

The *Florida's* young officers yearned to show off their natty gray uniforms trimmed with gold lace and bright buttons. But they could only lean on the rail and imagine the dark-eyed houris they would not meet, the kisses they might have stolen, the champagne that might have flowed copiously down their throats.

Arrayed in his sparkling best, John Maffitt stepped into his captain's gig to be rowed off by eight men in immaculate whites. He was something to look at, faultlessly garbed in Confederate gray. The admiring tailor at Mobile had done his best for the gallant captain. Maffitt's first duty was to present himself to the port *comandante* and make the *amende honorable*. When the *Florida* steamed past the Morro last night, she had breached port rules twice: entering the harbor after sundown and failing to obtain clearance from the health officer.

Many were the cheers that greeted "el capitán Maf-feet." He found the port dignitary most obliging, ready to bend backward for the Confederate wayfarer up to the point of flagrant violation of neutral restraints. The *Florida* could replenish her bunkers, but she must clear within the prescribed twenty-four hours. Of course, if the *capitán* needed a few additional hours . . . With a sly wink the official shrugged his shoulders. John Maffitt understood perfectly. What difference would it make if the *Florida* overstayed a few hours among friends? Maffitt caught the wink, but, wisely, did not return it.

Next, and not without pride, Maffitt betook himself to the palace of the Captain-general, Don Francisco Serrano, to pay his respects and express his appreciation of the kindness Serrano had shown the fever-ridden *Florida* back in August. News of the burn-ing of the *Estelle* on Havana's doorstep had reached official ears shortly before Maffitt came a-knocking. Coming on the heels of the *Alabama's* demolition of the *Hatteras*, it was profoundly im-pressive.

"El capitán! Welcome!" Cuba's ranking alcalde breathed hos-pitality.

"Your Excellency!" Maffitt bowed low. He was somewhat of a master at this business. He could hobnob captivatingly with the small and the great. "I came to express my country's appreciation of your courtesy and kindness to my stricken crew and ship."

"I only wish I could have done more, capitán," assured the dig-nitary, whose Southern sympathies were thinly disguised, notwith-standing his Queen's proclamation of neutrality. Had Serrano been able to do so without incurring the naval wrath of the United States, he would no doubt have been delighted to permit the *Florida* and *Alabama* to shelter their prizes in Cuban ports and thus put them—as he thought—out of reach of annoying Union cruisers. He resented having to swallow the kicking and cuffing given Cuba by Northern warships. Truckling to their highhanded violations of Cuba's "neutrality" was bitter medicine.

Serrano would shortly be superseded in his colonial post, and the Confederacy was to lose a staunch friend. Actually he was kicked upstairs. Returning to Madrid, he assumed the foreign ministry portfolio in the Castilian government, remaining a valiant but use-less ally of the South to the end. It is probable that the overly cor-dial exchange of missives between him and the Confederate presi-dent had induced his recall. More to the point, Spain had no desire to tangle with the mounting sea power of the United States. Cuba was her last sizable foothold, the most exquisite colonial gem left her. The United States had often cast covetous eyes on the Pearl of the Antilles. Gentlemen in the seats of the mighty at Washington had even proposed annexation, peaceably if possible, forcibly if necessary. Many was the American filibuster, intent on seizing the island, that had washed up in blood on her strands. The threat of aggression by her powerful neighbor had dangled over Cuba for decades.

Yet to John Maffitt, Serrano was frank, exuberant, and hopeful. "My hands will soon be untied. I will be free to say what I think and feel. My soul and heart are with you in your struggle. I will return to Spain as your minister and do all I can to cause your government to be recognized."

"What more could my country ask?" said Maffitt.

Regretfully, though, Don Francisco could not prolong the *Florida*'s stay. There was the little hurdle of neutrality. He must abide by it. Nor should the *capitán* forget Yankee cruisers were as numerous as sharks along Cuba's coast. He dropped his voice to impart a bit of warning that was really unnecessary: busybody American Consul Shufeldt was again telegraphing every port on the island, frantically imploring "any American warship in sight" to steam over and wing the Confederate hawk.

"And now, Capitán Maf-feet! Before you go."

From a decanter on his desk Serrano filled two stemmed glasses. Fine Spanish sherry it was, gleaming like topaz in the sunlight streaming through the patio window.

"*Viva la Confederación del Sud!*" They raised their glasses.

It was Maffitt's turn. "To his Excellency: friend of the Confederate States!"

By midnight, the *Florida* was coaled and shipshape. Lingering longer was out of the question. The Union pack would show up before dawn. Raising her anchor, the *Florida* headed eastward, lights out, on the hunt now. In the morning the red disk of the sun rose out of a placid sea. Skirting the shore, the ship kept a sharp lookout. Cuba's coastline was made to order for this game of hide and seek. Saw-toothed by inlets and crannies, the island's unfrequented hideouts offered fast sanctuary, if Union avengers pressed too hard.

At 9 A.M. the *Florida* sighted prey ahead, a likely bark gliding along over the bright waters. Streaking after her, the *Florida*'s gun summoned her to haul up, but the master of the would-be victim, *La Coquena*, was not so easily intimidated. He decided to run for refuge within the charmed three-mile league, which was luckily near at hand. He knew his neutral rights, and waters, too. He dashed off desperately and won. Maffitt might have cut her down with gunfire, but the three-mile line was questionably close and this was no place to take a chance of creating an unpleasant impasse for the gentleman at Havana, who had so lately toasted the great new Republic of the South. The *Florida* sailed on, out-maneuvered, but not for long.

Over the shiny waters, three hours out of Matanzas and bound for Boston, came the brig *Windward*, deep-laden with molasses and never a thought of danger. The *Florida* broke out English colors, but the master of the *Windward* took no chances. He took to his heels, but a shot that geysered near the brig's bow was inducement enough. Into the wind came Prize Number Two.

"I thought you were the *Alabama*," admitted the master of the doomed ship as he came aboard the raider.

"We're in the same business," replied Maffitt dryly, and almost in the same breath he gave orders to put the torch to the prize. In half an hour fire was licking her sides.

Smoke still billowed from the gutted hull of the *Windward* when the bark *Corris Anne*, chock-full of hogshead shooks, sailed un-suspectingly into Maffitt's arms. "Like taking candy from a child," he commented as the brig rounded to, a prisoner. By dusk she was a blazing inferno drifting into the harbor of Cárdenas, and gave the citizens the thrill of their lives. The war was flaring on their very doormats. Now to get out of the way and fast. Three bonfires in a row was practice enough for the *Florida's* torchmen. Maffitt wanted bigger game.

2

At this moment the South's bid for independence was rising. Her victory at Fredericksburg had resounded in foreign capitals. Lee was poised like a tiger to claw again at the Army of the Potomac. Lincoln was changing generals, searching, yearning for the man who could wrap up victory in Virginia. Congress was in a turmoil and the press was viewing with alarm the outcome of the struggle.

Gideon Welles was in double trouble with two Confederate "panthers" lurking about the Gulf and adjacent waters. For once his refusal to weaken the blockade and unleash a pack of his fleetest warhounds was relaxed. Panicky shippers were again knocking at his door. The excitement over the *Alabama's* ravages along the coast had subsided only to rise again in crescendo. Telegraph orders were flying to commanders of the blockading squadrons:

The *Florida* has escaped from Mobile, and the *Alabama* has destroyed the *Hatteras* off Galveston. Let the *Rhode Island, Lackawanna* and *Monongahela* be sent to sea with utmost dispatch.

He had already ordered the speedy *Vanderbilt* to hustle down to Cuba and sink the new menace. The commander of the *Shepherd Knapp*, a man with the ornate name of Hy. St. C. Eytinge, took off, vowing like a knight of old: "I shall scour these seas in hot pursuit, and God defend the right." It was Eytinge, be it remembered, who had sworn the year before, when chasing the *Sumter*, "I shall conquer or die at my guns." He did neither. Nor did he catch Maffitt. While scouring the seas—as he had proclaimed so valiantly—he failed to catch sight of a Cuban coral reef, which harpooned his ship as though it were a soft-bellied whale, providing the local salvaging gentry with a windfall. The *Shepherd Knapp* was a total loss. To cap off Welles's adversities came a dispatch from Key West. "Pirate Maffitt" had burned three American ships off Cuba's north coast.

Ringmaster of the Union gunboat rodeo on these tropic waters was Rear Admiral Charles Wilkes, whose elevation to flag rank was one of the promotion anomalies of the Civil War. It was his reward for involving the United States in a near-war with Great Britain. Wilkes had a flair for issuing orders. They flew out of his cabin like bats out of a cave. Having promulgated them, he waited around for the "boys" to make the kill, and wondered why they didn't. As commander of the independent West Indian Flying Squadron (seven or more ships), he was entrusted with the hunt: first, for the *Sumter*, then for the *Alabama*, and now for the *Florida*.

His flagship was the *Wachusett*, a new screw sloop, heavily gunned, sister ship of the *Kearsarge*. Wilkes was dawdling off Mujeres Island, on the Yucatan coast, when he received the news that the *Florida* had escaped from Mobile. Chagrined, he was suddenly fired up to do and dare. At forced draft, the *Wachusett* scurried for Havana. He reasoned correctly that the *Florida* would probably touch that port. It may have been just a hunch. Exactly twelve hours after the *Florida* decamped—at sunset, to be precise—the *Wachusett* steamed into the harbor, her guns run out and "a bone in her teeth." On the quarter-deck stood Wilkes, scouring the harbor with his glasses.

But far more startling news greeted Wilkes. The *Florida* had burned three ships, two of them off Cárdenas that same day. Opportunity knocked loudly at Wilkes's cabin door, but he refused to hear it. Had he sped off at once along the north Cuban coast, he could have secured his fame. Instead he began issuing up-and-at-'em orders for other ships, ships that would not reach Havana for days: the *Oneida, San Jacinto, Santiago de Cuba, Tioga,* and *Sonoma.*

After burning this third ship off Cárdenas, the *Florida* had run into trouble. The coal she bought at robbery prices at Havana would hardly raise a head of steam, barely five pounds, cutting down her speed to three knots. This fuel was the best Havana had to offer; but in a fight, low-grade coal would reduce the *Florida's* chance of survival by half. Unable to maneuver, she would be easy prey for almost any Federal ship. Maffitt no longer dared to stay in these waters. He could have been caught or sunk hands down.

Maffitt decided to get out of the way at once. Northing slowly, with double lookouts scanning every fleck on the horizon, the *Florida* crossed the Bahama Bank and ran up the Tongue of the Ocean, with Nassau as her objective. Green Key, of recent grim memory, slid by off to starboard. Reconnoitering carefully, Maffitt steamed into the Bahaman harbor "with the secession ensign at her peak and the war pennant at her main," to receive an ovation. The correspondent of a Liverpool newspaper sized it up: "The *Florida* became at once an object of interest. The secession sympathizers were jubilant, while the Union men went about in a depressed mood. Captain Maffitt immediately went to visit the governor, was received very cordially, and dined with his Excellency."

American Consul Whiting literally bit the air the moment the "late *Oreto*" appeared; but being a practical man, he hustled a schooner off to alert warships patrolling off Abaco Light to hurry over and crack down on the intruder. He was more incensed when Bahama's governor permitted Maffitt to have as much coal as he could carry. "Pretty neutrality, this, I must say," moaned Whiting to the State Department, citing the Union *Dacotah,* which was allowed only twenty tons recently, while Maffitt was permitted to fill his bunkers.

Desertion black-marked the *Florida's* brief sojourn at Nassau. Twenty-six of her crew vanished. "Our hard cases," Maffitt characterized them. Vexing to be sure, but his luck was on the rise. A

Negro crimp, who, amazingly, dealt in white flesh and blood, came aboard and agreed, for gold dollars, to deliver some eighteen men to the *Florida*, provided the deal was consummated three miles out, thus bypassing Britain's Foreign Enlistment Act. The crimp was as good as his word. He came alongside with a tugboat. Milling about her deck were various "gentlemen," equipped with rod and line, apparently out for a day's fishing. With little ado the "fishermen" straggled up the *Florida's* gangway, to make their marks on the articles of enlistment, and so be inducted into the Confederate States Navy.

Meanwhile, the side-wheeler *Sonoma* (one of Wilkes's pack) had picked up the *Florida's* trail soon after she left Nassau. Commander Stevens on her bridge had deduced that his quarry would probably head for Nassau and on up the Atlantic seaboard for a sweep at Northern shipping. His surmise was correct.

In the Queen's Channel he sighted a strange sail flying English colors. It was the *Florida*. The *Sonoma's* paddlewheels went into high beat, but Maffitt had sighted his pursuer at the same time, though his glasses mistook her for the ten-gun *Santiago de Cuba*. A fight was not on his agenda. "Our cruise had just commenced and its object was the destruction of commerce. I did not think it my duty to seek an engagement or run the risk of injury to our engine"—so he kept away.

He admitted the *Sonoma* outsteamed the *Florida*. Three times she had the raider almost under her guns. Each time an engine mishap crumpled her speed. Doggedly, though, she sniffed at the *Florida's* wake for thirty-six hours. Her game was to hang on until she met another Union cruiser and then gang up on the fleeing Confederate. Shaking off his pursuer, Maffitt stood northward with the idea of "giving the coast of New England a small appreciation of war troubles," but off Hatteras, Old Neptune rose in his wrath and drove him southeast to avoid the fury of the gale.

The next night a massive ship-of-war loomed out of the mist. Large, lengthy, the splash of her paddlewheels roared like waterfalls. She bore up close to the *Florida*, and Maffitt recognized the powerful *Vanderbilt*, whose eleven-inch guns could have splintered the raider like a match box. Her steel cutwater could literally guillotine smaller ships. Maffitt admitted, "To be rammed by this immense ship would have closed our career. She'd cut us in half."

Dousing all lights save a single lantern over the side, he shut off steam and stood end-on toward the *Vanderbilt*. It was his old lie-low trick—go dead and sit still. Gingerly, the mammoth sidled within hailing distance. Over the hazy waters came: "Have you seen a steamer go by?" Maffitt raised his speaking trumpet, "Yes, and going at great speed right astern." Then he held his breath and waited. Would she take the bait? After sniffing about for ten minutes, the *Vanderbilt* wheeled and sped off after the phantom steamer.

Flying along on the trades the *Florida* steered a course for the Spanish Main, though eager and ready to do business with any Yankee merchantman she might flush en route. The *Alabama* had passed this way three months before, leaving a trail of flame to set the pattern. Presently the *Florida* stood in the track of homebound East Indiamen and China clippers. Hope ran high.

Banking the *Florida's* fires and raising her propeller into its well, Maffitt ordered his sailors aloft to loosen sail. Under canvas the *Florida* bowled along, as if glad to abandon, though only temporarily, the new order of fireboxes and steam gages, propellers and paddlewheels, that was slowly relegating sail to a vanished realm.

Slanting southward under the cottony trade clouds, the *Florida* took time to beautify herself. Discipline, and pretty absolute at that, was the ship's watchword. Filched bodily from the old navy was the rigid code of the Confederate States Navy. Commanders of vessels were enjoined to be vigilant in suppressing insubordination, dissolute and immoral practices, drunkenness (which was a laugh); and to administer swift punishment. Divine services were to be held "in a solemn, orderly and reverent manner, twice a day and a sermon preached on Sunday." It is doubtful if ever the *Florida's* Jacks heard a sermon. There was no chaplain aboard, and John Maffitt was no preacher.

Instead of listening to appeals to the Almighty, the gunner and his mates polished their guns until they shone like mirrors. The engine-room crew worked like beavers, immensely proud of the burnished beauty of their twin powerhouse of steel and brass. Rigging was tarred and re-rattled, masts scraped and varnished, decks holystoned until they gave off a dazzling whiteness. "Youngsters" were given lessons in splicing and knotting. Midshipmen were introduced to the mysteries of navigation. Bright mornings—and

Sundays too—found them listening not to sermons, but to lessons in navigation, and shooting the sun under the tutelage of John Maffitt himself.

3

February 12, 1863. Longitude 65° 58′ W; Latitude 24° 1′ N— somewhere well east of the Bahamas and north of Puerto Rico. At ten A.M. the foretop sang down a welcome "Sail ho! Sail ho-o-o!" Yonder, five miles off the port beam, a clipper under vast spreads of canvas was winging along like a great white bird. The tips of her tall, raking masts seemed to scratch the blue sky above her. In a freshening wind she was a thing alive, knifing over the waters as if immeasurably proud of her ability to ride the waves with such speed and grace. Symmetry and precision marked her every movement.

Unable to restrain his enthusiasm, John Maffitt glued his glasses on her, appraising every feature. She was a Yankee, all right. It was written all over her. Who but a Yankee could build such a beautiful ship? Most likely she was heading for her home port, New York, on the last lap of her journey from the other side of the world—a guess that proved to be correct. Excitement beat a faster tattoo in Maffitt's breast. This dream ship would be his, *if* he could catch her. Breaking out the Stars and Stripes, Maffitt tried to coax the clipper to follow suit, but the lady was shy and not flirtatious. Obstinately, she refused to reveal her name, or rather, her nationality, though there really was no need for it. Instead, the clipper's captain, apparently scenting trouble or realizing that the vessel dogging him so closely was not a Union gunboat, changed direction and began throwing on sail.

Maffitt sent for Engineer Jackson, who hurried to the bridge.

"Mr. Jackson, stir your fires," ordered Maffitt. "We need every pound of steam you can raise. This is one we mustn't lose."

Then to the officer of the deck, "Raise every rag of sail."

The chase was on. All hands flocked topside to watch and thrill. Steam and sail pitted their power against one of the fastest things ever to cleave the seas under sail alone. John Maffitt climbed up the ratlines to get a better look. What a morsel for the raider, whose eyes lighted up like those of a huntsman who has sighted magnificent quarry. Deep in the engine room the fireboxes licked out red tongues at the volatile Cardiff coal, as if they too knew the part they were playing in this chase.

Two hours slid by. On fled the fugitive. Maffitt figured he was gaining half a mile an hour on her, but time was passing—interminably, it seemed. Obviously, he would lose this race if the clipper could stave off capture until nightfall, which meant keeping out of range of the *Florida*'s bow gun. Three hours, four, five. The ship's bell was gonging the sixth, when the clipper came in reach of Maffitt's long arm. With a warning boom the bow gun spat out her "heave to" that whistled across the waters three miles, to splash a ship's length astern of the fleeing vessel. Those one-hundred-and-ten-pound shots bore pressing, screaming invitations to haul up. The next might smash directly into her. Obediently, almost shamefacedly, the clipper clewed up, backed her yards, and quietly awaited her doom. She had tried and lost. It was four P.M.

Gliding up swiftly, the *Florida* hauled down her masquerade and ran up Confederate streamers. The raider's railbirds stared incredulously as the *Florida* described two complete circuits about her beautiful captive, much as a cat would toy with a mouse, after having made sure of her meal. On the bridge congratulations went round. This was the prize of prizes. God only knew how much she was worth or what her cargo might be.

But from somewhat-dazed Midshipman Terry Sinclair came this heartfelt outburst: "She rounded to, and as she lay thus, with black hull, gilt streak, scraped and varnished masts, and snow white sails, there was a general exclamation of admiration, coupled with regret that a thing of such beauty must be destroyed."

John Maffitt shared no such regrets. Setting fire to enemy ships was his mission, though he had never dreamed of winging one like this. As the *Florida* circled her magnificent victim, Maffitt read the name lettered artistically across her stern, *Jacob Bell*—a New Yorker, and one of the finest, fastest, and most renowned clippers ever to sail. She was famed wherever men put out to sea, and a record-breaker as well, having shown her heels to many a good ship. City bells had rung for her launching; hosannas had split the air as she dipped into her native element. Since then, painting, song, and story had immortalized her. She had weathered gales and icy winds off Cape Horn, had sweltered in tropic heat, and had ridden out rollers that seemed high as her tapering masts. She had braved all the terrors of the sea—successfully, until now.

For long moments John Maffitt stood, admired, and gloated. Richmond would be pleased with *this* burnt offering. Washington, on the other hand, would demand his immediate hanging for this act of "consummate piracy." Maffitt imagined the thrill it would be for the South were he to come triumphant into port, escorting the fastest clipper afloat.

The *Jacob Bell* was no stranger to John Maffitt. He had seen her before, had admired her prodigiously, as any true sailor would. Proud of her lineage, she was holding her own in an age that was passing from sail to steam, fighting it out with the white hot vapor that was revolutionizing navigation the world over. Yet, she was not to live to hear the requiem of the winds as canvas-driven ships sailed off into history. Perhaps it was just as well.

A captive, caught in the machinations of a bitter war, she was to be sacrificed on the altar of hate. As such, the *Jacob Bell* would go into history as the biggest bonfire ever touched off by a Confederate cruiser on the high seas.

Now to business. Maffitt summoned Lieutenant Charles Read. That young man was eager enough.

"Mr. Read, I want you to board her," said Maffitt. "Bring her papers and her captain, and, above everything, her flag."

"Aye, aye, sir," and off went the excited boarders. In a matter of minutes the tackles were whining as the *Florida's* cutter dropped to the water.

Meanwhile, having circled the clipper twice, the *Florida* ranged within seventy-five yards of her captive and lay to. Raising his trumpet, Maffitt hailed her. "Strike your colors!" The clipper demurred. Again Maffitt spoke. This time more sharply. Obediently, the *Jacob Bell* hauled down her flag—forever.

CHAPTER XVII

The Lady or the Pirate

LEANING ON THE quarter rail, Maffitt watched his boarders clamber up the clipper's glossy sides. His dark eyes flickered. It was hard to restrain his enthusiasm. He had made a catch that would resound throughout the North and South.

Captain Charles Frisbee, master of the *Jacob Bell*, met his visitors as they hopped over the bulwarks. This determined Yankee seaman knew no fear of man or wind or water. Forty years of combating the sea lay behind him.

Prize Master Read spoke first. Belted at his waist was a huge naval pistol. He barked out the historic routine: "You are a prize of the Confederate States Steamer *Florida*, Lieutenant Maffitt commanding."

Momentarily, the Northern mariner was stunned. His gaze flicked upward to the great sails flapping loosely, then he struck back.

"We're carrying English property. You have no right to interfere with this ship."

"I am Lieutenant Read, and simply obeying orders," replied the young officer. "Would you be so kind as to fetch your papers and come with us?"

"Is this the way you seize neutral goods?" demanded Frisbee with some belligerence.

"You and Lieutenant Maffitt will have to settle that. My orders are to bring you back with me, sir."

"There are ladies aboard my ship," riposted Frisbee. "My wife is in a delicate condition."

"We will make them as comfortable as we can," assured Read.

"But my ship!" Already Frisbee had sensed her fate. His face paled at the thought.

Read's voice was cold. "We'll probably burn her, but that's for Lieutenant Maffitt to decide. Tell the ladies to pack up such few articles as they'll need. You and your crew are prisoners of war. We'll come back for them."

Like a man in a trance, Captain Frisbee slipped down the ship's ladder to sit glumly in the cutter's stern sheets. With sturdy strokes, the tars quickly pulled alongside the *Florida*. Maffitt met them at the head of the gangway.

"I am Lieutenant Maffitt, sir," he said extending his hand.

"And I am Captain Frisbee."

"I regret meeting you under such circumstances," added Maffitt. Such courtesy. His torch was already lit.

"Maffitt! Maffitt! I never heard of you before," Frisbee's voice had a ring of unbelief.

"Well, you have now," said the Southerner, with a smile that died instantly.

Again the mariner spoke, "I thought at first you were the *Alabama*."

"My ship's the *Florida*," said Maffitt with pride. "She has no label. At least, none you can see."

"But we're carrying British-owned goods," asserted Frisbee. "You have no right to touch neutral goods."

"Perhaps not, but I think I have. Your ship's American. Lord Russell recently said if English subjects risk their property on United States vessels, they must look for compensation to the Confederate government. That's their privilege. But why dispute the point? Now may I see your manifest, if you please."

Maffitt's eyes bulged. Riffling through the clipper's declaration made him gasp. Sixteen thousand chests of tea. One thousand three hundred and eighty tons of it. Mountains. This was only the beginning. More tea packed in innumerable brightly-lacquered caddies and canisters. He read further. Camphor, cassia, matting. A thousand cases of firecrackers! Fans for my lady by untold thousands. Rainbow lacquerware of a hundred different shapes. Carvings of sandalwood, ivory, and shell. Temple bells. It beggared description. Seemingly, the Celestial Kingdom had contributed to the *Jacob Bell's* cargo tidbits to please every palate and fancy.

Maffitt's thoughts shot back to the Confederacy, where belts were tightening, and where the bottom of the bucket would soon be scraped.

And the value! Slightly over two million dollars! Duties on these importations were already figured up. The Federal Treasury would never collect this $175,000.

As for the clipper, she flew the familiar yellow, red, and yellow house-flag of A. A. Low and Brothers, who had pioneered the long runs to China. Tall ships to Cathay bringing back tea and silk had brought them fortunes and fine homes on Brooklyn Heights and Staten Island, where they could watch their ships sailing out and coming home.

Movingly, Captain Frisbee asked mercy for his ship. He might as well have appealed to the gales to stop their howling or the waves their tossing. The *Jacob Bell* was the rear-guard of the clippers, implored the mariner. That alone should reprieve her. But Maffitt remained hard as nails. This was the Confederacy's fight for life. Destruction of the North's means of making war, of her resources on the sea, which brought her wealth to fight with, could be a path to victory for the South. Spare the *Jacob Bell*? Hardly.

"I'm sorry, Captain Frisbee. The laws of war are hard. Your ship's a legitimate prize. I have no alternative. My orders are to destroy all I capture."

Unblinking, but game to the core, Captain Frisbee heard the death sentence of his ship. Maffitt's voice carried finality. Returning to the clipper, Frisbee summoned his passengers and crew, forty-one all told, to the main cabin. Without trimmings, he broke the news. The *Jacob Bell* was to be burned. His wife, six months gone with child, was game as he. Stoically his crew accepted their fate. Five of them, indeed, were to transfer their allegiance to the Confederacy after reaching the *Florida*.

But for passenger Martha Noyes Williams of Utica, New York, old Blackbeard himself had risen out of the sea in the person of her captor. It was unfortunate that this lady (whom Maffitt mildly designated as "something of a tartar") engaged passage on the *Jacob Bell*, which cleared Foochow, China, for New York on November 7, 1862. More unfortunate was it that the unpredictable fortunes of war had cast her into the clutches of "pirate Maffitt." It is not unreasonable to think that in olden times pirate captors, their patience worn thin, would have made the lady walk the plank.

Wife of an American customs official at Swatow, China, Martha Williams was not uncomely. Wielding a vengeful pen, she embalmed the capture of the *Jacob Bell* in a rare book (now long out of print), entitled *A Year in China*. To her travelog of Chinese habits she appended a "Narrative of Capture and Imprisonment when Homeward Bound on Board the Rebel Pirate *Florida*." Obligingly, poet William Cullen Bryant contributed a foreword. The author of *Thanatopsis* censured Maffitt for his "barbarities," accusing him of pilfering the lady's personal effects "among his other robberies." Snapped Bryant, "It illustrates the indiscriminate spirit of plunder with which this new class of freebooters exercise their profession."

Martha Williams' encounter with the "notorious Maffitt" flavored the book with war adventure and gave it a brief spell of best selling. The lady was even invited to Washington, where she related to President Lincoln the miseries suffered at Maffitt's hands.

But now, hurrying to her stateroom, she rounded up a few feminine necessities and tied them into "two emigrant looking bundles" in counterpanes. The long trip—it was the ninety-seventh day out of Foochow—had wearied her. Seasickness had afflicted her; but, like a woman, her chief worry at this critical juncture was:

> There was no time to give any attention to one's personal appearance . . . and my lady readers can readily imagine how they would look en *déshabillé*, with a loose gown of cotton print, an old shawl thrown about their shoulders, and a straw hat in place of a bonnet.

Hardly fetching enough to meet "pirates," who, tradition holds, preferred their females young and glamorous.

First to be packed off to the *Florida* were the two ladies. A ticklish task it was. The sea was running. Mrs. Frisbee was pregnant. She and Mrs. Williams had had a tiff, and as Maffitt put it in his *Journal*, "The ladies were not on terms."

But war recognized no such tiffs, and the two out-of-tune ladies were fastened securely side by side in a wide rattan chair, and hoisted overside to be lowered into the *Florida's* cutter by rope and tackle. Coming alongside the cruiser the operation was repeated, or rather reversed. Nerve-racking to be sure, but war was that way. Being suddenly snatched from the comfort of a paneled cabin on the finest clipper afloat and transferred to the comfortless hospitality of a commerce raider was not something to appeal to a lady's fancy.

To Martha Williams, "being lowered upon the deck of an armed vessel prepared for piratical warfare, amid the gaze of brutalized and vicious men, whose vulgar, jeering expressions of countenance was enough to make one shrink back involuntarily with loathing and indignation, was a severe test for a woman who, both in body and mind, was greatly weakened by a long voyage and months of disease in the tropics of the East."

The *Florida's* Jack hardly deserved this castigation. Had he jeered at these fair captives, John Maffitt would have ordered him ironed on the spot and consigned to the brig on bread and water.

But the Stars and Stripes came to Mrs. Williams' rescue, performing what she termed "doubtless the last honorable service of the flag of the ill-fated *Jacob Bell.*" Claimed as a prize by the "pirates," Captain Frisbee had folded the flag loosely over the ladies' laps as they began their flying-trapeze journey to the *Florida.* Averred Martha Williams, "The gleam of comfort and sunshine that flashed through my confused brain when my eye rested on one particular star in those folds can never be forgotten." It was probably the seventh star, New York's.

But, narrated the lady, "On being lowered to the deck of the cruiser, and freed from our chair tackline, I heard a rather cultivated voice on my right saying, 'Please take my arm, madam.' I saw nothing, for my first glance at the deck and the rough men with upturned faces rudely gazing as I hung in air, had caused my head and eyes to drop. But woman's natural instinct when in a position of fearful suffering and rude exposure, to readily and gratefully receive civility and protection—no matter from what source it may come—led me to accept the proffered arm."

It was the arm of the "pirate" himself, John Maffitt, "leader of the buccaneers," who graciously escorted her to his own cabin, which he had already vacated. Indeed, Maffitt had dressed scrupulously for the occasion. Ladies were coming aboard, and old habit was strong, even amid the rigors of commerce raiding. The dandy in him would out. Later the lady would mortify her conscience for even daring to touch the "polluted" gray of his sleeve. Hating was the vogue in war, then as now.

Overnight, manned by a prize crew, the clipper lay to near the *Florida*. Her crew was ironed by twos, and they slept that way with an armed watch for good measure. It was an imperative precaution. Maffitt had already relieved them of their long sailor knives, for which Mrs. Williams later flayed him as a thief. Thirty-odd men armed with knives, with half a chance, might easily seize the ship. A few stabs in officers' backs, and the *Florida* would sail off to New York a Northern prize.

In the morning Maffitt boarded the clipper, the only prize he ever set foot on, to watch his men break out her hold. Jack dived into the fragrant recesses as if he had discovered Abdullah's cave. Despoiling this treasure house was a day's task, but Jack reveled in it. Over to the cruiser went a hundred cases of tea for use in the messes. Eagerly seized was the exquisite set of ship china, adorned by the flowery kingdom's skilled artisans and given to the Lows by the son of old Houqua, famed Canton merchant; as well as her silver service, linens, towels, and endless knickknacks.

Maffitt ordered her fired at 4 P.M. How he longed to sail her into Mobile, or Charleston, or Wilmington! Live oak, locust, pine, and cedar had gone into her building. Around her waist, above her shiny black hull, ran a broad belt of gold paint. Her main cabin was testimony to the decorator's art, paneled in rosewood and birdseye maple, with intersticings of Chinese satin of varied hues. On her cutwater sat a life-size replica of Captain Jacob Bell, her builder, who appeared utterly unconcerned over what was about to happen to his namesake.

After setting her death hour and giving instructions to his "firemen," Maffitt returned to the *Florida*, where Mrs. Williams accosted him with a formidable list of crates and packages which she wanted salvaged from the doomed ship. Apparently she had brought a sample of everything China had to offer.

"But, Mrs. Williams," he replied, as kindly as he could, "there isn't room for them. We can't pile them on deck. We couldn't serve our guns if we did."

"But, Captain, it would be very hard to lose them," she protested. "The boxes in the hold contain my wardrobe, household goods, and many things of rare value. Your boarding officer promised to get them for me."

"Perhaps he did," admitted the officer, "but it's really impossible. I am allowing you far more than is customary. Didn't you take out insurance on your goods?"

She admitted that just before sailing from Foochow her husband had bought an insurance policy "just in case anything disastrous happened," though it had never occurred to her that the *Jacob Bell* might be waylaid by a Confederate man-of-war. The Union Navy had things well in hand.

On November 7, the day the *Jacob Bell* cleared for New York, the dread news of the *Alabama's* arrival in the Far East had not trickled up to Foochow. Off Java Head, in Sunda Strait, the *Alabama* had torched off her first prize. Terror-stricken American traders had spread their wings in flight to ports of safety. The *Jacob Bell* had glided past the very spot where the *Alabama* lit her first bonfire in the Orient. Malay bumboat vendors had informed Captain Frisbee of the *Alabama's* fiery visitation, but said the raider had continued north. There was no need to worry.

Maffitt examined her policy. "It's a war risk policy. If it's good at all, it should be good for this. But I am in no position to advise you, Mrs. Williams. Traveling with valuables in wartime is risky. It's my opinion your policy might be contested if you save anything."

"Then the rest, Captain Maffitt, must burn and go down with the ship," she moaned, fixing her eyes balefully on her captor.

"That is right, Mrs. Williams."

The lady seemed not to recognize the brutal fact that everything of value, personal effects and otherwise, including the money in her purse, were legitimate prize had Maffitt decided he wanted them. A Northern naval officer was later to write Maffitt, he "saw no reason why all the curios of China should be exempt, hence the lady's wrath at your spoils of war." Raphael Semmes had encountered this same dilemma when he captured the Indiaman

T. B. Wales in the same neighborhood. Cherished possessions simply had to go the way of the ship—into the flames.

For five days aboard the *Florida* the lady's rage mounted. She outdid old Gideon himself. Maffitt accepted it with good grace. His Journal reveals no ill will toward his recalcitrant prisoner. She could not get a bath. That was understandable. Abhorrent to her was the slaughter of the *Jacob Bell's* livestock, though it provided fresh meat for the raider's crew and prisoners. The *Florida's* happy-go-lucky middies had gone aboard the *Jacob Bell* and frolicked about the deck in her hoop skirts. This was a crime. But her ire was reserved chiefly for Maffitt, who longed to get rid of her as soon as he could overhaul a sail on whom he could pawn her off. Nor did she overlook the chance to pay her respects to Maffitt's "nine-year-old son,"[!] who, she said, was "a hopeful youth who had requested his father to send him a Yankee's head with the teeth all in it!!!" (The exclamation points are hers.) This was later read and believed like the gospel in the North, where hatred for Semmes and Maffitt had reached a high peak.

Rebutting her lambastings later came Captain Frisbee of the *Jacob Bell,* who accepted the loss of his ship as a casualty of war and presented to Maffitt the fine painting of the clipper that hung in his cabin. It was his wife who made the most earnest plea for mercy. Maffitt recorded, "Mrs. Frisbee pleaded with me to bond the *Jacob Bell.* I declined with regret. The ship belongs to the house of Low & Company, notoriously antagonistic to the South and its domestic institutions. I am glad they have had this misfortune."

2

4 P.M. February 13, 1863. Stout of heart, like one who has shrived herself and waits resignedly to be burned at the stake, the clipper rested on the waters. Her taut masts thrust skyward like imploring arms. If we must go, let it be otherwise! Give us to the gales, or the rollers, or set our sails and send us crashing to a grand finish on a roaring reef. But not like this!

On the *Florida's* deck the crew huddled along the rail, overwhelmed with a sense of sorrow. Each was deeply wrapped in his own thoughts. There was no gloating as they waited. Standing aloof, holding his wife's hand, Captain Frisbee gazed dejectedly on the ship that had weathered many a gale for him, carried him safely past many a menacing shore. Slightly apart from the Frisbees stood Martha Williams, watching, waiting. On the quarter-deck John Maffitt and his officers also watched and waited.

The incendiaries worked fast like old, adept hands. In the exquisite main cabin they piled hand-carved chairs upholstered with fine Chinese fabrics. Over them they poured buckets of melted butter and lard. In the forehold they heaped faggots of lightwood and other combustibles, anointing them with more lard and butter. Down in the main hold, amid pyramids of tea chests, they dumped a barrel of whale oil. Then, touching off the three pyres, they dropped into their boats and shoved off. From the *Jacob Bell* three billows of smoke ascended like darkling curtains soon to be drawn aside. Let Martha Williams draw the picture as she saw it:

> The distressing circumstances under which we were placed rendered it impossible for us to feel the sublimity of the spectacle she presented as the flames crept steadily up her sails, spars and rigging, until she became a pyramid of fire.
> To us the last sight of our noble ship a little before her masts fell, when all sails and rigging ablaze, she was quietly floating on, impressed us with a scene of awful and melancholy grandeur.

Night came on. The spectators were glued to the scene. The flames were dying down. Deep in the recesses of her hold, fire was eating her heart out. One touch of levity lightened the drama. With a mighty crackling and banging, the thousand cases of firecrackers exploded all at once like a massive Fourth of July celebration. The tension broke with an outburst of hoorays.

Filling away into the night, the *Florida* turned her head southward over waters red with the glow of the clipper's last flaring. She was in her death throes now, burned almost to the water's edge.

Five days later—on February 17—Maffitt joyfully disposed of his guests. The hour was late. The crew had been piped down and had gone to their hammocks. At eight bells the *Florida* overhauled the bark *Morning Star*, flying Danish colors. Actually, she was a Northerner turned Dane for protection, joining the exodus of American shipping to foreign registry. Her captain agreed to take off Maffitt's prisoners and land them at St. Thomas. Maffitt would have forced it at the point of a gun, if need be, but the bark's captain was a good-natured, sympathetic sea dog. The transfer was done then and there. Thirty-six souls. Five had cast lots with the *Florida*.

For Martha Noyes Williams, the *Morning Star* was "a whole constellation of light, hope and joy." Yet, not without a parting fling would she take leave of the "officers, the highminded gentlemen," the "so-called boasted chivalry of the South," the "Goths and Vandals." A sharp breeze was whipping the sea; the cruiser was pitching. With infinite care, under Maffitt's keen eye, the ladies were safely ensconced in the cutter that would ferry them over to the *Morning Star*. Only the stars beaming above and the unsteady gleam of a ship's lantern lit up this "touching" farewell. The boat loads of the *Jacob Bell's* sailors shoved off with cheers and thanks for being well cared for. Courteously, Maffitt took Mrs. Williams' hand and apologized for whatever inconvenience she might have suffered on his ship. Lastly, he wished her Godspeed.

"Captain Maffitt," she replied ambiguously, "if ever you are taken prisoner, I hope you may be treated as well as you have treated us."

"Madam," he said, "I shall do my best not to be taken prisoner." Then, divining her thoughts, he added with a touch of merriment, "But I suspect you really wish me to be captured."

"I shall not pray for it," she shot back equivocally.

For her readers she later admitted, "I dared not, amid such surroundings, say, as I must, if a reply were given, that I wished him taken." She classified his parting "Goodbye and God bless you" as a fine piece of acting.

Over the side of his "disgusting vessel" she went to sail off through the night and ultimately land at Boston where, instantly, she became a heroine, lionized by the press and pulpit as a second Barbara Frietchie, who had bearded the "ferocious Maffitt" and his blood-lusting banditti in their den. Martha Williams' dolorous tale of "Confederate brutality" on the high seas received a tremendous build-up. If nothing else, it sold scads of her books. Henceforth, the thought of Maffitt, like that of Semmes, would send Yankee captains scuttling to safe harbors the world over.

But Martha Williams acquired further distinction than jousting with "pirate Maffitt." In 1869, when the United States billed (two billion at first count) Great Britain for depredations on Northern shipping by British-built Confederate cruisers, Martha Williams claimed, and got, compensation for her losses. She and a fifteen-year-old boy were the only passengers on destroyed vessels whose personal property was listed on the celebrated *Alabama* Claims. You will find her name among the manifold claimants. She also received a slice of the proceeds of the sale of Maffitt's confiscated property in Washington.

3

The fame of the *Florida* leaped skyward with the flames that devoured the *Jacob Bell*. This holocaust, whose glare seemed to reach round the world, promoted John Maffitt to the Number Two spot on the Union Navy's roster of most wanted Rebels. The "club" was exclusive. Raphael Semmes headed the list. Both were to swing from the yardarm when caught—if caught.

On the nation the impact of the clipper's incineration was profound. A baffled public cried out: Where is the Navy? Why doesn't it retaliate? Why couldn't it catch the perpetrator of this monstrous act? The very audacity of the man galled Northern emotions like hot acid. The *Jacob Bell* was legend, a national pride. John Maffitt had burned her! Popular indignation exploded. Editor Horace Greely suggested hanging him in Union Square, New York, and inviting everybody to the party.

In February, 1863, the fiery slaughter of American shipping was rising to its peak, just as was the Confederacy herself. The *Jacob Bell* story erupted on front pages of Northern papers with an eye-jolting impact far out of proportion to its bearing on the outcome of the war. Nevertheless, it was the fiercest individual challenge yet hurled at the Union Navy, which, as Admiral Porter pointed out, refused to profit by its inglorious experience with the *Alabama's* raid down the Atlantic coast. Avengers dashed to the scene of the clipper's demise. The idea of spreading out like a pack of hounds seems never to have occurred to them.

No single vessel destroyed by Confederate commerce raiders played so much havoc with shipping morale. The wails of shipowners and insurance presidents rose in a chorus outside the office of Gideon Welles at Washington. At this juncture few, if any, dreamed of the day when Britain, almost at pistol point, would repay their losses. But the bedeviled Old Man of the Sea, blinking his rheumy eyes, puffing his inveterate pipe, sat tight, venting his spleen at Semmes, Maffitt, and his fellow cabinet members.

Nor did the editorial pundits, whose hate flared so rhetorically, realize that in Semmes and Maffitt the Northern navy was fencing with the most adept hands ever to play the game of catch-me-if-you-can. Semmes was past master of the in-and-out-and-vanish; Maffitt, a genius at getting into traps and getting out.

Ocean scorching by these gray whippets had an ominous feature. Armies might win land battles, but control of the sea lanes could, conceivably, bring ultimate victory. The pyre of the *Jacob Bell* drove this unpleasant thought home. Unless the *Alabama* and *Florida* were scotched, they could, within reason, threaten the whole Union cause. A brace of Confederate cruisers had all but disrupted the North's sea traffic. It was anybody's guess how many of these sea raiders would lunge out of Britain's shipyards. Estimates ran high as a score. Such a striking force, hacking away at vulnerable Yankee commerce, could pack wallop enough to stifle American trade abroad, and force depletion of the blockade. This, indeed, was the threatening, deadly intent of Confederate naval strategy—to siphon off the North's best ships to protect her commerce. Already hundreds of Northern merchant vessels had swapped flags for the safer umbrella of Britain's Union Jack. Nor would they ever return to American registry. These truants were to be a dead loss to the nation's carrying trade.

In the Confederate Museum at Richmond, Virginia, there are four small Chinese bird prints, done on rice paper, their subtle colors still vivid. Once, they adorned the main cabin of the *Jacob Bell*. Pasted in a scrapbook kept by the *Florida's* Assistant Engineer Quinn, they are the only mementos left of this once-glorious clipper.

CHAPTER XVIII

Scorching the South Atlantic

Ho! For the Spanish Main and Barbados! Over the broad Atlantic, with the Leewards to starboard, the *Florida* flew along before the gales. Her coal was down to ounces. Angrily, Old Neptune shook his trident in her face. Great combers swarmed over her bulwarks. She took their buffetings sportively, as if she liked them. The cut of her sails and the greediness of her fireboxes distressed John Maffitt; but, for all that, she was a good seaboat, as the saying went. Sailorlike, his heart warmed to her.

Tempest bowed out to fair winds. On sailed the *Florida*, skirting the islands that girdle the Caribbean like an emerald necklace. On these waters Yankee privateers had maimed British shipping in the American Revolution. Maffitt had come this way on the *St. Louis* and *Macedonian* way back in his midshipman days.

On February 25 the *Florida* stood in for Carlisle Bay, Barbados, easternmost of the Lesser Antilles, and first of Britain's rare jewels in the New World. She nosed into the Bridgetown anchorage "with the Confederate flag, until this day a total stranger to Barbados, floating from our gaff, the first herald of Southern nationality the inhabitants had seen."

Her arrival was the signal for an ovation beyond John Maffitt's fondest hopes. Southern prestige ran high at Barbados, but the actual presence of an armed outrider of the infant republic sent the islanders into ecstasies. Officially, there was silence. No salute to the Stars and Bars boomed from the fort, no delegation of port of-ficials came aboard offering civilities. But, as at Havana, the raider's engines had hardly stopped turning before admiring citizenry flocked to greet her, electrified by the thunderclap news of her de-struction of the *Jacob Bell*. It was a convincing demonstration of the long arm of the Confederacy. In his Journal, Maffitt gave way to nostalgic musings: "What a contrast to the last time I visited this place in the *Macedonian* in 1841. Then the Stars and Stripes floated over my head and the Union seemed as firm as the rock of Gibraltar. Abolition was considered treasonable, and the North and South were one; for nullification had died a natural death, and harmony guided the national association."

His naval cap ajaunt (as was his wont), he hurried ashore to ap-ply to Colonial Governor James Walker for permission to fill his bunkers. Gales had forced the *Florida* to use up coal immoderately, he pleaded. His boilers were gasping for fuel. If he could re-coal, he would depart at once for distant seas. He neglected to say that he had used considerable fuel chasing the *Jacob Bell* and over-hauling other craft suspected of being Northern.

But the apple of discord—belligerent rights—brought no crack-ling repercussions at Barbados. Only mildly did the governor pro-test against Maffitt's proposed infraction of international restric-tions, which permitted coaling but once in three months at a port of the same neutral nation. Now, less than ninety days after fueling at Nassau, the *Florida* had barged into another British port seeking the black jewels.

With stately indignation and threats of wrath to come from Washington, American Consul Trowbridge stalked into the palace to demand that the buccaneer "flying the so-called Confederate flag" be denied succor and ousted from the harbor. But the gentle-man's protest died at utterance. The governor politely waved aside Mr. Seward's irate minion. After all, reasoned the prefect, God himself had sent the gales that obliged the raider to burn coal ex-travagantly. Since the Almighty had taken a hand in the matter, what could a mere governor do but accede to Maffitt's request? Thus did Britain's sovereign functionary at Barbados ease his con-science and appease the Queen's proclamation of neutrality. The *Florida* could replenish her fuel, but she must put to sea within the specified twenty-four hours.

In a huff, Consul Trowbridge quitted the palace, though not before admonishing the governor to beware of consequences:

My Lord, I warn you, in the name of the President of the United States, from supplying or permitting any of your people to aid or abet the rebel ship. My voice is raised without power to back it; but the consequences will, one day or other, show themselves to the British government. Calling on all citizens to take notice of my declaration, my Lord, I take my departure.

Consul Trowbridge was no mean prophet. The "one day or other" was to come with a rush in 1869.

That night, revelry filled the governor's palace. On the terrace, under a twinkling canopy, rose the sounds of violins and guitars. Her Majesty's pronunciamento denied official salutes to the *Florida's* flag, tabooed exchanges of stilted courtesies; but it was conveniently silent as to social amenities. Colonial bigwigs, with Confederate leanings, could unofficially fete their gray-clad visitor as they wished—and Barbados was not lagging. That night hearts beat high. Confederate heroes were their heroes—and here was one of them.

Honored guest at the governor's was the *Florida's* captain. Tales of his exploits at Mobile had come before him. Naval prowess and glory was rooted deep in the island's traditions. From Barbados, buccaneering Henry Morgan had sailed off on the tortuous track that led ultimately to knighthood. Here Nelson's *Victory*, hounding after Napoleon's fleet, had anchored on the long chase that ended at Trafalgar. On the economic side, Barbados sugar had brought wealth to the planter and sweetened Britain's tea for two centuries. Her molasses had helped make New England rum-rich. On her waving fields of cane were laid the foundations of the old British Empire.

Ladies in Parisian gowns, aglitter with jewels, paid homage to this man of the sea who had appeared, as by magic, over the blue horizon. Compliments flowered; eyes flashed with admiration. Repartee and wit sparkled like the wine that bubbled in tall glasses. Toasted and huzzaed to the echo were Lee, the invincible; Jackson, the inimitable; John Maffitt, the uncatchable; the Confederacy, Queen of the South. It was Confederate night, that night, but it would never come again.

One wonders at this outburst of emotion. Perhaps it was because the South was fighting to hold on to something the Barbadians had lost and still yearned for. The rich planter class, stripped of their slaves a generation before, still gazed back on this outmoded institution as on a bygone golden era. It was this nostalgia that sent emotions and sympathies surging at the sight of the Southern banner floating serenely in the tepid airs of the harbor.

The military turned out en masse. Officers of the Barbados garrison, colorful in regimental regalia, "warmly Southern in sentiment," weaved in and out of the bright assemblage. Long would the ladies of Barbados remember this naval man *extraordinaire*, who certainly had a way with female hearts. For them he brought gifts to remember him by: beautiful canisters of tea and exquisite fans snatched from the ill-starred *Jacob Bell*. Little did they foresee the day in the future when John Maffitt's keepsakes would be written into the charges of the United States against Great Britain before the Geneva Tribunal.

Beguiling were the white shoulders, cherry lips, beaming eyes, words of adoration, but "hush! hark!" What Maffitt heard—or thought he heard—was not Byron's "rising knell," but the more pleasing rumble of coal tumbling into the *Florida's* bunkers. His was an inexorable business. At parting, many a lovely hand was held out for a touch of his lips, many a "come back again" echoed after him as he hurried off to the quayside. If nothing else, it was a gallant gesture. He represented a cause they loved but knew was doomed, refusing to admit it all the while. His gig was waiting. Steam was up. The Confederate ensign aflutter in the dawn light, the *Florida* pointed seaward. Standing by the rail, John Maffitt gazed shoreward. As the *Florida* bore him away, he seemed still to hear farewells ringing in his ears.

It was no time to tarry. Northern men-of-war had picked up his trail. Rumors of enemy ships-of-war, cunningly concealed outside the roadstead, persisted. Nor were the rumors idle noises. He knew that by now the *Morning Star* had reached St. Thomas with news of the *Jacob Bell's* demise. As luck would have it, Admiral Wilkes was trifling at St. Thomas, masterminding the hunt-and-kill for Semmes and Maffitt in the Caribbean. Orders flew hither and yon. This time Wilkes guessed accurately that Maffitt would be forced to duck into Martinique or Barbados for coal. Oddly enough, on the day the *Jacob Bell* departed from the registry of American shipping Admiral Wilkes had informed the Navy Department:

Maffitt is very well acquainted with this locality, having cruised here whilst in command of the *Crusader* in looking for slave vessels a few years ago. He frequented most of the West Indian ports and will probably select one of the nearest to be on hand to intercept vessels bound through Windward Passage.

So the *Oneida* and *Cuyler* were hustled south to Martinique, while the U.S.S. *Alabama*, a purchased side-wheel steamer, was sleuthing through the Leewards. Shifting his flag from the *Wachusett* to the speedier *Vanderbilt*, Wilkes took off like a bloodhound on a hot trail. He would show his pack how to make the kill. Doubling Puerto Rico "just in case," he eased through Mona Pass and hightailed down to Barbados.

But the bird had flown, vanished on the deep that told no tales, until she set another fire. Before leaving Barbados, Maffitt had spread the fiction of a foray into the Caribbean to cut out a California steamer on her way up from Panama to New York, with gold from Sierra diggings. It sounded logical. Admiral Wilkes accepted the bait at face value. But first, he charged into the governor's palace with accusations of conniving with the Confederacy to destroy Yankee shipping in the West Indies. He seemed obsessed with the notion that the governors of Barbados and the Bahamas had hatched up such a scheme, but he handled it ineptly. At the moment, the United States needed friends hereabouts, not enemies.

To give color to his bogus destination, John Maffitt stood southward from Carlisle Bay until out of sight of land. He then changed course to east by south, to run down the latitudes for the teeming hunting grounds off Brazil's great hump, where Yankee commerce streamed through the bottleneck between Africa and South America. Here he would stalk and run down Northern ships until Federal men-of-war showed up. Eight months at sea lay ahead of him, of which little more than ten days would be spent in neutral ports. There was nowhere else to go. For man and ship it was to be a grueling two hundred and forty-five days. Harried by wind and current, the *Florida* made easting too slowly. Turning her head north, Maffitt pointed for the thirties, where he could get aboard the northeast trades and ride them down to the Line.

2

March 6, 1863. Alas for the *Star of Peace!* Heavenly was her name, but peace was not her mission. In the early light she swam prettily into the *Florida's* ken like a toy ship on a millpond. Maffitt gaffed her with a single three-mile shot that went screeching over her. Her sails shriveled. A fine-sized ship she was, rolling homeward from Calcutta laden with a "hot" cargo—one thousand tons of saltpeter for the du Pont powder factories along the Brandywine. It was de luxe contraband. Commented Maffitt in his Journal, "This is a prize of national importance. Her cargo has been anxiously anticipated at the du Pont powder mills."

Glancing through her papers, Maffitt wasted barely ten seconds before condemning her to death. He smiled at the names of the four du Pont consignees on the manifest, and wondered how many gray-clad boys his timely haul would save from death.

Loudly did the master of the *Star of Peace*, Captain Francis Hickley, proclaim his hatred of war, his opposition to Northern legions trampling the South in the dust.

Maffitt cut him short. "The very name of your ship is a lie."

First, he took off her crew of twenty-seven. Because several were recalcitrant, he clapped irons on them, omitting only the skipper from his edict. Then, standing off half a mile, he ran out his guns and gave his marksmen target practice for half an hour. At dusk he dispatched his "fire laddies" to set her ablaze.

Afraid the cargo might possibly ignite all at once, he stood off several miles, but the *Star of Peace* burned obstinately. For an hour the flames refused to break through. Then the nitrate took fire. In a massive torch, it burgeoned up from the dark waters, as if hell itself were bursting out. Averred Maffitt, "Never was there a more beautiful panorama witnessed on the ocean. Although twenty miles from her the flames were so high and so brilliant that the focal rays illumined our sails and the ship did not appear more than five miles distant." At midnight, Maffitt turned in. He had done a good day's work. The dying *Star of Peace*, burned to the water's edge, was a dim flambeau on the dark horizon.

Next day, grateful for such a fine prize, Maffitt ordered an extra tot of rum served at mess call so that Jack could celebrate by splicing the main brace. The raider pushed southward. Overhead the star pattern was changing. The ancient stand-by of mariners, the North Star, was fading. Low on the southern horizon, serene and sparkling, glimmered the emblematic Southern Cross.

Seemingly, the stars were portents of good luck for the *Florida*. Near the fifteenth parallel a second mundane luminary flashed across her path. This big, handsome, Yankee-cut vessel was christened for what should have been a lucky star—the red and lustrous *Aldebaran*. Maffitt broke out Southern colors, which the Northern skipper saw only too well. Still, he decided to run for it. For an hour Maffitt toyed with her, letting her lead the *Florida* a merry chase over a choppy sea. She was making her getaway—or so her master thought—when the cruiser's pivot gun reached out and cut her short. And so fell Maffitt's second prize named for a star.

Bound from New York to Maranham, Brazil, she bulged like a Christmas basket—barrels of flour, interlarded with a fantastic, palate-tickling assortment of Yankee "fixins" (so said her log): beef, pork, hams, and live lobsters barreled in ice and seaweed, not to mention brandy, wines, rum, and whiskey. This windfall sent the stewards into high glee. The berthdeck mess had a gastronomic field day. Hardly one of the *Florida*'s Jacks had ever tasted New England lobster before. Another portion of the *Aldebaran*'s cargo was inedible: thousands of clocks, fashioned by shrewd Connecticut Yankees, on their way to tick off the hours in Brazilian homes. Nor was there a dollar of war-risk insurance covering this treasure trove.

Wrathily, the *Aldebaran*'s master, Captain Robert Hand, obeyed Prize Master Hoole's "come with us." He was still fuming as he stomped up the *Florida*'s gangway to meet a scrupulously polite naval officer whose smiling eyes belied his sputterings about "Southern piracy."

"I'll have to burn your ship, captain," observed Maffitt quietly, after inspecting the *Aldebaran*'s papers. "I see she's owned by you and Nehemiah Hand."

"He's my father," said the skipper, his face paling.

"He has a fine Old Testament name," commented Maffitt dryly, "but that can hardly change . . ."

Unable to restrain himself any longer, the Yankee mariner broke out, "We're both good Democrats. We voted for Stephen Douglas. The Bible doesn't say slavery's a sin. At least, that's the way we read it. We don't believe this is a fight to save the Union. Why should you burn our ship in a war we don't believe in?"

"That's the rub, captain," responded Maffitt to the skipper's moralizing on the evils of fratricidal war. "The innocent suffer with the bad. I have my orders."

So saying, Maffitt issued them, irrevocably. Ferry over to the *Florida* as much of the provisions as the stewards can handle—fetch the prize's chronometer—take off fifty barrels of flour. Iron the *Aldebaran's* crew as they come aboard. Thirty-odd prisoners from two prizes were too menacing to carry long, or unsecured. It meant a guard at all hours. Even manacles were no guarantee against seizure of the ship.

Next came the hot part of a cold-blooded war. In late afternoon Maffitt gave the *Aldebaran* to his torchmen. Writhing as if in agony, the ship burned like the star whose name she bore. Pitching and tossing on a rising sea, the wind-whipped flames wolfed her up to the last plank and spar.

Overhauling an English brig bound for Scotland, Maffitt induced her master to take off eleven of his captives, including the two Yankee skippers. A chronometer and several barrels of flour sealed the deal. This, at least, lessened the *Florida's* risk. Presently he fell in with an Austrian bark headed for New York with a cargo of coal consigned to "Mr. Cunard," whose steamships were then pioneering sea travel, forerunners of the fleet of modern liners that today bears his name. Maffitt doubted the propriety of letting her go. A flaw in her claim to neutral immunity brought her perilously near destruction. "But," as he admitted, "I, at length, gave him the benefits of the doubt on condition he relieve the *Florida* of her prisoners and land them in Yankeeland."

On the edge of the Sargasso Sea, in mid-Atlantic, Maffitt ran down a sizable Yankee bark, *Lapwing* of Boston, headed for far-away Batavia and Singapore. She had come in the nick of time. The *Florida's* bunkers were running low. Miraculously, the prize was glutted like a coal mine with smokeless fuel. Over a smooth, windless sea the *Florida* coaled ship.

One unique item of the *Lapwing's* cargo excited curiosity, as it still does. It was a fine family carriage, handiwork of Boston's leading chaise maker. Consigned to a gentleman in Java, it was diverted to play a rather unusual role in America's war: the chassis soon became the carriage for a Quaker naval gun.

Maffitt had toyed with the idea of converting a suitable prize into a bantam cruiser. The *Lapwing* seemed to answer his purpose. She was perfect for masquerading until within hailing distance. Water-tight (or so she seemed), well-found, she had Yankee written all over her. Seen afar or near, Northern skippers would welcome her as a friend, until it was too late. Thus would she double as commerce raider and collier until her coal ran out.

For armament, he gave her two twelve-pound howitzers, a few rifles, and ammunition. On this godchild of the *Florida* he bestowed the raider's original name *Oreto*, with the Roman suffix II. Next, he equipped her with a signal book and a chest of flags for make-believe. Of baptismal ceremony there was little save three hearty cheers from the crew of the *Florida*, who ran up the rigging and sounded off as the Confederate colors broke out at the *Lapwing's* peak. And so the Confederate Navy was richer by one fledgling commerce raider.

There was nothing wrong with the idea. It looked at this moment as if anything with a toy pistol and a few sails could snatch Yankee traders, but Maffitt had tabbed the wrong man for the job. Manning her with four officers and fifteen Jacks, he gave her command to Lieutenant Averett, his executive officer, whose wishy-washiness had not yet betrayed his unsuitability to the unrelenting rigors of the chase and of playing tag with Northern men-of-war. In parting, Maffitt ordered the *Oreto II* to hold on to the *Florida* at ten miles or so. This would double their range of vision. After setting a tryst for the ships on the Equator, the *Oreto II* stood away into the sunset. That very night, the *Oreto II* lost her hold on the *Florida's* apron strings.

But Maffitt's luck was soaring. Plowing along, he headed for the lush pasturage along the Equator. Next morning, as dawn came over the rim of the sea, he was greeted by the bark *M. J. Colcord* of New York, with a cargo of flour and bacon bound for Cape Town, Britain's colony at the foot of Africa. Maffitt speared her with a blank shot and a display of the Southern ensign. She came into the wind submissively.

The *M. J. Colcord* was a propaganda ship. With the blessing of President Lincoln, businessmen of New York and Philadelphia had

Captain John Newland Maffitt, Commander of the *Florida*.

The *Florida* standing by after making a bonfire of the famous New York clipper ship, *Jacob Bell*. From a contemporary drawing in *Harper's Weekly*

The Union sloop *Oneida*, which bombarded the *Florida* for two hours at pointblank range off Mobile Bay in September 1862. The *Oneida* and her consorts should have sunk the *Florida* in two minutes, and their failure to do so produced one of the *causes célèbres* of Navy annals. Official U. S. Navy photo.

James Bulloch, diplomat and secret naval agent of the Confederacy, for whom he secured the cruisers *Alabama* and *Florida* out of British shipyards. Official U. S. Navy photo.

An artist aboard the *Forest City* (on the right) sketched the blowing up of the revenue cutter *Caleb Cushing* off Portland harbor by Lieutenant Read and his small band of raiders in June, 1863. Reproduced by courtesy of the Maine Historical Society.

Lieutenant Charles W. Read, from a photograph taken in 1860 when he graduated from Annapolis. With a captured brig, a single brass six-pounder, and five Quaker guns, Read seized twenty-two Northern ships, burning thirteen of them, off the coast between Cape Hatteras and Portland. Official U. S. Navy photo.

The *Florida* chasing the *Star of Peace*, March, 1863.

This unique drawing by Frank Vizetelly, artist-war correspondent of the Illustrated London News, depicts the British-built *Lilian* running the blockade into Wilmington. Commander Maffitt, standing at the left on the paddlebox, is focusing his binoculars on the Union cruiser closely pursuing him. Vizetelly was a passenger on the *Lilian* at the time. This is the only contemporary on-the-spot picture of its kind.

The Union *Wachusett* ramming the *Florida* by night in the neutral harbor of Bahia, Brazil, in 1864.

organized a foreign aid "lift" across the Atlantic to relieve the plight of Britain's mill workers, who were reduced almost to starvation for want of the South's white staple. It paid big dividends, winning friends and influencing the common people's sympathies for the Union. A shipload or two were shunted off to Cape Town. In 1863, as now, the way to men's hearts was through their stomachs. British mill workers blessed America and President Lincoln, while at the same time they blessed out the Palmerston-Russell-Gladstone triumvirate that was working the Confederate side of the street for all it was worth.

But the *M. J. Colcord* was never to sight Africa and the grim old cape with its fleecy tablecloth cloud cap. The *Florida's* messes stacked their pantries with bacon enough to last Jack three months. Blazing from stem to stern, the *M. J. Colcord* bounded off for the port of missing ships.

Insatiable was the *Florida's* hot appetite. Astride the wide thoroughfare of commerce coming up from the South Atlantic, she roared into the torrid zone parceling out fire wholesale, strewing her trail with terror. The *Alabama* had recently scourged these waters, but now they were crowded again. Nor was there a shadow of protecting Northern warships. Where were they?

April found the *Florida* in the trades. She made the St. Paul Islets, a cluster of rocks that protrude from the bosom of the Atlantic in fantastic, clownish shapes; but paused only to take new bearings and correct her chronometer. Two days later she chased a sail. So like a Yankee was her quarry that she failed to recognize her own offspring, *Oreto II* (late *Lapwing*), whose crew were living like lords on the ship's well-stocked larder. But her commander, Lieutenant Averett, was mournful, full of excuses. On a seaway swarming with Northern commerce, he had not even smelled a prize. The *Oreto II* couldn't hold a wind. She leaked. To Maffitt the tender was "a perfect godsend as our bunkers were nearly empty." But he sent Averett off again with orders to meet him at Fernando de Noronha, Brazil's penal rock island.

Incredible was the *Florida's* take this next week of April 17. Thirty miles below the Equator she struck again. Over the Atlantic coasted the huge ship *Commonwealth* of New York. She was a catch of which a raider could be proud; and Maffitt's Journal exudes this fact. A thirteen-hundred-tonner, sweeping along under billowing canvas, she was bound round the Horn for San Francisco with a cargo insured for $370,000, though its actual value ran higher. One third of her cargo was consigned to the Federal military at San Francisco.

The day was "hot, very hot." Finding Captain McClellan of the *Commonwealth* "a most gentlemanly person" Maffitt invited him into his cabin for a cold drink while they chatted about things, mostly about fire. "The cool quiet manner which he exhibited under his peculiarly annoying position quite won my respect," said Maffitt. But it won no reprieve for his beautiful ship.

From the *Commonwealth* Maffitt eagerly gleaned New York papers as late as March 19, the day the ship sailed. Big doings in Yankeeland: Lincoln had a new general—Burnside had been sacked and command bestowed on the blond war-god, Joe Hooker, who was already blustering about, having Lee's army in the hollow of his hand. At the same time, Mr. Welles's gunboats were playing ring-around-the-rosy, with Cuba in the middle. As for Maffitt, hanging was too good for him. The object of this pointed diatribe offered this pithy comment, "The Yankees print lies with ease and indorse the most absurd statements in regard to the South." The wardroom went into guffaws over the fire and brimstone that was to be heaped on the *Florida* when they caught her.

Maffitt decreed the *Commonwealth's* doom with a single word: fire. In an incandescent welter the splendid ship faded from the dwindling roster of American ships on the high seas. Yet, on the *Alabama* Claims, the list of those claiming reimbursement for the *Commonwealth's* cargo led all the rest—in numbers, at least.

Next day, as if escorted by Lady Luck herself, a French transport bound for Pernambuco breezed along. Overhauling her, Maffitt persuaded her master to take over his prisoners. The American Consul at Pernambuco charged that the raider arranged the deal at pistol point, though Maffitt credited the magic of a Masonic sign passing between Captain McClellan and the French ship master. What difference did it make? He had gotten rid of his prisoners.

Seemingly, the *Florida* couldn't miss. Maffitt had hit the raider's jackpot, racking up a high score; and he knew it. How long his luck would last was something else. He wondered when Gideon Welles's gunboats would show up, and why they didn't.

Rolling down to Rio over a tumbling sea, close-reefed, her masts bending like buggy whips, came the tall bark *Henrietta* of Baltimore, with barrels of flour, innumerable kegs of lard, and thousands of candles to brighten the dark hours for Brazil's citizenry. Not an inkling had her master that his ship's name would so soon adorn the list of Maffitt's holocausts. A dyed-in-the-wool Down-easter was Captain George Brown, crammed with Biblical lore on slavery, and strong on the constitutional rights of the South. Maffitt found it hard to reconcile the sentiments of these New England skippers with the avowed purpose of the war.

Captain Brown was amazed when a steamer flying the American flag swept alongside, tossed the Southland's banner to the breeze, and ordered him to heave to. Even more amazed was he to find himself gazing into the muzzles of her starboard guns.

Countermanding his prize master's promise of reprieve, Maffitt's edict was peremptory: Burn her now. And burn her they did. If we are to believe Captain Brown, as he stood gazing at the destruction of his ship Maffitt turned to him and observed, "Doesn't she burn pretty? She belongs to Mr. Whitridge. He is a great Union man." With inconceivable rapidity the wind-fanned flames gutted the *Henrietta*, licking up the lardlike liquid tinder. Red tongues converted her masts into stupendous candles. The *Florida's* crew stared dumbfounded, amazed at their prowess. It was a spellbinding showpiece. Indeed, the forecastle was agog already. In no time these simple lads had become expert arsonists. More to the point, and the pocketbooks, was the sugar plum, prize money, that danced before their eyes. At the current rate of destruction, they were piling it up fast. They'd be rich, if and when they got home; and heroes to boot.

But it was dead certain that Yankee men-of-war would eventually whip southward to put an end to this blazing mop-up. At least, so it seemed. As for Maffitt, he knew they'd track him. Somewhere along the trail the *Florida's* luck would run out. Up to now he had not bonded a ship. Everything he caught had gone up in fire. Nor was the end in sight.

Amid his grisly business he wrote home, "The duty is very terrible upon one's mental and physical abilities; but I am doing all in my power for the benefit of the Confederacy." The *Henrietta* brought an all-too-brief respite from the harrowing exactions of his trade. Among the passengers taken from the ill-starred ship was a mother (identified only as Mrs. Flora), and her three children: a girl of thirteen, a boy of seven, and an infant in arms. "They became my guests," said Maffitt, who promptly ushered them into the comforts, such as they were, of his own cabin. It sent his thoughts homing back to long-gone days when his own brood pattered about the house.

Baby food was scant in the raider's pantry. Nor was there a cow handy. But amid the plunder taken from the *Commonwealth* were cans of a new product that ushered in a new vogue, Gail Borden's condensed milk. The baby lapped it up as if it were fresh from the point of origin. The two older children, who had come up the gangway whimpering as if they expected to walk the plank, permitted the fearsome "pirate" to take them by the hand, escort them about the ship, and show them her fine points. The forecastle went into stitches: the Captain had turned nursemaid. Later, Maffitt reluctantly consigned his small guests to a French transport bound for Pernambuco.

April 25, 1863. John Maffitt had a feeling everything was going his way as he stepped on deck this morning, drawn by the masthead's "Sail ho!" Maffitt's was an unpredictable business. It was like reaching into a grab bag. He never knew what he would get his hands on next.

Ninety-five days out of Shanghai, bound for New York, the three-sticker *Oneida* had surmounted every hurdle Old Neptune could put in her track. Gales off Cape Horn, snow, rain, heat, lightning, and even an iceberg or two had tried to impede her, but never had she swerved from her course. Now, on the homestretch, she was accosted by this impolite stranger, who appeared out of the blue and refused to let her alone. Surmising trouble, Captain Jesse Potter threw on sail and streaked away. Perhaps it was only a nosy Northern gunboat, so he raised American colors. Still, the impudent newcomer would not be shaken off.

Seeing his prey take to her heels, Maffitt ordered the propeller lowered. Banked fires were stoked and fed. Gongs rang in the engine room. In twenty minutes the steam gages were hissing "Let's go!"—and go she did. At a mile the *Florida's* bow gun heaved a *billet-doux* after the fleeing ship. A jet of water not unlike the "blow" of a huge whale geysered near her stern. Maffitt's gunners were pinpointing their shots with better accuracy. A little more practice and they'd be experts. At ten-thirty, the *Florida* closed quarters at a biscuit's-throw from her prey. Sweeping to leeward, he lowered his decoy colors and flicked out the emblem of the South. Maffitt gave his captive a fast count, setting her destruction for high noon.

"An odd fish" was skipper Potter, or so Maffitt characterized him. He came aboard muttering about pirates, greeting his captor with, "I suppose you'll want the rings on our fingers also."

"No," replied Maffitt cheerily. "We have the example, but we don't follow it, captain."

Opening up the *Oneida's* hold, the boarders drew back. An unforgettable fragrance smote their nostrils. More tea! Shades of the *Jacob Bell!* Nearly a million dollars' worth! A lot of tea in any man's war. But the *Florida* had enough of the delicate beverage to last as long as the ship herself. Prying deeper, they exhumed bolts of Chinese silk. Hundreds of every pattern and hue. On the spot, Maffitt decided to share this colorful plunder with Jack. To each he gave two bolts of silk to take home to his girl or his family. The berth deck was ecstatic. But Maffitt was strict. Only two to a man, and that included himself, who tucked his away for Florie and Mary Read. The Navy Department might frown at this. Then what? The whole shebang was going up in smoke anyway. They could hardly begrudge Jack a small dividend. It was the first and only "cut" Jack would ever get.

The *Oneida* was fine fare for flames. Captain Potter mournfully recorded, "Our ship was on fire from stem to stern by high noon." Her woodwork, dry as old bones, leaped into flame at the touch of the torch. Oft had she voyaged to the Orient and other faraway places; but her saga had run out.

A note of exaltation ran through a letter Maffitt wrote that evening to James Bulloch, the indefatigable Confederate naval agent at Liverpool, who had created the *Florida*. One could hardly blame him. He was exterminating Yankee shipping at an unparalleled rate. Unbiased appraisal would agree he was doing quite well at it. Northern ship owners and insurance companies would wail to the skies when the smoke finally blew their way. Maffitt's letter ran:

My escapes from great odds have been numerous, as no less than sixteen vessels were after us at the same time, and I burned vessels in the track.

The *Florida* has thus far done her duty. Six million dollars will not make good the devastation this steamer has committed. Will have to quit the line as quite a fleet is on the way to destroy her. 'Tis seventy days since we've seen land.

Bulloch did not see this letter until the Confederacy lay prostrate. Overseas mail traveled hazardous, zigzag journeys to its various destinations, and often did not reach them at all. The latter fate awaited most of Maffitt's letters to his children, and the official reports he meticulously wrote to Secretary of the Navy Mallory.

Intercepted on the high seas by Federal men-of-war, the Bulloch letter was packaged with evidence supporting America's demand for indemnity in the celebrated *Alabama* Claims.

On April 28, the *Florida* made the rock of Fernando de Noronha, which loomed up like a vast cloud. This stupendous granite cairn, created by nature eons ago, towers above the Atlantic two hundred miles off Cape St. Roque. Mariners of all ages have checked their bearings by this great milestone. But in the 1860's it was Brazil's delightful bastille, where she "entertained" her choicest felons, who had, until a few days before the *Florida's* arrival, enjoyed all the comforts of home. Overlord of Fernando de Noronha was genial, fun-loving Major José Basilio Pyrrho, whose pride in the artistry of his guests ran high. A jolly host was he. Under him, the keepers and their wards were just a happy family.

Then suddenly the *Alabama* bore up in the shadow of the precipitous rock. Pyrrho had been completely won over by the suave Semmes, who rewrote the rules of neutrality to fit his needs. Out of this neutral haven Semmes sallied forth to dragoon passing American ships and fire them for the edification of the governor and his guests.

Into this same hospitable retreat steamed the *Florida*. Sending a boat ashore, Maffitt learned to his disappointment that the *Alabama* had departed only the week before. He had hoped to meet his son, Eugene, a midshipman on the famed raider. Nor had the *Oreto II* kept the rendezvous—and the *Florida* was again famishing for coal. Denizens of the island unfolded tales of the *Alabama's* fabulous visit. Anticipating similar amenities, Maffitt dispatched a friendly letter to Pyrrho. But his missive elicited no reply. No fun, no parties at the governor's mansion.

Meanwhile, without waiting for permission, Maffitt had unceremoniously dumped his prisoners on the rocky shore. These castaways were at least on dry land. Now they could shift for themselves.

On the third day of the *Florida's* sojourn, a Brazilian man-of-war appeared bearing a new governor to replace the pro-Confederate Pyrrho. To the fresh incumbent Maffitt addressed another appeal for pratique. It brought fast repercussions—an order to: "Get out and take your prisoners with you." It was signed with a flourish by "Antonio Gomes Leal, Colonel, Commanding." The gentleman evidently meant business. He informed Maffitt that the easygoing Pyrrho had been deposed and that his hard-boiled replacement was ready to take summary action to eject the unwelcome visitor. If the uninvited *Florida* disregarded this warning, Brazil, speaking through Leal, would break off relations with a "friendly" cannon-shot; if the *Florida* insisted on remaining, the fort's guns would take "unfriendly" aim.

Taking no chances, Maffitt cast loose his guns. He was tempted to let fly a broadside; but after all, the Confederacy could ill afford to alienate a nation that could be most useful. Actually, Brazil's home government feared Northern warships would crack down on her in retaliation for Semmes's fandango at the island. Besides, the United States at the moment was too good a customer to antagonize. She was buying shiploads of coffee for her vast armies.

Fernando de Noronha was still in sight when the *Florida* met the *Oreto II* heading for the rendezvous. She had rounded up a single prize, the fine ship *Kate Dyer*, which she snared with a wooden gun ruse, a sawed-off spar mounted on the wheels of the carriage consigned to the gentleman in Java. Because of a neutral cargo, the ship was bonded. Taking as much coal as the *Florida* needed, Maffitt sent the *Oreto II* off again, commanded this time by Midshipman R. S. Floyd, acting master of the *Florida*, with orders to meet him at Rocas Island, midway between Noronha and the mainland.

Raising sail, the *Oreto II* soon integrated with the Atlantic mists, ultimately to make her exit in a ball of fire. Maffitt was never to see her again.

On May 6, off Cape St. Roque, the *Florida* nabbed the lusty brig *Clarence*, bound from Rio to Baltimore with ten thousand bags of coffee in her hold for the Union armies.

While Maffitt pondered the *Clarence's* fate, over to the *Florida* went three hundred sacks of Brazil's choicest. How welcome this prize would have been to the South that was already drinking ersatz coffee! But that was out of the question.

3

That evening Maffitt summoned Lieutenant Charles W. Read to his cabin. Under the gently swaying lamp, the raider and his second in command planned an enterprise that still makes one hold his breath. Generously, Maffitt granted Read the conception of the plan.

Read had proposed in writing:

> I propose to take the brig *Clarence* which we have just captured and with a crew of twenty men proceed to Hampton Roads and cut out a gunboat or steamer of the enemy.
>
> As I would be in possession of the brig's papers, and as the crew would not be large enough to excite suspicions there can be no doubt of my passing Fortress Monroe successfully. Once in the Roads I would be prepared to avail myself of any circumstances which might present for gaining the deck of an enemy vessel. If it was found impossible to board a gunboat, or merchant steamer, it would be possible to fire the shipping at Baltimore.

Maffitt's eyes glowed. He may have recalled the astonished look in Secretary Mallory's eyes that May day at Montgomery when he himself blandly proposed dashing in and firing the New York Navy Yard. The brig *Clarence* was a beauty, and Maffitt still cherished the idea of converting a prize into an armed tender to prey on the trade routes. Where the *Lapwing* had failed, the *Clarence*, under audacious leadership, might succeed. And that was where Read would take over.

Like the gallant Pelham, comparatively unknown to fame was this daring young man from Mississippi, who embodied the derring-do of all the bold captains ever to sail the seas against the foe.

Venturesome, resourceful, and with a flair for the hazardous, he filled the bill exactly.

In his Journal, while fuming at the inefficiency and delays of reconditioning the *Florida* at Mobile, Maffitt had written this entry: "This officer (Read) acquired a reputation for gunnery, coolness and determination at the battle of New Orleans. When his commander, T. B. Huger, was fatally wounded, he continued to gallantly fight the *McRae* until she was riddled and unfit for service."

The *Florida* must soon vacate the South Atlantic. That was obvious. The harpies were winging southward, and the environment would soon become unhealthy. Ranging northward, Maffitt planned to jog along, lighting "campfires" as he went, and head for the New England coast unless (always that *unless*) somewhere along the way the *Florida* met her comeuppance. If so, he'd shoot it out; but not until then. The *Clarence* would also work her way northward. Coming together off the Nantucket coast, they would sweep the Atlantic seaboard.

His imagination on fire, Read embellished his plan, though without any bravado: "Having the brig's papers showing her American registry I'm certain of getting inside the Virginia Capes and into the Roads jammed with Federal supply ships and transports. I'd wait till night and burn as many as we could. If I'm lucky, I'd cut out a steamer or federal gunboat, sail up the bay to Baltimore and set fire to the wharves and shipping."

Admiringly, Maffitt gazed at the eager young sailor. He was only twenty-three, and his sheer audacity was something to marvel at. He talked of assaulting this hornet's nest of sea batteries and Union warships as if it were a pleasant summer sail. It may have seemed like sticking one's head into the lion's mouth; but Maffitt knew his man. As for the *Clarence*: she was made to order to finesse her way into the vast enemy fold at Hampton Roads, crowded with maritime sheep. Every feature of her proclaimed her Yankee lineage.

"What men would you want to take?" asked Maffitt.

Read named them, good men all. Two he sought above all others: Assistant Engineer Brown and Quartermaster J. W. Billups, who had stood at the *Florida*'s helm the day she ran in to Mobile. For an hour they weighed the imponderables of the adventure, before Maffitt finished the conference with a word of caution: "If you find it impossible to enter Hampton Roads, you will continue up the coast towards Nantucket. The *Florida* should be there by July 4, unless [again that word *unless*] . . ." Maffitt smiled. One couldn't predict in this hazardous business. The *Florida* and *Clarence* might both be decorating the bottom of the sea by July 4.

Then he added, "unless something happens. We'd then sweep the coast together. I'll give you men, rifles, pistols, ammunition, and a six-pound howitzer. You might make a capture or two on the way up. You'll be on your own, no orders to hamper you. Your success will depend on yourself—and your sturdy heart." He couldn't hold back this last sentimental touch.

Now to give it official sanction. Admiral Porter said he doubted if Maffitt possessed authority to commission cruisers. What difference did it make? He was doing it. From his desk he fetched pen and paper. There was quiet in the cabin as his pen scratched over the paper.

"You might read that," he suggested.

Read read, in part:

Your proposition evinces on your part patriotic devotion to the cause of your country, and this is certainly the time when all our best exertions should be made to harm the common enemy and confuse them with attacks from all unexpected quarters. I agree to your request and will not hamper you with instructions.

Warmly, the two men clasped hands. This time Maffitt had picked a man after his own heart. Eight bells struck. Maffitt rose. Taking a decanter from his locker he filled two glasses. The liquid gleamed in the low glow of the cabin lamp.

"Here's to success. May it be yours."

Up came their glasses.

It might be well to look closer at this young man as he embarked on his meteoric cruise. Of slight build, his alert, boyish face was adorned with a close-clipped brown mustache and whiskers. His picture is that of a poet rather than a sea raider. One might find an analogy between Read and the German Count von Luckner of *Seeadler* fame during World War I, though Read possessed nothing in common with the physical lustiness of the latter. Both operated with sail against steam navies. Both acted with such daring vigor that their enemies refused, for the time being, to believe the reports of their captures. Read had graduated from Annapolis in June, 1860. From a naval fledgling, Read had leaped to the status of a seasoned officer in record time.

In the morning the *Clarence* was quickly armed and provisioned. Dipping her colors, she squared away. On the *Florida's* quarter-deck, John Maffitt raised his hand in salute as the brig bravely winged off over the squally sea for her great adventure. To the spectators it may have looked like a pitiful gesture, dispatching an armed brig with a tiny gun to raid the North's home waters. Yet, three thousand years ago a Roman named Terence had a word for it, or rather, three words: *Fortes fortuna adjuvat!* Thus was another Confederate commerce destroyer hatched upon the high seas with orders to burn, sink, and destroy.

Not for two months would Maffitt learn that on the day he hopefully launched the second of his brood, Secretary Mallory was writing him a long-hoped-for letter. It brought belatedly—or would bring—what he had ample reason to expect, though news of his spoils in the South Atlantic had not yet reached Richmond:

> You are hereby informed that the President has appointed you a Commander in the Navy of the Confederate States for gallant and meritorious conduct in command of the *Florida* in running the blockade in and out of the port of Mobile against an overwhelming force of the enemy and under his fire. . . .

Nor could he know that even at the hour the *Clarence* sailed away, the Confederacy was suffering heartbreak. Mighty Stonewall had fallen in the Wilderness. The South would see his like no more. It dulled the glow of victory at Chancellorsville. Never again would Confederate hopes beam so brightly—on the land, resounding victories; on the sea, Semmes and Maffitt leaving crimson trails of Northern merchantmen.

CHAPTER XIX

Blazing Interlude off Brazil

WITH HER ENGINES croaking, Maffitt swung the *Florida's* head south by west for Pernambuco. Dropping anchor, he courteously applied to Governor João Silveria de Souza for pratique and an extension of the twenty-four-hour rule to four days. Back came a bristling document, written in sweeping script an inch high, delivered by an officer dripping gold lace and red pipings. In effect it said: "Begone! Get out!"

The American Consul had stolen a march on the *Florida*. Dashing to the palace, he had deluged de Souza with protests and threats of reprisal if Brazil succored the "Confederate piratical wolf." Three United States warships were speeding down the latitudes. Resentful of any generosity shown the *Florida*, they might open their guns and reduce the palace to rubble. De Souza was duly impressed—outwardly, at least.

The governor, in fact, wanted to be good neighbor to both warring nations. As yet, Brazil was uncertain as to who would be the victor. Maffitt donned his finery and betook himself to the palace, where he turned on the charm. Caught between two fires, de Souza sought to edge his way out. Far be it from him to be discourteous to the "sovereign Confederate States." On the other hand, if Federal cruisers arrived, how could he protect the *Florida* from their attentions? The guns in the fort were antiques.

Maffitt smiled. "But, your Excellency, we really don't need protection. The *Florida* can take care of herself."

Shutting an eye, de Souza insisted the *Florida* must leave in twenty-four hours. It was the old story. Catching the wink, Maffitt lingered four days while Consul Adamson gnawed his fingernails to the quick.

From Pernambuco Maffitt wrote his children:

> I feel happy to tell you that the *Florida* has been doing a fierce business. Up to May 11 she has destroyed $9,500,000 of Yankee commerce, and eluded thirteen Federal men of war sent to destroy her and the *Alabama*. I cannot write what my plans are, but the duty is very terrible on me. I am doing all in my power for the benefit of the Confederacy.

Soon after, running northward for Rocas Island, the *Florida* was in full cry again. She struck fast. Three degrees below the equator, she picked up an acquaintance with the *Crown Point* of New York, who scampered away like a much-insulted lady. But it was an evil wind that blew her across the *Florida's* trail. After pillaging her "assorted merchandise," Maffitt fired her at midnight. And a fine show it was. The *Florida's* sailors crept out of their hammocks to occupy front seats along the rail.

From the *Crown Point* the *Florida* recruited nine men. Lured by the prospect of swashbuckling service on the cruiser, plus other considerations, they hurriedly cast lots with the bold buccaneers. To salve their qualms, Maffitt tossed in a bonus of a bolt of silk taken from the *Oneida*. It was a persuasive come-on, though mounting prize money spoke a more seductive language. Northern loyalties vanished like mist in the equatorial sun. Onto the Confederate Articles went their names and marks. It was laughable to watch these renegades despoiling their own ship. Northern newspapers would gnash their editorial teeth at this.

At Rocas Island the *Florida* loitered fifteen days, waiting for the *Lapwing*, for whom wind and fate had shaped a varied destiny. Maffitt concluded she had been captured or wrecked. Victim of winds and currents, she was, in fact, blown so far northward that her commander decided to shape his course for Barbados. Off that island she was fired by her crew, whose small boat was swept ashore where the wayfarers were received with cheering hospitality.

At Rocas Island, death's cold hand again shadowed the cruiser. Tropic fever claimed seaman John Johnson. Over him Maffitt read the burial service. With three volleys his body was committed to a grave on the barren shore. It called back sad thoughts of the much-loved Laurens Read, dead of yellow fever at Cárdenas. Here, too, Assistant Surgeon J. Dana Grafton gave his life for a shipmate. Tossed into the heavy surf by an upset shoreboat, Dr. Grafton gave the oar which was keeping him afloat to a young seaman who could not swim a stroke. Thus passed a loyal Confederate from Arkansas, whose professional skill and kindliness had won every heart on the ship.

While the *Florida's* tars frolicked on shore and recounted their multiplying financial blessings, three waterfront toughs shipped at Nassau were brought to book for insubordination. They were sentenced to be left stranded at Rocas Island, but Maffitt reprieved them, with stern warnings, the day the *Florida* sailed—for another breach of discipline he would set them adrift in an open boat. He could be hard as nails when necessary, dealing out precisely an eye for an eye.

Again the *Florida's* bunkers hankered for coal. Putting into Brazil's Ceará Island, Maffitt encountered another Mr. Big, José B. de Cunha Figueiredo. With decided Southern proclivities, the governor gave his official sanction, winding it up with a resounding "God guard you!"

Fire in hand, Maffitt wheeled the *Florida* northward for his amazing run up fifty degrees of latitude to keep his rendezvous with the *Clarence* off the Nantucket coast. He hated to leave these happy hunting grounds off Cape St. Roque, but common sense told him Gideon Welles's hawk-killers were winging south to put an end to his flaming jamboree. When they arrived, they would find burned spars and, perhaps, a charred hulk, but no *Florida.*

A stone's throw south of the line, fresh game broke cover. Down from aloft rang the welcome "Sail ho!" Up from the quarter-deck trumpeted: "Where away?", to be answered: "Off the port bow, sir." His prey seemed to sense that she had fallen in with an evil companion, and refused to haul up. Tossing out the Stars and Stripes, she whisked off defiantly. It proved a regatta, which took sail and steam to heave the fugitive to. Maffitt would have opened his pivot gun; but his glasses revealed a woman, the skipper's wife. A good-sized ship, one thousand tons, she was crammed with fancy logs from Mexico's west coast. As the *Florida* swept up and circled her captive, Maffitt raised his cap and bowed cordially to the lady, who acknowledged his greeting with a wave of her hand. Decorating the prize's stern were the stars of the *Southern Cross*, whose name she bore. But even this could not absolve her from the hot brand. She was Number Thirteen on Maffitt's ledger.

CHAPTER XX

The South's Jack the Giant-Killer

INEVITABLY, THE SPOTLIGHT must flash northward a thousand miles to the pint-sized *Clarence*, which Maffitt had commissioned off Brazil. The exploits of Lieutenant Charles William Read are inextricably bound up with those of John Maffitt, who dispatched him on his tumultuous mission.

On the day Maffitt burned the *Southern Cross*, June 6, 1863, his outrunner *Clarence* was opening the ball with her first prize off Cape Hatteras. The *Clarence* was a mediocre sailer at best. Futile chases had proved that. Failing to take a prize off the Windwards, with his larder running low, Read overhauled (with a shot from his brass six-pounder) a British bark whose master boiled over at the sheer effrontery of a Federal vessel, as he thought, daring to fire on her Majesty's flag. Lowering a boat, Read sent off a boarding crew in charge of Engineer Browne. The Britisher's captain met them in a rage as they hopped over the rail, "How dare you fire on her Majesty's flag?" Browne tried to maneuver his way out of the awkward situation by offering to buy cabin stores. But the captain stickled even at this. He was mad as a hornet.

"Then perhaps you will barter with us," suggested Browne.

Again, an obdurate no. Browne took another tack. "I appeal to you in humanity's sake. Won't you give us something? We are down to salt beef and salt pork, and threatened with scurvy."

"That's just like you Yankees," barked the irate skipper. "You'd beg your way across the Atlantic if necessary."

Facing this impasse, Browne went to the rail and signaled Lieutenant Read on the *Clarence*, whereupon the latter changed flags and ran up the Stars and Bars. Seeing Southern colors stream out, the captain recanted. "I'll give you the whole darned ship if you want it," he said, and ordered his steward to break out his stores. Read promptly reciprocated with three hundred bags of captured coffee. As a further neighborly gesture, the Britisher tossed in a cask of 'alf-and-'alf, plus a bundle of temperance tracts.

By the time the *Clarence* reached the American coast she was a ship-of-war, armed to the teeth; or such was her appearance at first blush. Her six-pounder had magically spawned five bristling offspring. In a twinkle, by simply opening her portholes, she could be transformed from a brig of innocent mien into a saucy man-of-war, ready for action. To relieve the ennui of the long voyage up from the Equator and compensate for his lack of armament, Read had improvised an imposing battery of Quaker guns. Sawing up spars in gunbarrel lengths, he and his men had ingeniously shaped them, painted them black, and mounted them. Hacking portholes, he trained his gunners to run out their "guns" and stand at quarters, lanyards in hand, as if ready to fire a broadside at command. His feat of legerdemain was a gem of deception.

For the arduous tasks ahead he had drilled his crew ceaselessly. Each man had his special duty. With a flair for the dramatic, Read had rigged up a bridge where he could take his stance and train his glasses on the horizon for possible victims.

First of Read's dupes was the *Whistling Wind*, which he captured about two hundred and fifty miles west of the Bermudas. The bark's master took one look at this tiny sea devil flashing Confederate colors and decided to haul up. Northern newspapers had warned that the rebels were concocting a "something" at Charleston that could swim above or below. Perhaps this was it. Whatever it was, the *Whistling Wind* took no chances. She was laden with coal for Admiral Farragut's blockading squadron in the Gulf, and Read joyfully burned her on the spot, clapping irons on her master and crew without delay.

Before breakfast next morning—June 7, 1863—he snatched the Yankee schooner *Alfred H. Partridge* bound for Matamoras, loaded "with arms and clothing for our citizens in Texas." But he didn't burn her. He was pleased, of course, to overhaul a ship flying the

Stars and Stripes; yet her mission was strange and gratifying. From her skipper he exacted an unusual bond that pledged the *Alfred H. Partridge* to complete her voyage and deliver the cargo "to loyal citizens of the Confederate States." This bond, incidentally, was faithfully performed. Read was evidently not aware of the vast sideline trade with the enemy through Mexico. Daily, vessels flying the Stars and Stripes were clearing out of Northern ports with cargoes destined, by way of Mexico, for transshipment across the Rio Grande to Dixie.

Working closer to Cape Hatteras, on June 9, Read gigged and fired the brig *Mary Alvina*, with commissary stores for the Union Army at New Orleans. That night in his tiny cabin, Read and his second in command revised their original plan for raiding Hampton Roads. Newspapers taken from his two prizes, and information obtained from his prisoners, convinced Read he must abandon his original design of infiltrating the Union lair and pillaging the supply flotilla. Fortress Monroe was intercepting all comers. Only ships carrying government supplies were permitted to enter the Roads. Gunboats were watchdogging day and night. It meant that the papers of the *Clarence*, which were intact, would admit him to Chesapeake Bay, but not into the Roads where the Federal supply ships were secreted.

At the moment, the *Clarence* stood directly in the track of Federal war vessels constantly shuttling between Hampton Roads and Union bases on the blockaded Southern coast. A small brig with a six-pounder and five mock guns was no match for anything; but her commander was as prolific and resourceful in expedients as John Paul Jones himself. Confident, cool as a New England autumn breeze, he asked only to stay afloat and uncaptured. Foiled momentarily, he "determined to cruise along the coast and try to intercept a supply ship with clearance papers bound for Fortress Monroe." He would transfer his "armament" and flag to her. Equipped with her credentials, he would enter the Roads and endeavor to carry out Maffitt's orders, wreaking all possible havoc on enemy commerce.

If anyone ever possessed the great actors' instinct for magnificent entrances, it was young Charles William Read. Yet, hardly did he envision the orgy of destruction he would inflict, or the panic he would set rolling from the Capes to Maine, within the ensuing fortnight. It is to be wondered why his story has so long remained in obscurity.

June 12, 1863, was a day to be remembered in Read's book. Off to port, just within sight, lay the Virginia Capes. At six A.M., out of the dawn mist swam the bark *Tacony*, in ballast from the Federal base at Port Royal for Philadelphia. Six miles off, she was running before a fair breeze. Read knew his nondescript "man of war" could never outsail her. The *Clarence's* portholes were closed. Her innocence was profound. The setting called for stratagem. At six miles his brass popgun was useless. Gifted with instant decision, Read hoisted the traditional distress signal of the sea—the American flag flying union down. If feigning mishap didn't fetch her, nothing would.

Something told the *Tacony's* skipper, Captain William Munday, to let the stranger alone; but the law of the sea was leavened into his Down-easter breed. Land was in sight and the sea placid; but "seeing men apparently in distress," he put toward them. A cautious man normally, he may have been lured by siren visions of fat salvage claims to reward him for his errand of mercy. Bearing up near the "distressed brig" he saw a boatload, ten sailors in rough seaman's clothing, shove off for the would-be rescuer. Coming alongside, they swarmed up the *Tacony's* hull, hand over hand, like old-time buccaneers. Not visible under their sea jackets were revolvers belted at their waists. Bouncing over the rail, they whipped out their weapons and jabbed them in the faces of the flabbergasted skipper and his mate.

"What's going on here?" stuttered Munday.

"You're prisoners of war! Take it easy, captain!"

It was Read himself speaking. He looked like a freebooter of days gone by. On the long journey up the latitudes he had let his reddish mustache grow until it flared outward into a true piratical adornment. In a jiffy, the members of the crew were rounded up and chained to the rail.

Read was blunt. "Pack up your stuff, captain. We're taking you with us."

A quick run-down of the *Tacony's* log confirmed what Read had already suspected: the *Tacony* was a far faster sailer than the *Clarence*. Another split-second decision. He would trade ships, burn the *Clarence*, coffee and all, after transferring his "armament" and flag to his prize. Back he went to shift commands, yet hardly had he reached the *Clarence* before the schooner *M. A. Schindler* hove in sight. Read bagged and fired her in half an hour. By now it was seven o'clock. The *M. A. Schindler* was ablaze fore and aft.

At this moment over the horizon hove the schooner *Kate Stewart*, whose captain was victimized by his own curiosity. Drawn by his desire to see what was up, he changed his course and ran down the wind straight into the raider's arms. He reached the scene at an embarrassing juncture. Read's only offensive weapon, his six-pounder, was in one of the small boats now plying between the *Clarence* and the *Tacony*. But Read was equal to the occasion. As the *Kate Stewart* sidled closer, the *Clarence's* portholes suddenly popped open and his "broadside guns" poked out their menacing snouts. There stood the gunners, lanyards taut, as if to let go a devastating blast. Jumping up on his cabin roof, the *Kate Stewart's* Captain Teague waved his arms frantically and bellowed through his trumpet, "For God's sake don't shoot! I surrender!"

"Come aboard and bring your papers," shouted Read. "You're prisoners of war."

Captain Teague obeyed with alacrity. Reaching the *Clarence's* deck, he gazed sheepishly at the wooden guns that had given him such a fright.

"Why, they're wooden guns," he gasped.

"So they are," snapped Read with a smile. "If you'd kept on your course, you'd have been all right. You deliberately stuck your head in the lion's mouth. You'll have to take the consequences."

Thus, before breakfast, Read had captured three prizes. But the *Kate Stewart* posed a problem. She carried passengers, twenty-odd ladies en route to Mexico, who were already swooning and melting in tears after the fashion of the day, the moment the "pirates" took over. But Read was not concerned with swooning women. Unfazed, he bypassed this temporary roadblock by bonding the *Kate Stewart* and transferring all his prisoners to her, for landing anywhere on the coast. It would be a dead giveaway, but he had no other choice. Yet, before releasing the *Kate Stewart*, he boasted of a Confederate high-seas fleet that would ravage the Atlantic coast and annihilate the blockade squadrons. To round out his morning's work, the brig *Arabella* came breezing by. Giving chase, Read overhauled her, though a neutral cargo forced him to bond her and send her on her way.

At noon he torched off the *Clarence* with over eight thousand bags of coffee beans still in her hold. Out over the bright waters floated the appetizing aroma of roasting coffee.

While he rested from his labors, Read took stock. Under his feet was a new, faster ship. Unencumbered with prisoners she could move as he pleased. He and Maffitt had agreed on a tentative rendezvous along the seventieth parallel of longitude; he had no way of knowing that the *Florida* had wasted fifteen days at Rocas Island, waiting for the ill-starred *Lapwing*. He was well aware that swarms of Union gunboats would dart out after him the moment the cartel *Kate Stewart* reached land and gave the alarm. Yet, up to this very moment, the Federal Navy had no inkling that a Confederate "pirate" was destroying commerce off the coast within one hundred miles of Washington. Until they caught him, he would work northward, torch in hand. How right was Admiral Porter when he said, "Read had in him the stuff to make a gallant naval commander."

CHAPTER XXI

Fire and Terror Sweep the
Yankee Coast

ON SATURDAY AFTERNOON, June 13, 1863, at 4:25, a wave of "alarums and alarums" swept through the Navy building at Washington. It blustered into the office of Secretary Welles to find that gentleman taking the afternoon off, listening to the Marine Band playing in Lafayette Park. Holding the fort, as the calamitous tidings rolled in, was Welles's able Under Secretary, Gustavus Vasa Fox.

Over the wire from Philadelphia had crackled an almost unbelievable telegram:

The pirate *Clarence* captured, within sight of Cape Henry, yesterday morning, brig *Schindler*, schooner *Kate Stewart* and bark *Tacony* of this port. They are using the *Tacony* for pirating further. E. A. Souder & Company

Fox acted promptly. Reaching out, he pulled every bell cord on the wall behind him. Gongs clanged furiously up and down the long corridors. Naval bigwigs came on the run. This done, he ordered a messenger to leap on a horse, gallop off to find Welles, and break the bad news.

To his breathless confreres, Fox spat it out: Confederate pirates were operating off the Virginia Capes, burning Union shipping and posing threats to the big army depots at Hampton Roads,

New York, and Boston. Anything might happen with these *hostis humani generis* (as Welles styled them) at large on the coast. They might even hoodwink their way into Chesapeake Bay, run up the Potomac, seize Federal officials and hold them for ransom.

By dusk, when Welles reached the office, Fox had launched the first batch of pursuit orders to naval commandants at New York, Philadelphia, Boston, and Hampton Roads.

For days, rumors of a combined strike by the Confederate cruisers *Alabama* and *Florida* had troubled the department. Something was up. What it was no one would hazard to guess. Perhaps this was it. Whatever, the Federal minister of marine had been caught off base. He had never heard of a ship named *Clarence*. Nor had news of her capture by the *Florida* in the south Atlantic reached the department. Welles's oft-repeated assurances of having the "pirate" situation well in hand had the sound of political soft soap. This fresh outbreak would be hard to explain to the watchdog Committee on the Conduct of the War.

But the telegram bearing the humiliating news was only the first of scores which would plague the harassed Secretary during the next fortnight. Welles feigned nonchalance over "this wolf that is prowling so near us," but the Official Records and his subsequent naval gymnastics dispute this.

In this age of atomic submarines, guided missiles, and weapons that threaten the very existence of man, it is not easy to comprehend the terror inspired by a lone, makeshift "cruiser," armed with a brass six-pounder and five dummy guns, trespassing the sacrosanct waters of the Atlantic seaboard. But such was the fact. The Washington state of mind at this juncture is best illustrated by Welles's confidence to his diary: "Something of a panic pervades the city."

Barely twenty-four hours had elapsed since Read's captures off the Virginia coast and the transfer of his flag to the *Tacony*. Toward noon this Saturday, the cartel *Kate Stewart*, bearing the prisoners he had released, touched at an obscure harbor on the New Jersey coast. Hardly had her anchor bit the mud before the *Tacony's* late master, Captain Munday, rushed ashore and caught a train to Philadelphia, where he poured out a tale of fear and fire to the ship's owners, E. A. Souther & Company, who promptly relayed the tidings to the naval secretary at Washington.

Newsmongers flocked in, almost mobbing the seaman in their eagerness to hear the last frightening detail. They drank in the skipper's repeat of Read's colorful fairytale about a flaming assault on the Atlantic coast to be made by the *Alabama*, the *Florida*, and his own peewee commerce destroyer. It didn't make sense; but that made no difference. The press fed it out in frightening chunks.

Read's coup had been dished up at a critical moment. Official Washington was aflutter. Lee and seventy thousand victory-flushed veterans were poised to lunge northward and dictate peace somewhere beyond the Mason-Dixon Line. The jump-off might come any day. Dispatches from the front were mystifying. Northern intelligence was groping. Lee's cavalry had screened off his front. Where was he? Where would he strike? Hooker didn't know. The setting was tailor-made for confusion. On this very day, June 13, Lee's legions began bypassing Hooker's massive army to duck through the Blue Ridge and streak up the valley in unending lines. To many a faint heart in the North it heralded the final grand march of the war.

The Official Records bear witness to Welles's zeal and diligence in this crisis; though, first, he scurried over to the White House to alert the President. Then, he bustled back to his desk. Old Gideon would show them how to catch a pirate! He went at it with a vengeance. Eighty-odd pages of the Official Records are studded with pursuit orders shot out to naval commandants at New York, Philadelphia, Boston, Hampton Roads; to warships, chartered vessels, tugs, yachts; to admirals and captains, commanders and lieutenants, ensigns and midshipmen.

To Admiral Paulding, commanding New York Navy Yard, sped this message, a sample of dozens: "The pirate *Clarence*, a sailing vessel captured and fitted out by the *Florida*, made three captures yesterday off the capes of the Chesapeake. Send what vessels you can in pursuit."

At 9:25 that evening came Paulding's reply: "Dispatch received. The *Tuscarora*, *Dai Ching* and *Adela* are ready and will proceed to sea tonight. We hope to get the *Virginia* and *Kittatinny* off tomorrow."

At 11:30 Admiral S. P. Lee, head man of the North Atlantic Blockading Squadron based at Hampton Roads, replied that five ships were on their way to waylay and sink the marauder. All night wires buzzed. Operators camped beside their keys. After a short, troubled sleep, Welles returned to the fray in the morning to find his desk covered with disquieting telegrams. Out flashed more orders for headlong chase.

Overnight, newspapers broadcast the news to the nation, and panic raced up the coast. Without reading the Official Records or conning contemporary accounts, one can hardly imagine the furor loosed by the little ship with its masquerade guns. Into the department surged a deluge of demands for naval protection. The outcry, "We are defenseless!" came from mayors of coastal cities and fearful citizens, as well as from boards of trade, committees on harbor defense, governors, politicos, lords of commerce, and merchant princes.

Little imagining the repercussions of his visitation, the object of Welles's steeplechase complacently set the *Tacony's* course for Nantucket.

By sundown, pursuit ships had blossomed like June roses. The fit and the unfit, the lame ducks and the moribund, were shaken out of their dockyard slumbers and hustled out to sea. In three days, no less than thirty-eight armed Federals were cruising the blue in a helter-skelter merry-go-round. Apparently, any semblance of a dragnet was absent. Had a dozen good ships fanned out up the coast at ten-mile, east-west intervals, they would have caught the disturber of the peace overnight.

Out charged the first cup-racer, *America* (now a Federal man-of-war), to win laurels for other than speed. Manned by twelve midshipmen on a training cruise, she skittered off bravely, only to limp back dejectedly in ten days, having lost her stays and about everything else that held her together.

The school-ship *Marion*, with a complement of more middies, sailed off to show the youngsters how to bag a Confederate pirate and win everlasting glory. Seasickness struck before they passed Sandy Hook. The middies, retching to a man, took to their bunks and stayed there. After tossing miserably on the Atlantic for days, she straggled back. Disgustedly her commander reported, "During our cruise we have neither seen nor heard of anything piratical."

With a naval view halloo the armed ferryboat, *Commodore Jones*, put out from New York, only to bounce back in five days after "bounding around like an india rubber ball from one sea to another, throwing water 50 to 60 yards ahead and on each side of her." The *Seminole*, leaking like a sieve (five or six inches an hour) bustled out; but her steam pumps could not compete with the water, and back she came. Even the *Kate Stewart*, which Read had captured and released, was chartered by Welles, given an old gun or two, and ordered out to redeem herself by capturing her captor.

Late in the day on June 14 Welles apparently became desperate. To Boston, Philadelphia, New York, went an all-out order: "It appears that the crew of the pirate *Clarence* have transferred themselves to the captured bark *Tacony* and have burned the *Clarence*. They have nothing but small arms. Charter or seize half a dozen moderate-sized, fast vessels; put on board an officer, a dozen men, plenty of small arms and one or two howitzers. Send them out in various directions. Take any vessel that can be sent to sea within the next forty-eight hours."

Taking the good Secretary at his word, the recipients obeyed with alacrity. Out scurried a nondescript squadron, unmatched in American naval history. One wonders why this armada of the good, bad, and decrepit, scouring the coast between Cape Hatteras and Boston, should have sighted neither hide nor hair of Read, who, on June 15, broke cover well out to sea off the Delaware capes, where he burned the brig *Umpire*, carrying Cuban sugar and molasses for the good folk of Boston town. On this same day Lee's grayjackets were legging it for the Potomac crossover into Maryland.

That night the *Tacony* was hailed by a Federal man-of-war asking news of the "piratical *Tacony*." With consummate nerve, Read gleefully trumpeted back, "Yes, we saw her at dusk chasing an East Indiaman." Then he tacked on a bogus latitude and longitude, and waited, tense, wondering. Would the Federal swallow it? Instead of boarding to verify what he had been told, the Union commander gobbled the bait and bore off to rescue the luckless ship. Before daylight a second Federal rose out of the mist with a similar inquiry, to receive an identical reply. This time, however, Read directed the hunter to a different location. Actually, he had sent them in exactly opposite directions, one northwest, the other southeast.

One by one, ships Read had intercepted and bonded reached port with accurate information of his ship's weakness, her lone gun and five make-believe cannon; but this in no way diminished the

consternation that greeted each newly-reported bonfire set by the
intrepid invader.

In the New York *Tribune* Horace Greeley jeered:

> This rebel cruiser, *Tacony*, in a few hours makes her appearance
> under the very noses of the Yankees and frightens them half to
> death. The New York *Herald* says "When the news first reached
> the Navy Department they should have ordered the chartering of
> every available steam vessel and sent them to sea, if need be, with
> volunteer crews shipped for a cruise of twenty days. Every
> available steam vessel! After one little cruiser!

2

Panic was mounting by the hour. Nor is this account exaggerated.
The Official Records and the contemporary press bear witness. If
one is to judge by the hysterical outburst, it would seem as if the
fate of the nation was riding in the cabin of the *Tacony*, instead
of on the feet of thousands of graylegs dusting north for a rendezvous with fate at Gettysburg. Men in coastal towns brought out
their muzzle-loaders and made ready to repel the invaders in
the spirit of Winston Churchill's dictum of a later war: "We shall
fight them on the beaches . . . in the fields . . . in the streets
. . . in the hills."

Pirate-spotters encamped on headlands, keeping vigil round the
hours. Ministers of the gospel led their flocks down to the beaches
to implore the Almighty to spare them from the fury of the
buccaneers.

New York was the sharpest thorn in Secretary Welles's flesh. "Are
you aware of the importance of this city to the nation? Do you intend to leave this great seat of commerce, art and learning naked to
the depredations of pirates?" an anxious editor demanded. As always, the politicians moved in to make hay out of the fears of the
populace. In the van strode stately U.S. Senator E. D. Morgan,
one-time governor of the Empire State. He would fend the city
from rebel brigandage. Hustling over to the Brooklyn Navy Yard,
he gazed delightedly on the new, heavily-armored, triple-turreted
Roanoke, a far more formidable monster than the diminutive *Moni-
tor* which cut short the *Merrimack's* destructive spree in Hampton
Roads. She was almost ready for sea, guns mounted, magazine

filled. If anything could terminate the career of Read's "dread-naught," the *Roanoke* could.

Armed with a resounding resolution from the New York Harbor and Frontier Defense Commission, Senator Morgan dashed to Washington, stalked into Welles's office, and demanded that the *Roanoke* be stationed off Sandy Hook "to defend this harbor from attack by a hostile ship or steamer." Welles blew up. He said no. He had no ironclads to spare. The *Roanoke* had another mission in life.

Not to be outdone by the glamorous conscript father, Mayor George Opdyke moved into the picture. He telegraphed Welles a flat order to leave the *Roanoke* where she was "until this city can devise other means of securing its safety from naval attack, which its importance to the nation imperiously demands."

Welles turned him down. Who was this uppity mayor of New York to order *him* around? His refusal to comply brought up big-gun Major General John E. Wool, commanding the Department of the East. Veteran of two wars (1812 and Mexican), he was loaded with years, prestige, and epaulettes. His sonorous voice rose above the hue and cry: "This great emporium from which you are supplied with money and almost everything to carry on the war against the rebels" must be protected at all hazards. Welles, more irate than ever, was still unconvinced. The General volleyed again: "I repeat that this great emporium from which both the Army and Navy receive their supplies, as well as pay, ought not to be left without means of defense. We shall be at the mercy of any privateers that may think proper to assail this city."

Welles finally soothed their fears (most likely at President Lincoln's instigation) by assigning the unfinished ironclad *Passaic* to duty in the Narrows until the furor subsided. This ridiculous cat-and-dog fight between Welles and the New York city fathers provided an incredible, though amusing, side show.

But other cities were taking alarm. As Read edged up the coast Governor John A. Andrew of Massachusetts fired an excoriating letter at Welles, pointing out the defenselessness of the common-wealth's coast and charging the Navy with dire inefficiency. He said he was being flooded with calls for help from seaside cities and towns. "A rebel vessel manned by as daring a crew as that of the *Tacony*, might burn half the towns along Cape Cod, and even lay, for a few hours, such ports as Salem, Marblehead, Beverly, Gloucester, Rockport, and Newburyport under contribution, none of which are defended by a single gun. The ignorance of the rebels as to our defenseless condition is our most effectual protection in the absence of action by the Navy Department."

Angry as a hornet, Welles hotly defended himself: "The alarm created by the reckless depredations of the *Tacony* is not surprising. Within two days from the time the *Tacony* was captured and appropriated to piratical purposes the Department had issued orders to send vessels in pursuit. . . . Yet your Excellency has thought it proper to say no vessels were sent until the *Tacony* had rioted along the coast for four days. It is not often that I devote a moment to controvert or correct undeserved censure or misrepresentation, but this seemed so gratuitous and even undeserved . . ."

To cap this tale of woe, the selectmen of Provincetown emitted a piteous caterwaul. Send a war vessel to halt this "rebel invasion that threatens to burn our town. We have no means of defense whatever. We also pray for 150 or 200 muskets that we may be prepared to meet any foe that may attempt to land on the back of our town."

So it went from Delaware to the tip of Maine. Even President Lincoln got into the act with a summary order to halt "rebel depredations on American commerce and transportation and capture the rebels engaged therein." He was at the moment, however, far more concerned with Lee's swift advance across Maryland and into Pennsylvania than with the turmoil created by Read and his one-gun fireball.

3

Meanwhile, the *Tacony* pursued her deadly course. Read seemed to revel in his orgy of fire. Newspapers seized from his captures revealed the panic he had created and the frantic antics of the navy pursuing him. To make it more pleasurable, he learned that Lee's veterans were racing across Maryland in what appeared an unstoppable drive. It must have looked to Read as if the gods themselves wore gray, for the weather and sea were in league with him. Soft, mild sunshine, smiling waters. Day after day, at the North's front door, he was burning prizes like clockwork.

Approaching Nantucket, Read straddled the New York-Liverpool track, fatback of American foreign trade. On June 20 he overhauled the huge packet *Isaac Webb*, with 750 passengers, mostly immigrants bound for new homes in the Western world. He cut down his prey with one shotless bark of his brass trinket. Over the rail the newcomers gazed down in terror on this pygmy manifestation of Confederate naval might. It was an awesome welcome for these optimistic aliens, lured to the land of the free by promises of high war wages, free land, and bonuses for enlistment in the Federal armies.

Read had caught a leviathan on a fishhook. He yearned to blaze off his magnificent prize. What a bonfire she'd make! His "firemen" gazed on her avidly. Their torch-hands fairly itched. But, like Raphael Semmes when he captured the gold ship *Ariel*, Read had no way of disposing of his host of prisoners. Nor was he, after all, in the cremation business. Going aboard to talk shop, Read forced her skipper to sign a bond for $40,000, a small fraction of her value. He was on his way back to his "flagship" when the fishing schooner *Micawber*, unlike her namesake, without waiting for something to turn up, sailed over to investigate. Read satisfied her curiosity quickly with his wooden guns. He had no ammunition to waste. To give an extra-special flourish to his technique, he promptly burned the schooner under the eyes of the *Isaac Webb's* petrified passengers, who fully expected his torchmen to come aboard and set her afire. Indeed, while the flames devoured the *Micawber*, groups knelt on the liner's deck, beseeching Providence to stay Read's brand.

Quickening his pace and hoping any day to sight the *Florida*, Read worked closer to Cape Cod. On June 21 the splendid new clipper *Byzantium* came dancing along with coals from Newcastle to New York. She hauled up at the yelp of Read's six-pounder and burned brightly, as did the three-masted *Goodspeed* which he nabbed later in the day. Hunting was just too good. The owners of the *Goodspeed*, a New York shipping firm, promptly sent a hot protest to Secretary Welles, charging that a Federal gunboat had stood by a mile or so off watching Read burn their bark. They based it on a cock-and-bull story told by the *Goodspeed's* skipper, whose excited imagination ran away with him the moment he got out of Read's clutches.

On June 22, with shotted gun and flaring torch, the *Tacony* pounced on the New England fishing fleet. This chapter of Read's activities was a retake of the *Alabama's* extermination of the American whalers off the Azores, but far closer home. It could be felt. The impact was harder, hotter, and it brought a wail of woe. At this season, the ocean was alive with Gloucestermen and Cape Codders out for the summer catch of cod, mackerel, and halibut. For three days Read and his crew luxuriated in a burning shambles. He roped in five schooners with his first day's haul. In three days he nipped off eight, all hailing from Gloucester. For a few hours the *Tacony's* forecastle deck resembled a prison yard. Burning six, he spared one and sent her off as a cartel to rid himself of his prisoners. He saved another for further use.

Unscathed, unchallenged, unseen by his pursuers, Read stretched northward. He was fighting the war without the least expense to the Confederacy. Day after day his ideas enlarged, and his brain teemed with schemes for Federal discomfiture. The Confederacy could mount dozens of these midget stingarees and send them out like swarms of mosquitoes to prey on Federal coastal commerce.

On June 24 Read plucked the massive *Shatemuc*, bound for Boston with hundreds of Irish immigrants who counted their beads vociferously as Read came aboard with a big pistol jangling at his belt. From her skipper he demanded a $150,000 bond in lieu of fire. Captain Oxnard's Yankee face reddened. He cussed up and down. He'd see the Confederacy in hell before he'd sign any such paper. He cussed everything, even Gideon Welles for not patrolling this vital ocean trade route. But Read was quietly uncompromising. Sign the bond or I'll burn your ship. Take your choice. He looked mild mannered, but the young sea raider was admirably suited to the task in hand. The skipper made a sensible choice.

Toward night, the mackerel schooner *Archer* of Southport, Maine, slid into Read's net. She was just what he wanted. To her—his third flagship and twentieth prize—he transferred his colors, armament, and stores. In his diary that night he confided the reasons for his swap:

The latest news from Yankeedom tells us that there are over 20 gunboats in search of us. They have the description of the

Tacony, and overhaul every vessel that resembles her. During the night we transferred our things on board the schooner *Archer*. At 2 A.M. set fire to the *Tacony* and stood west. The schooner *Archer* is a fishing vessel of 90 tons, sails well and is easily handled. No Yankee vessel would even dream of suspecting us. I therefore think we will dodge our pursuers for a short time. It is my intention to go along the coast with a view of burning the shipping in some exposed harbor and of cutting out a steamer.

Read's count of Federal huntsmen was off by eighteen. Actually, at the moment, thirty-eight armed ships were ranging the seas after him. Next morning, Read and his crew went through the motions of commissioning the new Confederate "man-of-war" *Archer*. After raising their flag and giving three cheers, they assembled in the little cabin to splice the main brace with the dregs of the 'alf-and-'alf the English skipper had donated off the Windwards. No downheartedness here. Not a croaker in the lot. They were going great guns and they knew it. How long the revelry would last was in the lap of the gods. On with the fire-dance! Under a fair wind, the *Archer* moved on to her destiny.

Read was seldom undramatic in his projects. Risky enterprise was the meat on which he thrived. Northern newspapers painted horrendous pictures of him; yet up to now he had not shed a drop of anyone's blood. His scorching of the fishing fleet was the last straw. New England fishing smacks had for centuries been interdicted as prize of war. Read had violated this tradition. Had he, at one fell swoop, eradicated the sacred cod itself, New England's indignation could not have been more bitter. But his star was rocketing toward its zenith.

June 26 found Read and his ninety-ton flagship bearing up for Portland, Maine. In his wake, crisscrossing each other's tracks like porpoises at play, without rhyme or reason, came Welles's *chasseurs*. About noon the *Archer* ran down two lobstermen who had been marooned in a dory outside all night. Taking the cold, hungry castaways aboard, Read fed them and then plied them with questions. When he announced they were prisoners of war, they thought it a huge joke. Their captors' rough fishermen's togs hardly comported with their ideas of how Confederate sailors ought to look. Nor did "Captain" Read, whose uniform had faded into a blue-gray blend. Readily, unsuspectingly, the two anglers agreed to pilot their benefactors into Portland harbor. Over a hot, succulent breakfast they chattered out vital details about the city's chief defense, Fort Preble, the frowning rampart whose gunners had loudly promised Read and his band of "cutthroats" a hot reception if they so much as dared look at Portland.

Whetting the raider's appetite (though not purposely), they blabbed about a new revenue cutter, the *Caleb Cushing*, a neat sailing warship mounting a 12- and a 32-pounder, and moored handily in the roadstead. She had only a fortnight ago emerged from the hands of the shipwrights and carpenters. Rambling on, they glibly divulged that the fast passenger liner *Chesapeake* was lounging at her wharf ready to sail in the morning for New York. Read's imagination caught fire. It was what he had dreamed of.

At sundown a light breeze wafted the *Archer* into Portland harbor, where she anchored innocently amid the shipping. Outwardly, she was merely another Down-easter snugging down for the night after a hard day's hauling nets outside. None would have suspected her of being a sea-wolf in fisherman's clothes. Through the falling dusk Read made a spyglass reconnaissance of the harbor and its battlements. Yonder was the *Caleb Cushing*, temptingly, it seemed, awaiting his ministrations. The more he looked, the more feasible the plan seemed. At this juncture, for safety's sake, Read ironed his two informants, Messrs. Albert T. Bigger and Elbridge Titcomb, both of Portland, who thus edged their way into Civil War annals.

Not until then did these two innocents come to believe that their captor was none other than the fearsome Read whose exploits had the coast in an uproar.

After nightfall, Read and his officers and men assembled in the *Archer's* dim-lit, fishy cabin, where he unwrapped the bold gamble his brain had trumped up. It is doubtful if Henry Morgan mapping a raid on Spain's gold coast ever went at it with more aplomb than this cool-headed Mississippian in scheming his sortie in Portland harbor. Without the flicker of an eyelash, the star of this audacious show briefed his men for their roles. By now, they would have followed him to hell itself. To them he was the "Captain" nonpareil. Their fantastic adventures had left them spellbound by the ingenuity of their leader and their own apparent infallibility. Weather-beaten, unshaved, unshorn, they looked like banditti.

"We looked like pirates must have looked" admitted a participant in after times. It was an understatement, if contemporary accounts are accepted.

"I have decided to capture the steamer *Chesapeake*," announced Read as calmly as if proposing a stroll in the moonlight. "Then we'll fire as much shipping as we can and head to sea."

It was a big order. Eyes bulged. Up spake able, devoted Engineer Browne, "Captain, I doubt if I can handle the *Chesapeake* alone, without another engineer. She's a big ship. Steam would be down. It'd take hours to get it up. Dawn would find us still under the fort's guns."

Read made a split-second decision. "Very well, sir, we'll capture the cutter and sail her out. There's a good offshore breeze blowing. After getting beyond the fort, we'll go back and fire the shipping."

Lastly, a short prayer. Read was a powerful praying man—and cusser to boot, when need be. He could reel off invocations to the Almighty like a circuit rider. All knelt. Impressive was the silence in the cubbyhole cabin while Read implored heaven to bless his enterprise and cooperate with him in lighting more fire on the altar of Confederate liberties. Fervid Amens followed. To each man Read assigned a role in the big scene.

At 1:30, moonset, "Captain" Read and nineteen men, in two small boats, oars muffled, rowed silently across the dark harbor toward the sleeping *Caleb Cushing*. He left three men to sail the *Archer* out to sea and wait for the cutting-out party with the swag.

Lady Luck still held Read's hand. The captain of the cutter had died shortly before. His successor, Lieutenant James H. Merryman, was not expected to reach Portland until morning. Command of the ship overnight had devolved on youthful Lieutenant Dudley Davenport, a Southerner, who had cast lots with the old flag in the great disruption. Half the cutter's crew were in Portland on liberty. The deck watch was a lone bluejacket. In fact, the cutter was under orders to put to sea on the morrow and join the search for Read. The set-up was tailor-made for the raider.

Stealthily, the Confederates sidled up to the revenue cutter. First over her rail was Read himself, brandishing his pistol. In two minutes, nineteen boarders had bounced over the bulwarks. All the trimmings of old-time pirate stuff! The deck watch dashed below to rouse Lieutenant Davenport. Read chased after him to meet the two men as they emerged from the cabin.

"I'll kill you both if you make a sound!" Read's Southern drawl had a hard, deadly inflection. "Don't speak a word."

Read had them ironed together to the mast. The crew were captured in their hammocks, half asleep, and shackled on the spot. The cutter was Read's. Not a sound of alarm had reached shore. The job was perfect so far. It was a thrilling moment for these ship-snatching adepts. Shipshape, clean as a new pearl, the *Caleb Cushing* even smelled new; but this was no moment to indulge in such small pleasures. Read stood at his high-water mark. But, just here, his star began to decline. The stiff offshore breeze had died to a whisper! The tide had set in.

But his ability to brush aside setbacks amounted almost to genius. Undismayed, he manned his two small boats with oarsmen and began towing the cutter at a snail's pace against the tide for the open sea. Back-breaking work, reminding him, as he said later, of the day Captain Hull saved "Old Ironsides" from British capture by an identical maneuver. Fort Preble was fast asleep. The sentries on her parapets saw nothing, heard nothing. Daybreak found Read five miles out, beyond gunshot. But more heartening, the offshore breeze had suddenly freshened. Raising sail, he steered seaward to join the *Archer*. So far so good, but it was too late to go back and ravage shipping. By now it was broad daylight. He dared not tempt Fate too far.

He had a new ship under his feet. He could sail her off to meet Maffitt or embark on a fresh rash of burning. He first considered disguising his schooner-rigged captive, but how? That could come later. Calling in his oarsmen and posting a sharp lookout, he ordered all hands below for a well-earned, sumptuous breakfast on the cutter's ample larder.

With unfailing Southern hospitality, he invited his prisoner-guest and Annapolis classmate, Lieutenant Davenport, to a leisurely repast with him in the wardroom, taking occasion to rebuke him for deserting the South.

"Look what's happened to you now," observed Read between mouthfuls of New England bacon and eggs.

4

The city of Portland awoke that morning with a shudder, to be thrown "into a state of excitement bordering on consternation." The news swept the city. Church bells were ringing. And at such an early hour! It wasn't even Sunday. The citizenry leaped out of bed to see what was the matter. The pirates had come! By eight o'clock the waterfront was swarming. "Women and children filled the streets and were rushing hither and thither in aimless fright." In the night the *Caleb Cushing* had vanished by some "unauthorized external force." It was mystifying, frightening. The warden of the harbor knew nothing.

The Portland *Argus* had for days predicted Read's probable descent on the city. Nobody had taken it seriously. If he came in the night, nobody knew anything about it, nobody had heard a sound.

Man of the hour was Jedidiah Jewett, Collector of the Port, who mounted the stage unbidden and nominated himself "commander-in-chief." He apparently made a good choice, for he seems to have been the only Portlander who kept his head. In the first shock-wave of the *Caleb Cushing*'s inexplicable departure, "Admiral-General" Jewett unjustly concluded that Lieutenant Davenport, whose Southern background had caused some eyebrow arching, had sneaked the vessel out to sail her into the Confederacy; but a sleepy-eyed dock prowler, who had witnessed the cutting-out party's neat operation and then gone back to sleep, came up with the first clue that the cutter was victim of a *tour de force* and not of treason. Later, a fisherman volunteered that he had seen a ship being towed seaward by two small boats.

Jewett acted with commendable dispatch. The *Caleb Cushing* belonged to the United States Treasury. As highest ranking representative of that department, he delegated authority to himself and began dishing out orders at once. Messengers galloped off to Fort Preble for men and guns from the Seventeenth Infantry (regulars), and to Camp Lincoln for a detachment of the Seventh Maine Volunteers. Next, he commandeered two large steamships: the *Forest City* of the Boston line; and, over the protest of the local agent, the New York liner *Chesapeake*, which Read had originally planned to seize. To protect the *Forest City*'s vulnerable engine

room high on deck, Jewett armored her with a barricade of cotton
bales. He then manned her with one hundred men of the Seventeenth Infantry and two brass field guns. On the *Chesapeake* he
stationed the Maine Volunteers and a score of Portlanders fired
with patriotic zeal to avenge the infamous theft and run down the
dastards. These last were armed with ancient muskets, squirrel
guns, and even cutlasses. The rear guard was a steam tug armed
with nothing.

At ten o'clock "Admiral General" Jewett's formidable fleet got
underway. In its wake ribboned a motley rabble of small sailboats,
crowded with owners, friends, and fight-fans intent on occupying
front row seats at the coming combat. Sweeping the outer harbor
with his glasses, Jewett discerned the *Caleb Cushing* about fifteen
miles out, beating down Casco Bay for the open sea.

Read sighted the posse bearing down on him at about the
same time. The chips were on the table, and he cleared for action.
He had fought one blasted ship at New Orleans until she sank
under his feet. Now he was ready to repeat the performance. At
two miles the *Archer* opened fire with her 32-pounder, letting fly
at the *Chesapeake*, which had outsteamed the *Forest City* to shooting range. The projectile screamed off to splash only fifty yards off
the steamer's port bow. It was an uncomfortably accurate shot.
Venturing closer, the *Chesapeake* was treated to three more shots
that bracketed her, one tossing up a geyser at her waterline. These
were enough to squelch the war ardor of the citizen volunteers, who
suddenly realized this was no lark. Their valor promptly capitulated
to their discretion. So poignant were their outcries that the steamer's captain hauled about to wait for the *Forest City*. By mega-
phone the two ships held a council of war and decided to continue
pursuit. They would run down the cutter before her long gun
placed a vital shot.

With the two Yankee ships pressing after him, Read summoned
his little band.

"Men, this is our last chance. You have written a glorious chapter in Confederate naval history. We have our choice: fight or
surrender. Which shall it be?"

"Fight!" exploded from twenty-two mouths.

"Fight it will be!" assured Read grimly. "Go to your stations!"

Read took his battle station beside the 32-pounder on the forecastle deck. For an hour he fended off his attackers with well-placed shots that screeched menacingly through the rigging of the steamers. Then, all at once, he ran out of projectiles! Five hundred pounds of powder lay in the cutter's magazine, but no solid shot, or shell. The shot locker with a reserve supply, eighty-odd, was ironbound, and his prisoner, Lieutenant Davenport, had tossed the key overboard, or so he said. The Official Records and on-the-spot reports are at variance in explaining the shortage of ammunition at this crucial moment.

With scraps of metal picked up about the deck, Read continued a desultory fire, but his game was up. The raiding saga of Charles William Read was hurrying to its end. He would at least make it long remembered. To brighten his exit, fate supplied a bit of humor. In the officers' mess Engineer Browne discovered a "projectile," a round, ancient Dutch cheese that was gleefully rammed home in the 32-pounder. Boom! Off galloped the cheese to splatter on the Chesapeake's deck with a stench that induced a recipient to remark, "The pirates are firing stink pots at us like the Chinese." With this smelly blast Read's guns went silent. His ship was a sitting duck, wings clipped.

Coolly, deliberately, in a manner worthy of his metal, Read decided to end the game. At bay, his bluff was called. Further "effusion of blood" was pointless. Nor would he keep the rendezvous with the Florida. But he had a last decision to make: Yankee prison or Davy Jones' locker? The steamers cautiously edged nearer. Read could see their decks packed with soldiers, field guns run out, ready to open fire. First, he bundled his prisoners into a small boat. After them he tossed the keys to unlock their irons. Now to play out his last act: destroy the ship. While his firemen set the Caleb Cushing ablaze, fore and aft, Read lit a slow fuse to the magazine. Hardly had they taken to their small boats before flames burst up from the wardroom and companionways to run up the mast and fire the sails. Rapidly pulling away from the burning ship, they rested their oars three hundred yards off. Five hundred pounds of powder needed only a spark. Slowly, the Chesapeake ran them down. Read and his company were flying white handkerchiefs, which fluttered from oars.

In his official report, Lieutenant Merryman, who had arrived just in time to join the chase, had this to say:

We now observed a crowded boat leaving her, which proved to contain Lieutenant Davenport and his crew who were picked up by the *Chesapeake*. A few moments later two more boats left her, and instantly smoke and flames were seen bursting from her wardroom and cabin companionways. By the aid of my glasses I perceived that her decks were deserted and that the *Cushing* was doomed to destruction. Expecting every moment to see her blown to atoms, for I had learned that her magazine contained 500 pounds of powder, I advised Captain Liscomb to bear away for the boats containing the pirates and run them down.

But even in defeat Read was no broken reed. Up the gangway, his men trailing him, he strode, pistol and sword at his side, with the grace and dignity of a man who had fought to the last ditch and lost. He was as cool as if standing on his own quarter-deck with the tables reversed.

Bowing, he addressed Lieutenant Merryman, "I am Lieutenant Charles W. Read of the Confederate States Navy. Your prisoner, sir!"

With a gesture of finality he handed over his sidearms.

Not until this moment, indeed, did Portland's saviors know they had captured the redoubtable arch-raider, who with twenty-two men, one gun, five Quaker guns, and an appalling amount of nerve, had strewn the coast with wreckage and for whom, by now, forty-seven Union war-vessels were combing the seas.

At 1:48 the *Caleb Cushing* blew up with a sheet of flame and vanished below the chill Maine waters. The explosion, reverberating across the bay, scared the already frightened citizens of Portland half out of their wits. A short chase by the *Chesapeake* overhauled the *Archer* and her skeleton crew beating out to sea. Back to Portland, with their "trophies" securely handcuffed, steamed the triumphal procession, to be greeted by frenzied crowds who literally tore the clothes off Read and his men. It brought from Read the complaint, "Our clothing was distributed as relics to the people of Portland." From the Portland *Transcript* came this suggestive comment: "Our citizens could hardly reconcile themselves to the idea of not hanging somebody."

Colonel Andrews, commanding the detachment of the Seventeenth Infantry, offered a wise suggestion in his report to the War Department: "I would respectfully suggest that the prisoners be sent from here as quietly and expeditiously as possible, as I do not think it safe for them to be placed in the custody of citizens while the present excitement continues." This was done. Closely guarded, fettered hand and foot, Read and his bold, bad crew were hustled off to Boston's Fort Warren and incarcerated for a year before being exchanged as prisoners of war.

Read's pennant—"the new flag of the rebels"—which had flown successively from the *Clarence, Tacony,* and *Archer,* was seized and dispatched triumphantly to Secretary Welles at Washington. Two days later it was unfolded across President Lincoln's desk at the White House. Old Gideon was in his glory. He had caught the "pirate"!

In reporting from prison to Confederate Secretary Mallory, Read paid high tribute to his second officer, his petty officers, and his seamen, commending them to the generosity of the South. "They are good seamen, brave and patriotic men," he said. If Read made a mistake, it was in not taking stock of his powder and ball before engaging his enemy.

From John Maffitt came the well-deserved praise: "Daring, even beyond the point of martial prudence," but Admiral Porter supplied the caustic tagline. "A single Federal gunboat, under an intelligent captain, would have nipped Read's whole scheme in the bud."

Look at the box score of Read's dramatic assault on the North's home waters. In twenty-one days he had taken twenty-two prizes, a staggering average. He burned thirteen of his captures—and this under the very nose of the United States Navy.

CHAPTER XXII

Where Was the *Florida*?

READ'S JOURNAL, captured on the *Archer*, revealed that he had expected to meet the *Florida* off Nantucket. Often had the daring young man scanned the horizon for his mother ship, but it is hardly probable that Maffitt believed he could keep the rendezvous. Yet it seemed as if the fickle goddess at least tried to synchronize the operations of the *Florida* and her granddaughter, *Tacony*.

Eight degrees above the Equator, in the vast gateway between Africa and South America, the huge *Red Gauntlet* barged across Maffitt's track. Far off, she resembled a swan, wings outspread. It was June 15, the day Read fired the brig *Umpire* off the mouth of the Delaware. The *Red Gauntlet's* cargo was ice and pianos for the Chinese! Lacquered in red and yellow flame, she made her exit in style.

Well east of the Windwards, Maffitt sent an iron calling-card whining across three miles of water after the three-sticker *Benjamin F. Hoxie*. She was the only treasure ship ever captured by a Confederate raider. (Raphael Semmes had captured the *Ariel*, which should have been a treasure ship—but wasn't.) Bound from Mexico's west coast, her hold was a mine of silver ore. Breaking open a steel-barred cabin, the *Florida's* boarders stepped back and "looked at each other in wild surmise," speechless, as if gazing into the fabled coffers of the Incas. Silver ingots! No pieces of eight, but bars of solid silver worth $105,000. This was the payoff. Excitement swept the berth deck. Jack was rich! Or so he thought. Nimbly, hopefully, he figured it up. One thousand dollars a man from this haul alone. Spellbound, he watched the shiny stuff come aboard. It was consigned to a Liverpool bank. Topping off this haul, the ship's strong box yielded seven thousand dollars in gold.

Claims of neutral cargo failed to dovetail accurately enough to fireproof the *Benjamin F. Hoxie*. She crimsoned out in a red festoon. She and the *Red Gauntlet* gave the *Florida* eight volunteers. Pay: twenty-two dollars a month, Confederate money; a bounty of fifty dollars and a share of the prize money Congress had voted. And maybe a "cut" of the silver just seized. What better bargain could a recruit ask?

On June 27, the day Read snatched the *Caleb Cushing* in Portland harbor, Maffitt pounced on the whaler V. *H. Hill*, which slithered out of the dark at eight bells like a specter, passing two ship's lengths or less to starboard. Maffitt had turned in; but he was out of his bunk and ran on deck, buttoning his jacket.

"She's running away," said the quartermaster at the helm.

"Well, tell her to stop," ordered Maffitt.

The night watch leaped to it. With a crash, the pivot gun tore a hole in the night. Its booming voice uttered an unmistakable "Halt." The whaler came out of her dream of racing away, and lay to. The V. *H. Hill* of Providence appeared in good time, because the *Florida* was all but overrun with fifty-four prisoners. Eight tough recalcitrants had to be kept shackled and ironed. It was perilous. Bonding the whaler, Maffitt sent her off in the night to land his captives at her home port.

Veering west by north, the *Florida* steered for Sandy Hook. The weather was thickening and heavy combers climbed over the freeboard. Lookouts were doubled, guns shotted, crews briefed, for these were hostile waters. Anything could happen here. Welles's tireless vigilantes were stalking every mile of the coast. Newspapers taken from the V. *H. Hill* estimated seventy-odd on the hunt. Front page news carried the terror created by Read's depredations; and so Maffitt learned what had happened to his lieutenant, and why the *Clarence* was deflected from their original plan. That night, round the wardroom table went Maffitt's toast: "To Charles William Read, *sans peur, sans reproche!*"

The Boston Board of Trade had sent Gideon Welles a bristling reproof for leaving the "hub of the universe" naked to her enemies. Welles himself had renewed his vow to tie halters round the necks of Semmes and Maffitt, when he caught them.

Featured also was a letter to Secretary of the Treasury Salmon P. Chase from the Collector of the Port at Bath, Maine, pointing out: "You are aware that the ports and harbors of the coast of Maine are in imminent danger of attack by the rebel cruisers now off and near the coast, and that a successful attempt has been made to cut out the revenue cutter in the harbor of Portland."

July 7 saw the *Florida* in the mainstream. New York lay just over the port bow, and Maffitt was tantalized by the old dream of a hit-and-run pounce on the packed harbor. The city was jittery; the time was now. Ranging closer shoreward, he overhauled the packet *Sunrise*. His latitude was that of New York; his longitude that of Boston. It was deep night and the packer's running lights were aglow. Sighted afar, she resembled a bright-eyed nightbird gliding over the sea. Barely eight hours out of New York, she carried late papers that the *Florida's* boarders seized eagerly. Heartbreaking news was bannered across the pages. Maffitt's heart sank as he read it. Lee bloodily repulsed at Gettysburg—Vicksburg capitulated under Grant's hammer blows. Packed with passengers, he bonded the ship and sent her off into the night.

Noon, July 8. On a boisterous sea the *Florida* hovered forty miles off Sandy Hook. Maffitt decided to wait for night before dashing in to despoil the anchorage. He knew the harbor by heart. He'd give the coast a repeat performance of Read's whirlwind. At one bell, out of the haze, loped a four-pipe sidewheeler—and the picture changed.

Eagerly Maffitt studied the newcomer, then sent his men to quarters. Fires were stoked, guns cast loose, sails furled. A fight! Jack was spoiling for one. It looked as if he would get it right here almost within earshot of the metropolis. Pointing the *Florida's* head directly at the Federal ship, Maffitt hauled down his British colors and broke out the secession flag.

Three miles off, the stranger was standing east under Yankee colors and steering for the *Florida*. Maffitt could see her clearly in the circle of his telescope. Her ports gaped. Her big paddles raced and her walking beam upsidaisied like boys on the end of a plank. She maneuvered uncertainly before deciding to close.

Nearer, nearer, the two ships cut down the distance. At twelve hundred yards the *Florida's* fore pivot blazed out with a blast and a puff of white smoke. Arching across the water the shot ricocheted and sliced off half the Yankee's foretop. First blood. Up went a yell from the *Florida's* gunners. With a sheet of flame, the *Florida's* broadside roared off. Shells splashed round the enemy ship, but no hits. No reply, either. Maffitt hoped for a crippling shot in her paddle box. She was near enough now for him to identify her. The *Ericsson*, without a doubt. He'd gamble on it. Perhaps he could capture her.

Into the speaking tube he bellowed down to the engine room, "Give her all you've got."

Up rumbled, "Aye, aye, sir, all we've got!"

At that moment, the *Ericsson* hauled about and headed for New York. Catch her! But the old ocean herself intervened. In came a curtain of fog, blanketing the hunter and the hunted. Not for half an hour did the veil lift. Yonder, five miles off, the *Ericsson* scuttled for Sandy Hook and safety. Into the *Florida's* fireboxes went coal taken from the *Red Gauntlet*. Low grade it proved, and the *Red Gauntlet* had her revenge. The fireboxes hardly sniffed at it.

Again Maffitt spoke to the engine room, "Fifteen hundred dollars for fifteen pounds of steam!"

Firemen began tossing in the last resort, pitch and rosin. The old blockade-running legerdemain had its virtues; but this was the *Florida's* off day. Eight pounds. Nine. Ten. The indicator stopped dead, while the *Ericsson* flew off like a frightened deer.

To Gideon Welles her commander reported, "Confident we would soon be captured if we attempted to engage her, I concluded to take advantage of the fog to escape."

A letter home from one of the boys on the Rebel raider's berth deck had this to say: "All hands were anxious to catch her, for she had been sent to catch rebel cruisers, but she nearly caught a tartar this time. However, we had the pleasure of burning two vessels under her nose. We showed the crew of the W. B. Nash the *Ericsson* making tracks for New York."

Tucking in her guns, the *Florida* tacked away. New York, alerted by the *Ericsson*, was out of the question now. But Fate made fast amends. At dark, the brig W. B. Nash of New York, with 650,000 pounds of lard, came a cropper. Unceremoniously, Maffitt fired her. To make a bigger show, the whaler *Rienzi* hove in sight, homing for Provincetown, her hold glutted with whale oil from the South Pacific. Maffitt seized her in less time than it takes to tell it. No need to examine her papers. She was Yankee to the marrow. New York just beyond the horizon, and prizes wrapped in flames. Grease-fed, the fire soared two hundred feet. Sails shriveled and spars tumbled. The red reflection could be seen fifty miles off. Where were Gideon Welles's hawkshaws? A double bill for Jack. If not a Federal warship to bear off in triumph, Maffitt had at least given his men a two-ringed spectacle.

Turning about, the *Florida* bore off southward. On July 16 the raider sighted Bermuda's glistening white strand with her pennons of palm and her pink and white houses. Slowly, the cruiser nego- tiated the narrow channel to come to rest over the shimmering coral gardens of Five Fathom Hole. Lounging at their nearby moor- ings were a dozen blockade runners; others nuzzled at wharves, taking on war munitions to run into the beleaguered Confederacy. For Maffitt, it was a nostalgic scene.

But for the Confederate wayfarer there was niggardly welcome. The fort gave no sign of recognition. It was no more, or less, than Maffitt expected. He had other motives for his visit: good Cardiff coal for his empty bunkers, and caulkers with buckets and bales of oakum to pay the *Florida's* gaping seams, pried apart by the equa- torial sun. The big Atlantic rollers had relentlessly climbed over her bulwarks, and her deck leaked like a sieve. Her engines needed tinkering again. Fifty days at sea up from Brazil had racked them.

By now he was an old hand at fencing for favors with airy, stiff- collared colonial officials. So far he had been lucky. This was the third time he had come seeking indulgences at British colonial ports. He had found out that belligerent rights were what you make them, with the right methods.

His get-up was impressive as he stepped into his captain's gig to go ashore. Dame Rumor's heralds—also the Nassau *Guardian*—had trumpeted his arrival. With formality as thick as cake icing and enough gold braid to decorate a dozen lieutenants, the Admiral of the Port, William Munro, received Maffitt with a deep bow and obvious awe. To Maffitt's request for pratique, the dignitary brusquely reminded the raider that Britain—and therefore Bermuda

—was strictly neutral in the tragic broil of the American states. Tapping his desk, stickling at this and that, the port functionary evaded Maffitt's direct request for permission to refuel his vessel. Apparently, the gentleman had something else on his mind.

"I am astonished, Captain Maffitt," he said, "that a former officer of the American Navy should be guilty of a breach of etiquette on entering her Majesty's harbor."

The raider's eyes widened. He was caught unawares. "How so, sir?"

"You steamed into our harbor without saluting her Majesty's flag," replied the official gravely. It was unpardonable, but, Maffitt sensed, not irreparable.

"That is true, your Excellency," he admitted. The old winning smile broke over his face. "But I could hardly do otherwise. I had no reason to expect our salute to be returned. England has not yet recognized the independence of the South."

With a twinkle the admiral replied, "Captain Maffitt, you can never tell till you try. You didn't try."

The interview was over. The hint was sufficient. Elated, Maffitt rose, saluted, and bowed out. Two hours later an emissary from the governor's palace, clothed in glorious raiment, stalked up the *Florida's* gangway bearing an official communication. It was done up in fine style, red sealing wax and all. Breaking it open Maffitt read:

Sir, I shall be happy to return any salute that Commander Maffitt may be desirous of ordering in compliment to Her Majesty the Queen. Ten or twelve o'clock tomorrow forenoon would, either of them, be convenient hours. In fact, any hour would suit if I am informed a short time previously. I am, yours obediently, William Munro.

Accompanying this formidable open-sesame was a copy of her Majesty's proclamation of neutrality; but this was for the record at the Foreign Office at London.

Next morning, the *Florida* dressed ship and manned her yards. Decks holystoned, guns slicked, brasses agleam, sails neatly furled, she looked fetching as a young lady in a fresh spring dress. Immaculate on the quarter-deck stood Maffitt and his officers. The dress-up contagion had overtaken Jack, too; he was ordered to don his Sunday best, sennit hats and whites. While twenty-one guns boomed slowly from the *Florida*, the English ensign wriggled its way to her peak to break out in the languid breeze. Now it was the Stars and Bars' turn. Down slid the Union Jack. Up sped the Southern bunting. From the fort boomed twenty-one resounding gun salutes. On the *Florida's* bridge her three-piece band played the inevitable "Rule Britannia" and "God Save the Queen."

Thus was the Confederate flag accorded its first and only foreign salute. It was implicit recognition of Southern independence, and its echo would be heard one day in the future *Alabama* Claims against Great Britain. For Maffitt, deep student of naval history, it was reminiscent of the first recognition of the Stars and Stripes, when, in 1778, John Paul Jones sailed the *Ranger* into Quiberon Bay, France, with the new Stars and Stripes at her peak.

Then, picking up her skirts, the *Florida* swished into St. George's harbor, with the Stars and Bars fluttering out her pride in the new nation she so ably represented.

"Lionized" was the best word the Bermuda *Royal Gazette* could find to describe the ensuing love feast. For Jack the welcome was uproarious. Wherever he turned, a hand was held out to welcome him. In her jubilation Bermuda all but turned Confederate. Tidings of Gettysburg had reached the islands, but few wanted to accept its prophetic impact. But letting down the bars of neutrality would have repercussions. The guns that shattered Lee's charging grayclads on the slopes of Cemetery Hill were echoing in London. The South had reached her crest. Mortally stricken, she would reel on to her finish. Britain must consider the future.

But, at Bermuda, away with melancholy! The Confederacy was still afloat and here was "the glorious *Florida*" with gallant Captain Maffitt and his gallant band. Elatedly, one of his lieutenants wrote home, "We are received with open arms everywhere we go."

American Consul Allen transmitted a depressing report of the fêting and banqueting to Secretary of State Seward. But the correspondent of James Gordon Bennett's New York *Herald* seems to have succumbed to Maffitt's glamour. Before his readers in New York he paraded the unpalatable facts:

> Captain Maffitt is no ordinary character. He is vigorous, energetic, bold, quick and dashing, and the sooner he is caught and hung the better it will be for the interests of our commercial

community. He is decidedly popular here and you can scarcely imagine the anxiety evinced to get a glance at him. Nobody, unless informed, would have imagined the small, black-eyed, poetic-looking gentleman, with his romantic appearance, to be a second Semmes, probably in time to be a more celebrated and dangerous pirate.

For eleven days the *Florida* dallied in Bermuda. The twenty-four hours accorded her magically spun out from day to day. Meanwhile, coal barges snuggled up and dumped tons of black jewels into her bunkers. Caulkers swarmed over her decks. At the height of the jubilee the Federal *Wachusett* crashed the party. Unwanted, she came in and anchored near her quarry. Bermuda's governor ejected her fast. She could have coal; but she must anchor and give the *Florida* twenty-four hours' leeway before putting to sea. Strict neutrality for the North; overtime and feasting for the South.

Old friend James Wilkinson, skipper of the blockade runner *Robert E. Lee*, came a-visiting. Quite amused was he at what he saw: "The *Florida's* deck when the crew were at their meals, was a curious scene; the plain fare of the sailors being served on costly china, captured from homeward bound Indiamen, and the scamps had become fastidious in their taste about tea."

To the *Robert E. Lee* Maffitt entrusted a dozen bags of captured coffee and chests of tea for the hospitals at Richmond. To Secretary Mallory he dispatched twenty-one chronometers taken from his prizes, and the flag of the *Jacob Bell*.

Sad-eyed Jack watched the silver bullion from the *Benjamin Hoxie* being ferried ashore. On turning it over to the Bermuda representative of Fraser, Trenholm, it was taken into custody by the colonial prize court. Maffitt was confident it would be adjudged legal prize of war; but he was mistaken. Shipped to England, it was returned to the claimants to whom it was originally consigned.

On June 25, rejuvenated, re-coaled, and re-caulked, the raider steamed seaward. But ere she raised anchor, up the gangway came a bevy of ladies with armfuls of flowers to say farewell to the *Florida's* captain. And perhaps—though he does not record it—to bestow a goodbye kiss or two in this delightful interlude. For John Maffitt was never averse to feminine attentions. After all, he was a sailor. Only forty-four, fascination still lingered in his eyes. Nor were his bits of gallantry, his witty sallies, unacceptable to female hearts. About him clustered irresistible, almost legendary glamour. At Bermuda he wore fresh laurels: his brush with the *Ericsson,* her swift retreat.

But he would come again, he promised. Yes, one day he would return—when the Confederacy was falling like a burned-out star and the sound of mourning was rising over the ashes of her would-be glory.

Caressingly the *Florida* dipped her prow into the Atlantic swells. Overhead, blue sky and the smile of the sun. She was off to sweep the European sea lanes where American merchantmen waited like tinderboxes. Common sense told Maffitt these cisatlantic waters were fast becoming untenable, haunted by Union men of war in full cry. Unfurling sail, banking his fires, and cradling his propeller, he pointed the *Florida* easterly over a stormy sea. In mid-ocean he ran down the packet *F. B. Cutting,* crammed with passengers for New York. He bonded her for $40,000 and turned her loose. Near the English Channel the *Anglo Saxon* obligingly materialized on the horizon, giving him a chance to display his hot wares for Britain and France. Maffitt meted out short shrift. Over a tossing sea the *Florida's* cutter with her torchmen and prisoners took an hour to pull up under the lee of the cruiser. As dusk was falling, a vivid red glow leaped from one wave crest to the next.

Four days of howling gale took the heart out of Maffitt. Like the *Florida,* he was wearying. Nearly eight months at sea and little respite had robbed the cruiser of much of her fleetness. She cried out for docking. A careful inspection revealed her propeller shaft out of line and the sleeve leaking badly. But where could she go? Maffitt had his choice of refuge—France or England. That is, if he could outwit Federal cruisers now ganging up in French and British waters. He considered striking for the Mersey. There, perhaps, Bulloch could get his first child repaired and out to sea again. It was tempting, but too risky. He picked France as his haven. He hadn't touched at a French port; but he knew that his Imperial Majesty, Napoleon Three, was playing both ends against the middle, and giving the Confederacy the better deal. Brest had docking facilities.

Just where the Channel entered the Atlantic, the *Florida* caught the New York-bound packet *Southern Rights,* whose name gave the Floridians a laugh. Southern rights were a thing of the past. A million men in blue were trampling them out. His prize was crowded with four hundred emigrants, half of them with Federal enlistment papers. More foreigners to pull triggers and jab bayonets into Southern bodies. Maffitt saw red. He was sorely tempted to remove her passengers and send her flaming to the bottom. He could make shore in several hours. He would dump his human cargo anywhere on the coast of France. But the lamentations of the travelers beat down his yearning to burn this Union army carryall. Upbraiding himself for weakness, he bonded her, raised sail, and sped away.

CHAPTER XXIII

Farewell to *La Floride*

BREST! *La Floride* had come! Excitement swept this Breton town as
her fisherfolk rushed to the waterfront to see the raider that had
peppered the Atlantic with charred hulks and spars. Outrider of
the Confederate Navy, she was the first of her breed to display the
colors of the Southern Republic in the airs of France. She had
saluted the tricolor as she came abreast of the fort on the point,
but had received no answer from the iron-throated guardsmen of
the port. Yet the exploits of *La Floride* and her sister *L'Alabama*
were themes that electrified many a French heart.

Captained by the audacious "Old Salamander," her unan-
nounced appearance out of the Atlantic gave rise to sensation and
mystery that resounded through France. For two days she lay in
the harbor, black, rakish, silent, with the unfamiliar banner of the
South flapping at her mizzen.

Then, amazingly, curiosity to see her gave way to ugly myths,
which made tempting morsels for the excitable French temperament. Fantastic tales were hawked about. Parisian newspapers repeated them. Embellished with horror, these stories spread fast;
and the welcome for the Confederate seafarer died to a whisper.

The *Florida* was depicted as a *corsaire* whose decks were stained
with blood and infamy. She was not a Confederate naval vessel.
Her tars were pirate vultures—"the refuse of the earth"—who sliced
jugulars for the fun of watching the blood spurt. Maffitt and his

officers were sea wolves. Several corpses were reportedly dangling from her yardarms as she entered the roadstead. Maffitt had cremated a shipload of women and children in the English Channel. The *Florida's* hull was filled with gold ravished from Northern ships.

Up went the cry: *La belle France* should refuse shelter to these accursed desperadoes and expel their ship from her waters. The simple mariners, who had rushed to greet her, now stood at the quayside shaking their fists.

A pretty kettle of fish, to be sure; but John Maffitt sat tight. With a seaweary ship and a crew famishing for a rollicking carouse on shore, he could do nothing else. Anchored in a strange harbor, in sight of a city that was cold and hostile, he might as well have been shut off from the world. Meanwhile, his crew was growing unruly. France, in Jack's imagination, meant oceans of wine and bedding down with lovely ladies. Maffitt had weathered many a storm. He could outride this one, too. First he dispatched a lieutenant, who had to run a gantlet of threats, to Paris to notify Confederate Commissioner Slidell of the *Florida's* condition and her request for pratique. He then went ashore to pay his respects to Port Admiral de Guedon and formally request docking for his ailing vessel. At his heels tagged a crowd hurling imprecations and murderous glances. The naval dignitary received him with marked respect and exuberant courtesy. The raider's sweep of the seas had excited his Gallic love of glory.

"I have followed your cruise with deep interest, Capitaine," glowed de Guedon, as he bowed deeply and grasped Maffitt's hand. "I have admired the courage and devotion of your men. I am happy to inform you that my government has instructed me to extend to you the hospitality of Brest."

As for the wild tales of the *Florida's* bloody excesses on the high seas, the admiral had only a "Poof! poof!" These villainous sensations had originated in the fertile brain of a Bordeaux merchant whose goods had gone up in the flames that consumed one of Maffitt's prizes, and who now demanded indemnity on threats of legal seizure of the ship.

But Maffitt was disturbed by the tempest of gossip investing the *Florida*, and was determined to scotch it if he could. Would the admiral come aboard and attest the falsity of these rumors? The flattered dignitary agreed with delight. He would visit the *Florida* officially the next day. Hurrying back to his ship, Maffitt issued orders: haircuts and beard-trimming for every officer and Jack, and pronto. At sea he was indulgent in this matter. Beards had flourished like weeds on the long cruise. Unearthing a box of scissors snatched from a prize, the forecastle was converted into a huge barbershop. All day amateur tonsorial artists plied their trade in a you-cut-mine-and-I'll-cut-yours marathon. Then the ship was tidied up. Mustering his men on deck, Maffitt had them double the capstan while he inspected each man's new-shorn look.

Next day, with ruffles and salutes that frightened the townsfolk prodigiously, Admiral de Guedon and his staff clanked up the gangway. Not even a French man-of-war could boast a nattier crew. The *Florida* had been prettied up, and Maffitt was at his captivating best.

"Excellent!" exclaimed the Frenchman as he noted the fine points of the ship. "Vraiment excellent, Capitaine Maffeet!"

Then into Maffitt's cabin, where *La belle France* and *La Confederacy* received broadsides of flowery fanfares over bumpers of champagne.

From this moment obstacles fell away as by enchantment. The ugly rumors quieted down. The admiralty issued an official communiqué: "The steamer *Florida*, now undergoing repairs at Brest, is not a *corsaire* as has been at first supposed. She belongs to the navy of the Confederate States of America." Once more the fisherfolk flocked to the waterfront to cheer and clap hands, as a tug nuzzled the weary *Florida* into dry dock. *La Floride* was *sans pariel*, *sans tache*, *sans* everything but what was fine and admirable.

Maffitt then made a grandstand play. He showed himself and his officers in public at the opening of Brest's theatrical season, with this result:

> Their appearance at the performance was quite an event. They were steadily gazed at during the whole evening, and they came out victorious from public scrutiny. When the curtain fell on the last act the men declared that the Confederate officers were too gentlemanly in their deportment to be pirates; the women swore they were too young, and too handsome, and looked too modest to be guilty of the crimes with which they were reproached. The following day they were invited to the different clubs in the city

and called upon to relate their dangers and their many narrow escapes from the enemy.

Meanwhile, a cold war was raging on the diplomatic front at Paris. American Minister Dayton demanded that France expel the Confederate pirate. With threats of retaliation, he protested that the *Florida* was fully able to raise sail and put to sea. Engine repairs were not necessary to her well-being. But the Emperor of the Second Empire was still hypnotized by the glory of the South's struggle. His sympathies were thinly concealed. With a historic comment he capped off and quashed the diplomatic furor: "Because a duck can swim is no reason to clip her wings."

The Federal *Kearsarge*, mousing along the coast, slipped into Brest roads to anchor near the *Florida*, as if to take her measure before sending her to the bottom. She was ordered out. The good Bretons again shook their fists, this time at the effrontery of this stranger who had come to do harm to *La belle Floride*.

Yet this diplomatic tempest answered a vexed question. Insofar as France was concerned, a Confederate man-of-war could enter her ports and claim the immunities and privileges of a warship of a sovereign nation.

Drawn by the fame of the *Florida*, the London *Times* dispatched a correspondent to Brest, where the cruiser now basked in the haze of her restored glory. Coming aboard, the newsman found Maffitt "a slight, middle sized, well-knit man of about forty-two, a merry looking man, with a ready, determined air, full of life and business —apparently ready equally for a fight or a jollification." The *Times*' news hawk seems to have overlooked the streaks of gray creeping into Maffitt's dark hair.

"We never seek a fight, but we don't avoid one," said Maffitt. "You see, the Confederacy has only two vessels on the high seas, the *Florida* and the *Alabama*. The Federals have almost a thousand. Our object is to destroy commerce. It's the quickest way to peace. Altogether the *Alabama* and *Florida* and their tenders have taken seventy-two prizes. The *Jacob Bell* alone was worth two million dollars."

"Do you take gold and precious articles?" asked the scribe.

"We have the right to," snapped Maffitt. "We'd do it pretty quick if we needed it. It's legitimate prize. But we make war only on the United States government. We are trying to destroy the

Federal merchant marine. We've cost our government little, for
we've lived on the enemy. You're drinking tea now from the
Jacob Bell. The finest hysong."

"Prize tea," observed the reporter.

"None better," smiled Maffitt. "We treat our prisoners well. They
eat the same food as my crew. We've had some ungrateful rascals
and we dealt with them accordingly. When we reached Brest the
Florida had been at sea nearly eight months with only a bit of
patching here and there. Two hundred and forty-five days on the
ocean without repairs or replenishing our provisions. Our prizes
were our pantry and we've lived high."

Pointing to Brest's single narrow outlet to the sea, the reporter
wondered how Maffitt expected to escape the Federal cruisers
clustering off the port.

"Well," he replied philosophically, "I imagine there'll be seven
or eight of them out there before long. But we'll get out. I've run
a dozen or more blockades already. It may be hard, but I'll run this
one, God willing."

The reporter then twitted Maffitt on a touchy subject: the bullion
he had snatched from the *Benjamin Hoxie*.

"I left it at Bermuda for your prize court to adjudicate," said
Maffitt. "I believe it belongs to us legitimately, but the Confederacy
will abide by your court's decision. Now one thing more: There
are no bags of gold on the *Florida*. The gold we took from the
Hoxie's strongbox belonged to the ship. We took that for ourselves. Our men work on faith in the ultimate independence and
solvency of the Confederacy. In the meantime we pay them well.
No better wages on the high seas unless on the *Alabama*. And
they've lived on the fat of the land. Look at them."

Maffitt's black steward, Charles, entered, immaculate in white
apron, bearing a cold, just-uncorked bottle. The *Times* man gazed
in surprise at the smiling, polite Negro.

"He's Charles, who's taken good care of me since we ran out of
Mobile. No one could have done it better."

"And what's your score, up to now, Captain Maffitt?"

"Twenty-two Northern ships captured, most of them burned.
We lit our last bonfire, the *Anglo Saxon*, right at your front door.
And this doesn't count the burnings by my tender, the *Clarence*,
with Lieutenant Read commanding."

But the cold war at Paris must give Maffitt a last jab. Who fired it was a moot question. Maffitt was a drunkard who spent most of his time in his cabin tippling! What a pity, ran the canard, that such a gallant man, who had outwitted the entire Federal Navy, should succumb to the enemy, John Barleycorn. But France was not impressed. A Paris newspaper polished off this slander in pointed fashion, "Apropos of Captain Maffitt's use of liquor it may be well to point out that President Lincoln is reported to have told a delegation that came to complain of General Grant's intemperance, he would like to know what brand the general drank so that he could send a barrel of it to his unsuccessful generals. If Captain Maffitt, whose deeds of pluck, skill and daring have excited the admiration of the world, makes too free use of spirits, it has only sharpened his nautical abilities and his genius in burning Northern ships."

That settled that.

One fine September day, after the *Florida* had emerged from drydock, came a blow, a stabbing pain in the chest that sent Maffitt reeling to his bunk. Breathing hard, he lay there wondering. The debilitating effects of yellow fever, the hard grind of the sea, the unremitting tension and danger of his business, had sapped his fine physique. Ages had gone by, it seemed, since he had known a carefree moment. The French heart specialist who hurried down from Paris shook his head and tapped his breast. Le capitaine must rest. Three months, at least. Perhaps travel on the Continent when he got back on his feet.

News that Maffitt was stricken spread fast. Boats came hourly with messages of condolence and flowers. From a café on the Place de la Madeleine in Paris, where he often sipped excellent wine, came a rapturous round robin, bearing the signatures of the entire staff, cooks and all, and many a customer who had admired the man of fire and elevated him to the stature of Lee and the lamented Jackson.

John Maffitt chafed under inaction as he got better. The Confederacy was more deeply embattled with her back to the inevitable wall. He would idle a while, sit in the sidewalk cafés, travel a bit in Holland and Sweden, and then, a new ship and more bonfires. Behind him stretched an electrifying fusion of pestilence, danger, hurricanes of shells, death in a hundred forms, escapes by the skin of his teeth, nights and days of struggle with wind and wave—but now, for awhile, surcease.

To Commander Matthew F. Maury, Confederate Naval Agent at Paris, he wrote, "I regret to inform the Department that in consequence of impaired health I shall be under the necessity of applying for detachment from the *Florida*."

Not until the day he was to say good-by, one day in October, did he realize how deeply he loved the ship or how tight were the cords that bound him to the men who had served him.

At noon he invited his officers into his cabin for a parting word. Pale-faced, he spoke with obvious emotion.

"I regret more than I can say leaving you and the *Florida*. But you will go on to greater fame. That I know. Serve Captain Morris as ably and faithfully as you have me and all will be well."

But a bit of humor must creep in. Maffitt was that way. His eyes brightened and a smile ran along his lips as slowly he quoted:

> *Whether sailor or not, for a moment avast!*
> *Poor Jack's mizzentopsail is hove to the mast;*
> *Though the worms gnaw his timbers,*
> *His hull a mere wreck,*
> *When he hears the last whistle*
> *He'll jump up on deck.*

With the crew lining the rail and the ship's band blaring *Dixie*, he stepped over the side. Holding tight to the manropes, he went down the gangway. Never again would he tread her quarter-deck, or gaze in pride on her shapely hull. As the gig swept shoreward he stood in the stern sheets looking back, his hand raised in a long farewell salute. About his shoulders—and incongruous it must have seemed—was a faded naval cloak.

CHAPTER XXIV

Under the Guns Again

LONDON. NOVEMBER, 1863. There was no discharge in the war for John Maffitt. The long fight was in his bloodstream. Sojourning in Sweden and Holland were delightful interludes; but, health improved, he couldn't remain inactive for long. In Britain's capital, as in her colonies, he was much sought after. To this man, "whose sea adventures beat romance in her own domain" (as a London paper stated it), arms were outstretched in welcome. His legendary escapes, his blazing passage over the seas in the *Florida*, were told again and again, while Southern sympathizers flocked to greet him.

In the privacy of a quiet room, presumably at the old Adelphi Hotel, he again met James Bulloch, who had just lost what had looked like a winning hand in his touch-and-go game of evading British neutrality. As they clasped hands, Bulloch gazed admiringly into the steady eyes of the man who, for the moment, was the toast of Mayfair.

Britain's Foreign Office, said Bulloch, had impounded the two Laird rams that between them might have vanquished the Northern blockade. The outcries of the American press, and the heated exchanges of notes between Minister Adams and Lord Russell, had at last brought John Bull to his senses. In the sobering news of Gettysburg, he read the handwriting on the wall. The concentrated indignation of the United States was too alarming. Britain was shying away from deeper entanglement. No longer was "every South victory welcomed as if it had been won by an English army; every Southern defeat spoken of as if it had been a national reverse." Yet, her upper crust and the various Southern Independence Associations and Societies for Promoting Cessation of Hostilities were just as impassioned as ever. Parliament still rang with cries of the Southern claque.

Eighteen months had elapsed since Bulloch and Maffitt parted at Savannah. One can easily surmise what they talked about. Certainly, Bulloch inquired after his firstling, the *Florida*, née *Oreto*. His sea dog's pride in his two cruiser offspring, *Alabama* and *Florida*, reads eloquently through the lines of his memoirs. Yet, if he was downhearted at the flip of the dice, his official correspondence does not indicate it. The whole Confederacy was a gamble. Until now he had managed to keep an ace or two up his sleeve; but the inexorable turn of events defied his amazing capabilities.

There was much Maffitt wanted to know. Was Bulloch building a new cruiser in a hideout shipyard somewhere in Britain? Unfortunately, said Bulloch, Britain had plugged that loophole permanently, forcing him to transfer his ironclad schemings to France, where he was to fare little better. He was, however, angling for a merchant steamer he could arm and dispatch to knock off America's whaling fleet in the Pacific. But no more British-built cruisers would saunter down the Mersey incognito.

News from behind the wooden curtain off the Southern coast was sparse, though orders for Maffitt had seeped through from Richmond. He was to return to blockade running. As for Bulloch, he would henceforth devote his talents to procuring ships to carry munitions through the blockade. His magic touch had already conjured up a brace of speedies whose faces were being lifted at a shipyard on the Clyde in Scotland. The hierarchy at Richmond had decided to officer and man these ships with Confederate naval personnel. Ownership was vested outwardly in Fraser, Trenholm & Company, the South's omnipresent fiduciary agents; but this simply was subterfuge. Maffitt was to command one of them, sail her across the Atlantic to Nassau, and then through the cordons to Wilmington.

Bulloch had ornamented one of the pair with the name of a young lady named Florie, who was "as sweet as she was brave." Maffitt's eyes kindled. Was it for *his* Florie? Who else? smiled Bulloch. He then related the story of her capture aboard the blockade runner *Nassau*. Her gallant behavior under fire on this occasion had inspired the New York *Herald* to express admiration of her coolness and to dub her "a chip off the old block." The second ship would be named *Lilian* for a friend.

What of the *Florida*? She was still at Brest, champing at frustrations. Diplomatic roadblocks had piled up. Repairs had come grudgingly. Lieutenant Morris, commanding her, hoped to get through the encircling Federals outside the roads. With returning health Maffitt yearned to get to sea with a fast, fresh-built commerce destroyer and sweep the European sea lanes with his blazing broom. Yet he bowed uncomplainingly to orders from Richmond. He had learned duty the hard way. Nor was he one to inveigh against it.

2

Meanwhile, English shipping interests and manufacturers were growing rich from the war. Her industries ran night and day, save for her cotton mills, where the operators were starving. But blockade runners were not loafing. Many were nipped; but in the first nine months of 1863, over one hundred thousand bales of cotton reached Liverpool. Valued at over four million pounds, they brought gold enough to buy masses of powder, shot, and shell.

Britain had two capital customers on her hands; the North and, *sub rosa*, the South. Her Foreign Office might halt the building of war vessels, but it had no intention of impeding the flow of British munitions. Trading surreptitiously with the South, or even directly, brought protests, but no imminence of war. So it was business as usual in everything that took human life, except camouflaged cruisers to pillage Northern merchantmen, and undisguised ironclads to devastate the blockade.

Revived—in a sense—was the golden age of the eighteenth century, when merchant adventurers financed swashbucklers to roam the ocean and reap harvests where they found them. It differed from the past only in the method of operation. And the profits were much higher. Gentlemen, merchants, bankers, and even lords of the realm bought shares in long, narrow side-wheelers that could outwit and outrun the big, surly cruisers of the Federal network.

The year 1863 saw blockade running at its zenith. Never before were the fast Clyde-built steamers so numerous. They came and went in droves. Observed a contemporary British commentator: "Everyone in London and Liverpool who has capital enough to purchase a share in a steamer, invests in that way, and looks with composure upon the prospects of running a valuable cargo into some rebel port and a return trip with the accompanying profits. Hence a cloud of steamers mottles the seas, bearing cargoes of valuables to the rebels, and we find them daily, or nightly, dashing through the blockaders."

To help things along, the *Alabama* and *Florida* had already destroyed a prodigious amount of America's merchant marine, while frightening far more of it off the seas. British bottoms would soon have the oceans to themselves, if these two fireballs stayed afloat to roam as they pleased.

3

Three thousand miles from the comfortable lodgings where Bulloch and Maffitt chatted in low tones, the coils of the blockade were slowly squeezing the breath out of a bleeding South. Yet, this was the year of her biggest bid for victory.

Traffic through Welles's sea-chain was brisk, but the gamble was double what it had been when Maffitt was doing business. And the profits were even more fantastic. One hundred and fifty blockaders now patrolled the approaches to Charleston and Wilmington, though runners came and went as if invisible. On the Gulf, Galveston, Mobile, and a few lesser ports still plied their trade. Ceaselessly, long runners weaseled through the Federal dragnet. Nassau, Bermuda, Havana, and Matamoras were merely stopovers through which Britain "traded" with the South. Farragut would soon plug the Mobile gap for good.

The year was waning when Maffitt accompanied Bulloch to Greenock, Scotland. There, at the wharf on the Clyde, lay the brand-new, identical *Florie* and *Lilian*. Light craft, they possessed the grace and lines of steam yachts. Below decks were engines with big tubular boilers capable of standing what was then a tremendous pressure of steam which shot them along at fourteen knots or better. They were shaped to the queen's taste for wriggling through the blockade. Into their holds stevedores were dumping cargoes of death-dealing stores. Scotch pilots and crews (signed on for an innocuous voyage to Bermuda or Nassau and paid in gold in advance) were waiting. Bulloch had overlooked nothing, not even the well-stocked captain's cellar.

New Year's Day, 1864, found the *Lilian* in mid-ocean. It was the year of blood. In late January, the *Lilian* ran into Nassau to refuel. Three nights later she bore up off the Wilmington bar, but there were no welcomers with red-flashing greetings. Maffitt had not forgotten his old tricks. He slid through like a wraith and up the Cape Fear River to the city.

After a brief, joyful reunion with his daughters, he boarded a rickety train for a flying trip to Richmond. Twenty-four hours' racking over a decaying roadbed and worn out rails landed him in the capital. Secretary Mallory was still optimistic. Gettysburg? It was only a bad dream on the Confederacy's hard road to independence. When Lee's spring campaign blazed out, Lincoln's new general would go the way of those who had preceded him, disillusioned and defeated.

Elixir to Maffitt's soul was his two-day sojourn in the citadel of the South. Escorted onto the floor of Congress, he was huzzaed by legislators and packed galleries. To the presidential mansion on Shockoe Hill came throngs to pay tribute to him. With elegant phrases, the chief of state wreathed him in verbal laurels. Top-flight politicos in broadcloth vied with fighters in battle-stained gray in praise of his skill and daring. From the ladies, as always, showers of attentions. Nor was the press reticent. "Commander Maffitt has come to town and captured many a heart," gushed an admiring newsgatherer. In the years ahead, these scenes would unroll like bright tapestry against the background of a dead and gone Confederacy.

4

Freed from the lingering chase, in devious ways
Upon the swelling tides
Swiftly the Lilian glides
Through hostile shells and eager foeman past;
The lynx-eyed pilot gazing through the haze,
And engines straining, "far hope dawns at last."

> *Now falls in billows deep the welcome night*
>   *Upon white sands below;*
>   *While signal lamps aglow*
> *Seek out Fort Fisher's distant answering gleams,*
> *The blockade runner's keen, supreme delight—*
> *Dear Dixie Land, the haven of our dreams!*

Standing on the airy-fairy *Lilian,* John Maffitt was making ready to cast off for the outrun. The runner was moored at the cotton press. Her hatches were battened down. A mouse could hardly have squeezed through her jam-packed hold. The loaders were at the moment lashing two last tiers of bales on her deck fore and aft, leaving runways to the cabin, engine room, and forecastle. She bore a ridiculous resemblance to a huge bale of cotton with two sticks (her masts) protruding from the middle. Her cargo totted up to eight hundred and fifty-odd bales.

Maffitt was perplexed. Two of his seamen had taken French leave since the *Lilian* ran in several days ago. They might be basking in one of the brothels that added to Wilmington's wartime attractions, though he felt certain they had deserted to the enemy— for a price. It was probably good riddance, but embarrassing. Capable seamen were getting hard to find. He needed every man he had. He had picked the *Lilian's* crew carefully, and over the last four months trained them to a nicety.

In an hour or so the *Lilian* would shove off, pause at Smithville to be searched and smoked for runaways, deserters, and spies, bank her fires, and wait for night to get out. Maffitt's annoying reverie was cut short by a loud conversation on the wharf directly below him. He listened.

"Ah! the top o' the morning to ye, Mister Sullivan. And have you any news by way of divarsion?"

"Indade, I have, Pat Murphy, but it's nothing divarting, me jewel. Just a bad spirit of the divil's invention—the telegraph."

"Spit it out, me boy. Never mind how bitter it tastes."

"I will. It sets like a sour pill on me stummick and won't be kept down. General Hood's been beaten in Tennessee, and, bad cess to the telegraph, it says one of our countrymen, General Pat Cleburne, is wounded. Pat, me jewel, what do you think General Jackson would say to such infernal bad news?"

After a puff or two of his odorous pipe, Murphy replied, "And what would he say? Bejabers, he'd say he was glad he was dead."

Recognizing the voices of two shipmates of former days, Maffitt invited his Celtic friends into his cabin, where he broke out a bottle of the "breath of the morning." Nor was it long before he had filled his truants' places, with assurances from his visitors that "like true Irishmen they would stand by me, if every foot of the salt sea spawned a Yankee gunboat."

Darkness fell. Silently, the *Lilian* steamed past Fort Caswell, making for the Western bar. Clear of the channel, she met the swelling greeting of the Atlantic. She was soundless save for the moaning of a northeast wind and the unavoidable dash of her paddles. Night glasses scanned the bleared horizon. Then out of the spindrift emerged the inevitable specters. She sprinted along unseen. In Maffitt's own words: "How taut, like harpstrings, every nerve is strung, anxiously vibrating with each pulsation of our throbbing hearts."

As the *Lilian* emerged to windward between two blockaders, pilot John Laughlin observed in a muffled voice, "Captain, according to my logic them chaps ain't going to squint us this blessed night."

Maffitt's reply was stifled by a broad-spread flash of light that blazed from the Yankee flagship. The *Lilian's* paddles had betrayed her.

"Full speed!" ordered Maffitt down to the engine room.

There was no waiting. As if Pandemonium were discharging evil spirits, guns roared. Shot and shell screamed at the *Lilian*. An explosion and a shock told Maffitt the ship was hit on the port bow.

"What's the damage?" he called out cheerily to his boatswain.

"Five bales knocked overboard, sir. Nobody hurt."

The sea was brightly illuminated. Half a dozen blockaders were trying to ring the ship, at the same time ripping the sea with missiles. At the height of the melee, a government V.I.P., traveling on the *Lilian* under special orders, dashed onto the bridge, wringing his hands in terror.

"Captain Maffitt, you'll have to surrender! You must!" he insisted. "We'll all be killed."

Much provoked, Maffitt summoned the irrepressible Murphy, whom he had stationed near by.

"Murphy, take the lubber below!" ordered Maffitt above the din.

"Aye, aye, Sir," said the delighted Celt, who apparently was reveling in the threats of annihilation hurtling through the air.

Unceremoniously seizing the unhappy, protesting individual by the collar, he hurried him to the cabin while reeling out a stream of invective, "Shut your flytrap, or by the powers of Mollie Kelly, I'll hould ye up as a target for the divarsion of thim Yankee gunners."

As the menace multiplied, wrote Maffitt, "our mazeppa's speed increased and gradually withdrew us from the circle of danger. At last we distanced the party." The *Lilian* had made it again, her tenth run through the curtain of fire.

The delighted Murphy, whose spirits no danger could subdue, waved his hat as the last abortive shell screeched overhead. "Farewell, me jewels! Indade, you are charming companions at a convenient distance. Present me compliments to auld Father Abe and thank him for his flattering attentions to King Cotton."

Day dawned under a soft blue sky and a bluer horizon. Maffitt wrote: "Over the broad expanse hovered a profound calm. It seemed difficult to realize that such serenity was ever tortured into the most wild and frantic commotion by rude storms and hurricanes that often held high revelry where not a ruffled wave appeared, or a gentle ripple bleared the mirror'd surface." For awhile, he flattered himself into thinking the *Lilian* would reach Nassau without hindrance. Yet at five o'clock, the masthead's "Sail ho!" dispelled this pleasing notion.

"Can you make her out?" he trumpeted up as he sent his pilot aloft to double check.

"Yes, sir, a large steamer heading for us fast."

Maffitt changed course. The stranger followed suit.

"A monster," reported the pilot as he came out of the rigging. "I think she's the *Vanderbilt.*"

"Well," said Maffitt drolly, "I outfoxed her once with the *Florida.* Maybe we can do it again."

He knew that the big million-dollar side-wheeler had recently trundled back from her fruitless chase of the *Florida* and *Alabama* through the complexities of the West Indies and the South Atlantic. Now, attached to the North Atlantic Blockading Squadron, she was hanging off the Bahamas hoping to snare any unwary runner that came along. When the Vanderbilt bobbed up on the horizon, the Lilian's enginemen were cleaning her fireboxes. Her boilers were lukewarm. Steam was down. But these considerations were dismissed instantly. Get up steam fast or else. In twenty minutes white vapor was hissing at the valves.

Twilight was brief. Night came down as steam came up. The Vanderbilt was pounding nearer. Her Captain Baldwin (old friend of Maffitt's) was no mean sea sleuth. His chase after the Alabama was a naval classic. Now he held on, grimly determined to overhaul the fleeing Lilian. Maffitt zigzagged. So did the Vanderbilt. His glasses now plainly revealed the Vanderbilt, none other. Maffitt felt admiration for her size and shapliness, though he knew the Lilian would be knocked apart by a rap from her eleven-inchers. There wouldn't be a splinter left. Maffitt admitted his "thermometer of hope fell below zero." He sent for his engineer.

"Have you plenty of coal dust?"

"Aye, aye, sir!"

"Be ready to feed it in fifteen minutes. Then, have clean coal ready that won't smoke. I'll give you the order shortly."

Following a bloc-runner's smoke in the dark (by the nose) was a Federal trick of the trade that had brought doom to many a hopeful. It was like a hound following the scent of a hare. Maffitt waited. The Vanderbilt wasn't near enough to let go gunfire.

Presently Maffitt barked into the speaking tube, "Throw on your dust."

Out of the funnels gushed volumes of dense sooty vapor that, snatched by the wind, swirled across the bosom of the ocean, and into the nostrils of the Vanderbilt's men.

Again, Maffitt waited. Then, "Now feed clean coal."

Instantly, he changed course "and left the Vanderbilt to capture the Lilian's shadow."

At sunrise the Lilian crept into Nassau's crowded harbor to wait her turn at the wharves. Next morning Maffitt was awakened by the serenade of a ship's band, fife and drum. It was playing "Yankee Doodle." Stepping on deck, he beheld a Union gunboat sailing blithely into the harbor, bedecked with a gorgeous array of red, white, and blue bunting. Hardly had her anchor chain ceased rattling before she began spreading her glorious news. Fort Sumter had fallen! A Federal ironclad attack had reduced the hated fortress, and the Stars and Stripes now floated over her battered ramparts. The Northern contingent at Nassau went into hysterics of joy. And as John Maffitt put it, "bad news is no sluggard but travels with seven league boots." Gloom fell over the Southern sympathizers. Maffitt's breakfast was tasteless.

At noon, at the zenith of Federal hilarity, a blockade runner, direct from Charleston, steamed in with news that changed the picture instantly. The attack on Charleston had miscarried. Battered and torn, Fort Sumter had proved invincible. Like magic, the Yankee gunboat stripped off her joyful manifestations. Averred the delighted Maffitt, "She quietly put away her cheerful regalia."

Boredom seldom assailed Maffitt, even in port, where waits for "moons" or weather were often exasperating. That same afternoon an English naval officer came aboard to renew an old friendship.

"Captain," he asked presently, "have you any friends among the officers of the Northern gunboat over there?"

Maffitt thought not.

"How would you like to visit her, incognito?"

Maffitt expressed reluctance. It might be judged as indelicate spying.

"What have you as a blockade runner to spy about? You're not in uniform. No one will know you. It's merely a harmless visit to indulge your nautical curiosity."

So off to the *Winona* (one of the pack that had greeted the *Florida* so warmly at Mobile) he went. At the head of the gangway the commanding officer received them courteously, little dreaming that "Mr. Russell, my nom de plume for the occasion" (whose hand he shook) was the somewhat notorious "Pirate Maffitt."

After a brief turn about the deck the Yankee skipper remarked with some pride, "I've just come in from the squadron off Wilmington. I am happy to be able to announce the end of the pirate Maffitt's career."

"How so?" inquired the amused Englishman, flicking a glance at his companion.

"Well, with his customary audacity, he tried to run through our squadron two nights ago. We had the satisfaction of sinking his vessel."

"Wonderful, wonderful!" exclaimed the Britisher. "But how do you know it was Maffitt?"

"Quite simple. Our agents on shore had notified us he was ready to run out with the *Lilian*. We knew exactly when to expect him. We just about blew his ship out of the water. We searched for hours but couldn't find a survivor. A few bales of cotton floating on the water told us his ship was at the bottom."

The Englishman was unable to hold back further. "Why, Captain, you must be mistaken. I saw Maffitt on his own quarter-deck not two hours ago."

The Federal's face fell. "You amaze me, sir. We surrounded the buccaneer, poured broadside after broadside into him. Then, he vanished. Every officer was positive he had gone stubbornly to the bottom."

This disconcerting conversation was interrupted by a ridiculous altercation at the nearby gangway.

"Get off this ship, you infernal Irish secessionist! How dare you intrude your rebel impudence on board an American man-of-war?" The watch officer was raging. "Throw the rascal overboard!"

"You may save yourself that divarting exercise," came the fast-fired reply. "It's me own legs that can function for me carcass and relieve your agitation."

Maffitt recognized the voice instantly. It was his newfound shipmate, Murphy.

"Punch his head in!" roared the exasperated officer.

Several burly bluejackets moved to comply. Disregarding the numerous fists preparing to demolish him, Murphy would have his last fling. Grasping the gangway manropes, he shot back with unblushing effrontery, "Upon my soul, Mister Leftenant, you are as polite as a French tomcat and spake their language like a native. A beautiful paycock show you had the other night. Wasting your powder for nothing. Bejabers, you didn't get the *Lilian*. And you didn't get John Maffitt either."

So saying, he plumped into a small boat and, with a look of triumph, pulled away for the *Lilian*. Transfixed, fearful that Murphy would espy and accost him, Maffitt decided to tempt fate no longer and return to the hazards of blockade running.

As he came aboard the *Lilian*, he found an obviously British visitor armed with credentials vouched for by Major Heyliger, Confederate overlord at Nassau, permitting the holder to embark on the runner for Wilmington. Into his cabin Maffitt ushered Francis

Lawley, war correspondent of the London *Times* and later eminent editor of the *Daily Telegraph*. Lawley was on his way to Lee's headquarters in Virginia. Later, from his pen came a classic account of his trip on the fast-flying *Lilian* with John Maffitt on the bridge. He wrote in part:

The *Lilian* was commanded by Captain Maffitt, an officer of the United States Navy before the war, who, however, being a North Carolinian, had followed his State when she seceded from the Union. I knew that Captain Maffitt was a favorite of General Lee, who was always glad to relieve the strain upon his mind by listening to his old friend's sea yarns, and one glance at his resolute, straightforward face made me determine that I would go with him. He was, in truth, a fine specimen of a Carolina sailor, and the more I saw of him during our short three days and four nights voyage, the more I liked him.

It was impossible at such a moment to withhold one's admiration from the fitness of the vessel under our feet for the purpose for which she had been built, and also for the perfection of the system under which she was handled, and which experience had already shown to be necessary to give her and her consorts every chance of success. When night fell, not a single light was visible in any part of the ship, and no one under any circumstances was allowed to smoke, lest his cigar or cigarette or pipe might be seen by a lookout on board of one of our vigilant enemies. Steam was blown off under water, our coal made no visible smoke, and our feathering paddles no noise; our hull rose only a few feet out of the water; our only spars were two short lower masts with no yards, and only a small crow's nest in the foremast. The forward deck was constructed in the form of a turtle back to enable the *Lilian* to go through a heavy sea. Our start from Nassau was so well timed that a moonless night and high tide were secured for our running into Wilmington. For the rest, we trusted to our speed, which, as will shortly be seen, saved our vessel next day from capture, and ourselves from the distinguished honor of passing a few months as prisoners in the Old Capitol, or in a fort off Boston or Baltimore harbor. The blockading vessels, too, were admirably managed. No lights were carried by them except on board one vessel, that in which the Flag-Admiral sailed. She changed her position every night, and the absence of strong lights on shore, discernible two or three miles away from Fort Fisher, greatly augmented the difficulty of hitting New Inlet, a narrow channel leading into the Cape Fear River. Moreover, the vessels which maintained the blockade were provided with calcium or other incandescent lights, which they flashed forth on the slightest provocation, and also with rockets which they let off in the direction a blockade-runner was taking,—talking to each other, in fact, with colored lights at night as effectually as they did with signals by day.

It will readily be imagined that during our third night out from Nassau, going to bed was far from our thoughts. The night wore rapidly away; 2 o'clock, 3 o'clock, 3:30 came, but no eye peering through the thick gloom could descry the light on top of the mound at Fort Fisher. Then, as morning dawned, Captain Maffitt stopped his engines and prepared to lay to for the day between the outer and inner cordon of blockaders. It was too much to hope that for sixteen or seventeen hours of broad daylight we could escape observation in that cruiser-haunted neighborhood; nevertheless from four in the morning till 1:30 P.M., we were unmolested. Then the tall masts of a big steamer, her immense paddle wheels and lofty, black hull hove in sight from the direction of Wilmington, going at full speed, and by the keen eyes on board her, the little *Lilian* was instantly descried. Before we could get up steam fully, our gigantic enemy drew uncomfortably near, and orders were given to have all the mail bags carried by the *Lilian* made ready, in case of capture, to be dropped with weights attached to them, into the all devouring ocean. Several shots flew over our heads or dropped by our side, but going at such a pace it is not easy to hit a little vessel with projectiles fired from the unstable platform of a pursuer going fifteen knots an hour through a lumpy sea.

Presently our beautiful little craft began to answer in earnest to the driving power within her, as a thoroughbred horse gallantly responds to the spur of his rider. As the pressure of steam ascended from fifteen pounds to twenty, from twenty to twenty-three, from twenty-three to twenty-six, and as the revolutions of the paddle mounted from twenty-six to twenty-eight, from twenty-eight to thirty-three per minute, the little vessel flew out to sea swift as a startled wild duck. Before two and a half hours had passed the hull of the big Yankee was invisible and her topgallant sails a mere speck on the distant horizon. As, however, she and doubtless others of her sisters lay between us and Wilmington, it became necessary to run around them. Our helm accordingly was changed and as the sun dropped into the sea our pursuer, though a long way off, still hung upon our rear. There was nothing for it but to stick to our course; but such had been the speed of our flight that the inside blockading squadron was clearly sighted by us before the close of the day. Grim and forbidding enough in all conscience the black hulls looked and so close did they lie to each other that it seemed hoping against hope to expect that a little craft like ours would pass unscathed between them or among them, taking the fire of two or three broadsides at little more than pistol range, or that she could eventually escape destruction at the hands of such formidable antagonists. But in command we had a captain who, in broad day, had braved the worst that the blockaders off Mobile could do to the little *Oreto*, without being scared or sunk. It is at such moments that you realize how paramount is the influence of a dauntless chief upon all around him; and it is felt more in so confined a space as the deck of a ship than in a great battle on land. Nevertheless, we could not but perceive—indeed, Captain Maffitt's anxious face plainly told us so—that our position was far from comfortable, pursued as we were by a vessel a few miles off to the rear, which clearly saw us, and, swiftly approaching a powerful squadron of heavily armed blockaders, which had not yet caught sight of the *Lilian's* two masts, but might do so at any moment.

Fortunately for us, before we got close in, night fell. The crews on board the blockaders were taking their evening meal as we approached them, and I suppose the lookout were not quite so sharp as they undoubtedly became before the end of the war. Not a moment was lost by Captain Maffitt, or by our excellent pilot, a Wilmington man, when darkness had fairly settled upon the face of the deep. Silently, and with bated breath we crept slowly in, passing blockader after blockader so close that at every moment we expected a brilliant light to flash forth, turning night into day, and followed by a hurricane of shot and shell, which might easily have torn the little *Lilian* to pieces. It was destined, however, that upon this occasion she was not to receive her baptism of fire, for the shots sent after her by her big Yankee pursuer hardly deserve the name. Just as we approached the big mound, close to which Fort Fisher stands, a dark spot was discerned on the bar. It was a Federal launch groping for secrets, or perhaps sinking rocks and other obstructions into the channel immediately under the fire of Fort Fisher's guns. I am afraid that if Captain Maffitt had seen her a little earlier he would have run her down. As matters stood, the launch escaped, and those on board were either too much scared to fire a musketry volley into us, or reluctant to do so, as Fort Fisher would doubtless have opened upon them, and, as I had many subsequent opportunities of ascertaining, her guns were seldom fired without effect upon any object within their range.

Another moment, and we lay safe and sound below the mound, eagerly asking for news from within the Confederacy, and as eagerly questioned in our turn for news from without.

Hardly had the Lilian cushioned up to the wharf at Wilmington before a dock officer handed up orders for Maffitt to proceed at once to Plymouth, North Carolina, and take command of the ironclad ram Albemarle that had recently played such havoc with a Federal squadron in Albemarle Sound. Maffitt accepted the new duty philosophically. Richmond called the tune. He danced to it. Command of an ironclad somehow appealed to him.

This was June, 1864. It is pertinent to record that within two months after Maffitt vacated the Lilian's bridge, she was a Federal captive. Chased five hours by three Federals (one a captured blockade runner turned to Union employment and bearing a name of ominous import, Gettysburg) she hauled up, a prisoner, with a shell hole below her waterline. Repaired, equipped with two big guns, the Lilian, too, soon turned her speedy talents on her former playmates off the Wilmington bars. She rendered her last service in the second bombardment of Fort Fisher, which reduced that great bastion.

Built without benefit of a shipyard, near Edward's Ferry, up the Roanoke River, that homemade sea-horse, the Albemarle, was a naval absurdity; but she packed a villainous wallop. Spit and image was she of the slant-backed, queen-for-a-day Merrimack. Plated with railroad iron ransacked from the countryside, heavily gunned, she shed ball and shell like birdshot. In May, 1864, she waddled down the river, took on nine Federal ships, rammed one to the bottom, and badly messed up eight others. Cheers from the gray! Groans from the blue! Another such whack, and the Federals would skedaddle out of the Sound.

Since then, the Albemarle had dozed on her laurels "in glorious inactivity" at Plymouth, where she posed a threat to Federal encroachment up the rich Roanoke valley. Should she blast her way

to sea, she might raise hob with the blockading squadrons. Yankee
Admiral S. P. Lee issued a stern ukase: "At all hazards the *Albemarle* must be destroyed by shot, ramming or torpedoes."

Meanwhile, Secretary Mallory at Richmond became dissatisfied
with the inertia of her commander, the man who had built her and
led her one successful foray against the Federals. He decided to
give command to a man of action, John Maffitt, who the moment
he mounted her deck announced he intended to fight her "till the
last Yankee galoot" had tucked tail and left the Sound. His fiery
pronunciamento brought fast repercussions. Panicked by Maffitt's
determination to steam out and engage the Federal fleet, the military command sent hurried protests to Richmond. Suppose she
went out and was sunk? Leave her where she was. Official feathers
were riled and ruffled; and Mallory yielded to pressure. Maffitt was
removed.

For Maffitt, it was a much desired relief. Fencing with petty-
minded military officials was not his dish. He knew but one way to
fight a war. Said he, "As the duty enjoined on me was nothing
more than that of a river guard, I was not sorry when the Secretary
of the Navy ordered me back to blockade running."

But the epilogue of the *Albemarle* must be told: on a thick rainy
night, five weeks after Maffitt relinquished her command, a daring
young man in blue, William Barker Cushing, glided noiselessly up
the river and exploded a torpedo that blew a hole big as a barrel at
the ram's waterline. In minutes the South's last dread monster had
gurgled down to a wet valhalla to commiserate with the *Merrimack,
Louisiana, Mississippi, Tennessee,* and other gray ironclads rusting
out the years and, perhaps, sighing over what might have been. It
is conjecturable that the *Albemarle* would not have made such an
inglorious exit with John Maffitt on her bridge. Far better, he
averred, for her to have gone down with guns blazing than squatting on the edge of a swamp inviting what happened: a sneak torpedo in the dead of night.

On September 20, 1864, Maffitt reported at Wilmington for his
last command. The Confederacy had begun her downward spiral;
the blockaders off the Cape Fear bars were just as hair-triggered as
before—only more so.

Awaiting him was a letter somewhat delayed in transit. It was
acknowledgment of a sword belt he had purchased in London for

an old friend whom he greatly admired. Dated "Camp at Petersburg, August 11, 1864," it ran:

My dear Captain: I have received the sword belt you were so kind as to send me. It is very handsome and I appreciate it highly as a token of your remembrance. I recall with pleasure the days of our association in Carolina—with equal admiration your brilliant course in the defense of your country. Wishing you all happiness and prosperity,

I remain, most truly yours,
R. E. Lee

CHAPTER XXV

Dies Irae

NORTHERN NEWSPAPERS were sounding doleful warnings. "Pirate" Maffitt, commanding a new, faster, harder-shooting commerce-destroyer, would soon be ravishing the Atlantic seaways again. From the Navy Department alerts flicked out to naval commands along the coast, to the blockaders sealing off the Southern ports, to the squadrons tracking down gray incendiaries. Maffitt was on the loose again! His bag of tricks apparently had no bottom. But where on earth did he get his new ship? Jocularly, the New York *Herald* suggested: perhaps "Aladdin" Bulloch had rubbed his lamp and sleight-of-handed it out of a peasoup fog on the Clyde.

But—glory be for the Union Navy!—the two most feared and destructive sea-rovers actually were no more. Like mad dogs they were hunted down and expunged. Riddled by the guns of the *Kearsarge*, the *Alabama* rested at the bottom of the English Channel. In the mud of Hampton Roads the *Florida* had reached journey's end, victim of an atrocious violation of Brazil's neutrality.

Only half right were the press forebodings. Actually, Maffitt had a new ship. Not a cruiser, as the newspaper scareheads proclaimed; but perhaps the speediest blockade-runner ever to cleave the seas. With engines powerful enough for a steamer four times her size, she could, in a pinch, click off seventeen knots with the ease of a greyhound, and turn on a dime. Her oversized bunkers gave her a cruising range double that of others of her ilk. *Owl* was this one's name. Sisters three had she: *Stag*, *Deer*, and *Bat*. Bulloch had adorned them with names comporting with their jack-o'-lantern mission in life: keeping the Confederate war gods supplied with grist for their mills.

Take a look at the *Owl* before she wings off in the night. One of the paddle-wheel quadruplets openly purchased on the Clyde by James Bulloch for the Confederacy, she was lean and long (230 feet, nine times her width), bluish gray, with two rakish, tele-scoping funnels. She mounted a small pivot and a brass carronade, just in case. She could load almost nine hundred bales of cotton, or a staggering tonnage of war goods. Stripped for running, she could really make speed.

On September 14, 1864 Secretary Mallory wrote Maffitt:

> The *Owl* is the first of several steamers built for the Con-federate government and which are to be run under the direction of the Secretary of the Navy. Naval officers are to be placed in command, and you are selected to take charge of the *Owl*.

Five days later, Mallory amplified these instructions with an ap-prehensive telegram:

> It is of utmost importance that our steamers should not fall into the enemy's hands. Apart from the specific loss sustained by the country in the capture of blockade runners, these vessels, lightly armed, now constitute the fleetest and most efficient part of his blockading force off Wilmington.
>
> As commanding officer of the *Owl* you will please devise and adopt thorough and efficient means for saving all hands and de-stroying the vessel and cargo whenever these measures may be-come necessary to prevent capture.

Mallory need not have worried. Maffitt was no novice. He knew the Federals were arming captured runners and turning them loose to prey on their former companions. Capture had never entered his mind. Yet it wasn't always as easy to abandon ship as Richmond seemed to think.

More urgent and pointed was Mallory's later communication: "Circumstances must govern you in the destruction of the *Owl*. When capture in your judgment becomes inevitable, fire the vessel in several places and embark in the boats, making for the nearest land."

But, again, more easily said than done.

2

December, 1864. Inexorably, Wilmington's hour was about to strike. The port still flourished. With its dual entrances protected by Fort Fisher and Caswell, the most formidable defense works in the Confederacy, the town seemed to lead a charmed life. The Southern press maintained that only one runner in ten was being captured off Wilmington. Obviously, unless this gap in the Great Blockade was plugged, the war might be prolonged.

Deeply chagrined, the navy's face grew red. Apparently, it was unable to cope with the eely procession that slipped through the Wilmington portals. Rumors were bandied about that the navy was shutting one eye. Commanders of the blockaders—so 'twas whispered—were running a bootleg business. They had bought shares in highly profitable runners.

In the summer of 1864, the Washington high command pronounced Fort Fisher's doom. With the right combination of men, guns, and leadership uniting in a huge pincer movement, this tough nut could be cracked.

At Petersburg, back door to Richmond, Grant was stalled before a barricade that would not be breached until spring. Torch in hand, Sherman was sweeping across Georgia. Savannah would be his by Christmas. But at Wilmington, runners cavorted over the Cape Fear bars with timetable regularity. Incomers moored beside the port's wharves to discharge guns, rifles, drugs, saltpeter, and ammunition, plus cigars, silks, perfumes, and wines for the carriage trade. Emptied, the runner shuffled cross-stream to the cotton press, where lines of grinning stevedores packed their holds and decks with bales for the outrun.

Fort Fisher! This battlement was the key factor in the formula: to take Richmond you must first take Wilmington; but to take Wilmingon, you must first take Fort Fisher. Lee had warned prophetically, "If Fort Fisher falls, I shall have to evacuate Richmond." Thus, Fort Fisher held the fate of Lee's army, and hence of the Confederacy.

With Fort Fisher liquidated, the Cape Fear gateways would be sealed finally. For the North, it became the Carthage that must be destroyed. Up to 1864 the storming of Sevastopol in the Crimean War was considered the master warpiece of its kind, but taking Sevastopol was child's play (so said Union officers who had observed the Crimean War) compared with the problem posed by Fort Fisher's imposing ramparts. Federal engineers, who inspected it from afar, pronounced it unassailable; called it the Malakoff of the South. Its sea-face was 1,898 yards long and fifty feet high. It was built to withstand the heaviest fire the Federal Navy could bring to bear, even considering the penetrating power of the Union's new fifteen-inch shells. It was erected for a single purpose—to keep the lifeline to Wilmington open.

In September, 1864, supreme Union commander Ulysses Grant called a conclave at his headquarters at City Point on the James, behind the lines at Petersburg. Here the assault on Fort Fisher was blueprinted. Admiral David Dixon Porter had been brought east from his campaign on the Red River and given command of the North Atlantic Blockading Squadron, whose arc of operations included the North Carolina coast and, hence, Fort Fisher.

Porter was no shrinking violet. Able, aggressive, rough and ready, he had bulldogged his way from lieutenant to flag officer since 1861. Chesty, and a braggart to boot, he got results. This was what Lincoln wanted. Porter's big hunt for Raphael Semmes and the Confederacy's first raider, Sumter, had brought him into the limelight. Since then, he had forged to the summit of navaldom. Summoned to Petersburg and asked point-blank if he could take Fort Fisher, Porter refused to go off half-cocked. Before venturing an opinion, he would take a look. Boarding his flagship Malvern, he coasted down and reconnoitered. It was feasible, he reckoned, but only by amphibious assault: naval guns against the bastion's sea-face, and a flanking column to land up coast and strike at its unprotected belly.

Getting bolder, Porter predicted he could wipe Fort Fisher off the map in three days, if given what he asked for: eight thousand troops, enough warships to fire 150 guns in broadside (meaning three hundred in all), and carte blanche. Fort Fisher mounted seventy-five seacoast guns. This meant Porter's armada would have four guns afloat to one on shore, not too great a preponderance for wooden ships against heavy earthworks, where cannon could be sighted more accurately than on water. Grant agreed to Porter's demands, but said the troops would be drawn from the Army of the James, commanded by General "Beast" Butler, whose military abilities were less than nil. Porter didn't like Butler, and vice versa.

Thus was bombastic, muddle-maker Butler ushered onto the scene. Lincoln had once cracked: Butler is as full of poison as a dead dog. Yet Grant, and Lincoln, too, shied off tangling with this powerful political whatnot. Butler abounded in ideas. He affected a uniform decorated with enough gold embroidery for a king's mantle. He swashbuckled about his camp barefooted. In uniform, he was the spit and image of a Central American general. Also, he had read somewhere of a successful general who wore no shoes.

Take Fort Fisher! A piddling job, ejaculated Butler. He had a brilliant idea that would pulverize Fort Fisher and gobble up Wilmington at one fell blast. Oceans of blood and money would be saved. He proposed creating a mighty bomb: loading a ship with 150 tons of gunpowder and exploding it off the sea-face of Fort Fisher. In one big poof the bastion would vanish. Butler's knowledge of explosives was limited, but he was so eloquent, few could contradict him. He harped on the story of an illustrious Chinese general, Chi-Fung, who had blown up an impregnable enemy fort in this manner. Porter was lukewarm to the scheme, and Grant said pooh! pooh! Back in July Grant had tried to crack Lee's lines at Petersburg with a man-made earthquake. Its backfire was costly: five thousand dead and wounded and a ghastly crater reeking with blood and smoke.

Traipsing up to Washington, Butler sounded out President Lincoln, over whom he seemed to exert a strange mesmerism. Lincoln gave his half-hearted blessing to the scheme: "We might as well explode the idea with gunpowder as anything else." Gideon Welles took a dim view of Butler's gimcrack, but he went along with it, mainly because the navy had oodles of gunpowder and a lot of rotting ships he now wished to get rid of. The "scientific" naval officers were deeply impressed, but the down-to-earth ordnance experts said Butler's volcano would have about as much effect on Fort Fisher as a broadside of feather-dusters.

Given the go-ahead, Butler became so expansive that even the distrustful Porter fell in with the scheme. The rickety, beat-up

Louisiana was trundled out of her slumbers at Hampton Roads. Carpenters disemboweled her in a hurry. Negro troops, doubling as stevedores, stuffed her hold full of powder. Gomer fuses, like huge tapeworms, crawled through the piles of powder-bags, entwining every bag so there could be no doubt of its going off. In the cabin a peculiar clock was installed to set off the master fuse at a given hour. There were candles that would burn so many minutes and then explode; there were hand-grenades that would fall at a selected hour and fire the vessel. There was every known contrivance. Doubting them all, Porter had half a cord of pine-knots piled in the cabin to be ignited by the last man to leave the ship. (This was what finally touched her off.)

The concussion of so much exploding gunpowder—averred Butler—would displace so much air so rapidly, it might kill every living thing within a score of miles. Fort Fisher would be a mass of rubble. A section of North Carolina's coast might even be blown into the sea. A tidal wave was a possibility. The bombarding fleet had better stand miles off. Boilers might burst, magazines go off. As for the mighty fortress, no one would ever know it had been there.

Meanwhile, Wilmington held its breath. Suspense gripped the town. The good folk were well aware there was a plan afoot to annihilate their mainstay, Fort Fisher; but not until a Philadelphia newspaper ran an "exclusive" account of it did they realize exactly what was up. Until then, Butler's powderboat was top-secret, as were his predictions that the town would be blown to kingdom come. But confidence in the fort's ability to beat off the Porter-Butler combine ran high. Runners continued to slide through the Cape Fear inlets with miraculous immunity.

Inside the fort, the garrison was serene. Fort Fisher was untakable. That was that. All the ships in the world, with "Beast" Butler to help them, could not crack this case-hardened nut. The fort's commandant, Colonel William Lamb, had constructed the work for just this purpose: to withstand the heaviest fire the Union navy could bring to bear.

In the bombproofs, around the tallow dips of evenings, rose the strains of violins and accordions, or perhaps a quartet harmonizing on "Lorena," "My Maryland," and other Southern campfire melodies. A few read Bibles. One thing was obvious. The South had robbed the cradle to bring Fort Fisher's manpower up to its needs. "Brave little boys," Lamb called them, "torn from their firesides by the cruel necessities of the struggle."

Meanwhile, the grapevine relayed southward every move in the vast chess game. Over Wilmington hung a dark curtain of foreboding.

3

On December 21, 1864, the *Owl*, bulging with cotton, dropped down the Cape Fear River to anchor off Smithville at sundown. The hurrahs of sister blockade runners, tethered at the wharves, gave her a cheery, steamy sendoff. Hardly had she cast off when another runner warped up to the cotton press in her place. Her departure was hastened by baleful tidings. Porter's fleet—"75 or 80 well-armed vessels"—had cleared Hampton Roads and turned south. Runners were ordered to load and put to sea at once. If Fort Fisher succumbed to the vast Yankee machinations, Wilmington would be cut off. Only God himself could predict the outcome.

From Smithville, through the gathering dusk, John Maffitt reconnoitered and chose his gantlet. He would slip out by the western bar. The grim sentinels outside were already taking their stations, as if to announce "The channel is closed for the night." Maffitt counted ten, lurking in a five-mile crescent off the exit he had chosen. Well, he had done it before. He could do it again. It was all in the day's, or rather, the night's, work.

For him, the leave-taking was gloomy. Gazing at the darkling land, he wondered if this was his last look at the Dixie he had known and loved. Despondent thoughts. Shades of impending doom hovered over the South, even deeper than those settling on the ocean. The Confederacy was caving in, and he knew it. John Maffitt wondered: Was so much blood and treasure, so freely spent, to go for naught save the sadness of a lost cause? Yet, like Scott's *Marmion*, which he sometimes quoted, the South would fight on:

> With dying hand above his head
> He shook the fragment of his blade
> And shouted "Victory!"

But this was no time for poetry. Beyond the bar, blockaders were waiting. Biding his time until midnight, when the moon slid below the horizon, Maffitt turned the *Owl's* prow seaward and ordered, "Full speed ahead." Fort Caswell, warder of the western bar, blinked him good-by and good luck. He would need the latter. Blacked out, her throttle opened wide, the frail vessel shot ahead, racing for the channel and the open sea. Within moments her paddles began their rhythmic slap-slap.

Maffitt stood on the bridge, his glasses combing the blackness, appraising every wraith imagination could devise. He was not given to seeing things. Long ago he had mastered that often fatal tendency. Clipping along nimbly, the *Owl* was logging her best, over sixteen knots.

Not a wisp, not a twinkling light, did Maffitt see of Porter's men-of-war that three days later would anchor a mile off Fort Fisher and deluge its ramparts with a spiteful twenty-four-hour avalanche of destruction: 20,271 projectiles of every caliber from three- to fifteen-inch.

Just ahead rose the somber silhouettes of the Federal coil. Picking a "hole" between two murky bulks, Maffitt whispered orders to his pilot. Soundless save for the whip of her paddles, the *Owl* skimmed between two shapes. Yet, no blaze of Drummond lights, no "Heave to!" no gunfire cut through the night. Maffitt's Journal stated that the blockaders awoke after he had outdistanced them and "presented me with a few affectionate souvenirs at long range."

Christmas Eve—Fort Fisher's zero hour. While Admiral Porter's squadrons were moving up in gigantic, three-ringed array, the *Owl* steamed into St. George's, Bermuda, without the loss of even a rope yarn. Idling at the wharves, loaded to the gunwales, lay a dozen runners awaiting the outcome of Porter's assault. On December 30 the *Chameleon* brought heartening news. Fort Fisher had breasted Porter's iron hammering. And Butler's harebrained powderboat had gone off like a big Christmas firecracker, an ignominious failure. The imbecilic Butler was finally relegated to the military scrapheap. Needled the New York *Tribune*, "It was so terrible, so awfully grand, so-o-o dreadful it woke up everybody in the fort," which about summed it up. The fort's defenders actually thought a blockade runner, filled with munitions, "had grounded near the fort, set herself afire and blown up."

Yet first reports flashed to Washington had proclaimed the fort "demolished," the carnage "frightful." Porter actually thought so.

He congratulated himself by sitting down to a Christmas dinner of turkey and champagne in his comfortable cabin and gazing on the "ruins" of Fort Fisher in the distance.

The South was exultant. The fleet's "overwhelming" barrage had killed three and wounded sixty-one graybacks. "Where is the vaunted Yankee armada?" chided the Richmond *Whig*, to which the Richmond *Dispatch* replied: "Beaten, scattered, sunk, dispersed. It is a matter of impossibility for the Federals to stop our blockade runners at the port of Wilmington."

So thought Commander John Maffitt, who, on January 17, cleared St. George's with a cargo of food for Lee's half-starved, ragged veterans holding the tenuous lines at Petersburg. Trailing the *Owl* came three more runners: *Charlotte*, *Blenheim*, and *Stag*. "Joyfully anticipating a speedy reunion at Wilmington," said Maffitt, "we parted at sea, and met not again."

Two nights later, the *Owl* bore up off Lockwood's Folly, downcoast from the western bar, where for two years a signal station had kept vigil for incoming bloc-runners, and flashed the cherished *passe-parole*. Beaming his code light, Maffitt's signalman blinked out: "Steamer *Owl* bound in. Protect me. Set range lights." It brought immediate reply: "All right, *Owl*. Lights will be set."

"There's something up," whispered Maffitt to his pilot. "They answered too fast."

Going aloft he searched the dark shoreline with his night glasses. Far north, beyond the sand spits above Fort Fisher, he saw a red glow against the night sky, which he little suspected to be the campfires of Union soldiers. The moon would not rise until eleven, but high water was due on the bar at eight. He would take it at the flood and venture in. Feeling her way with the lead, the *Owl* gingerly approached the channel to find a single blockader waiting to dispute her entrance. It didn't make sense. Where were the others? Eluding the lone sentinel, the *Owl* sprinted over the bar and ran into the stream. The range lights flared up, one after the other. The Mound Light, at Fort Fisher, was already burning. A huge fire on Bald Hill made Maffitt more apprehensive. His cipher flash to Fort Caswell brought no response, though the bastion looked "natural and quiet" save for a rumble of muffled sounds echoing down to the water. Mystified, he edged on at half speed, and anchored off the fort's wharf. Nearby, Smithville was dark, deserted looking. He had no way of knowing that on January 14 Union forces, in a second coordinated land and sea attack, minus Butler, had swept over Fort Fisher and were now moving on Fort Caswell, which was at this moment being evacuated under cover of darkness. Nor could he know that Fort Fisher's signal book had fallen into Union hands. With some pride, Porter later related how he baited the trap for incoming runners not aware of the fort's demise, by setting the range lights when they signaled for them and luring them to their doom with phony all's-wells. To make sure, he ordered the Mound Light kept burning, as in the heyday of runner traffic.

The splash of oars told Maffitt a small boat was coming alongside. Up the gangway hurried Captain E. S. Martin, Fort Caswell's ordnance officer.

"Captain Maffitt," he reported sadly, "Fort Fisher is captured. A second attack on January 14 was successful. Our troops are leaving Fort Caswell now. We've laid a powder-train to the magazine. We'll light the match in half an hour. Fright and confusion are everywhere."

"What about Wilmington?" asked Maffitt anxiously.

"Going up the spout like the Confederacy," replied the officer with brutal frankness. "Porter's forces control the river."

Maffitt was struck dumb. The bright banners of Dixie were falling! Added the officer, "The Federal fleet crossed the North Inlet yesterday. A dozen ships are anchored upstream almost within hail of you."

Maffitt winced. He was under their guns. Obviously, this was no time to stand on the order of going.

"Are any other runners coming in?" inquired Martin.

"Three left St. George's behind me. They should be in shortly."

"Too bad. Porter's trap's waiting for them, as it was for you. What'll you do, Captain Maffitt?"

"Get out, if I can," said Maffitt flatly. "I've been trapped before."

"So I know, Captain."

With a salute and a "God be with you," the officer vanished down the gangway. For Maffitt, as he said later, "To depart instantly became an imperious necessity." It must be before the moon rose, or not at all. At this juncture, his pilot came to him.

"Captain," he pleaded movingly, "I have to go ashore. My wife's ill. She has no money. I will return in twenty minutes."

Maffitt wasted no time deciding. "You can go on one condition: you come back in exactly twenty minutes."

In poignant distress, "my sorrowing mind foreshadowing the fate of Dixie," Maffitt waited. Fort Fisher gone! Fort Caswell doomed! Wilmington at the mercy of the invader! Again he climbed to the masthead. Now he discerned giant shadows of Porter's fleet riding at their anchors. Near by, a patrol boat was mousing about in the dark. It was inconceivable that they had not discovered the *Owl*. Presently he heard the pilot's foot on the deck.

"Here I am, Captain," he reported. "My wife's better, thank God. I'll do as much for you some day, sir."

"All right, let's go," said Maffitt.

The boat was hooked on and run up the davits, the chain slipped. In the dark narrow channel the *Owl* made an oxbow turn. As she crossed the bar—so said Maffitt—"the solitary blockader awoke from his lethargy and pursued me with avidity. Yet his artillery palled under the sudden reverberation of an explosion that rumbled portentously from wave to wave, in melancholy echoes, enunciating the fate of Fort Caswell."

Hugging the water, with shells splattering after her, the *Owl* scampered away. Three dark objects slid past, clipping along for the New Inlet, where Fort Fisher huddled, silent and bloody. In apple-pie order the *Charlotte, Blenheim,* and *Stag* were dashing for the bar—and doom—decoyed by the still beaming Mound Light. First to glide in was the *Charlotte.* She anchored off the Mound to bide the usual visit of Fort Fisher's inspection officer. In the dark, unwittingly, she had moored several cable lengths from the *Malvern,* flagship of the doughty admiral, who found keen delight in the discomfiture of his "visitors." Aboard the *Charlotte* were three distinguished British army officers in search of adventure in the Southern ranks.

From John Maffitt's pen came this graphic, semi-humorous account of the welcome accorded the vanguard of the three wayfarers who dropped into Porter's deadfall one after the other:

> Waiting for some time without receiving the official call, the captain naturally concluded it had been deferred until daylight. He therefore directed the steward to serve the entertainment

that had been elaborately prepared to celebrate their safe arrival in the Confederacy. The gastronomic hidalgo flourished his baton of office, and escorted his guests to the festive board. In shouts of revelry and with flowing bumpers the jocund party huzzaed for Dixie, and sang her praises in songs of adulation that made the welkin ring, and aroused the sea-mews from their peaceful slumbers. A pause from exhaustion having occurred in their labor of justice to the luxurious repast, gave to an English captain a desired opportunity to ventilate in appropriate sentiments his appreciation of the joyful occasion. Mysteriously rapping to enjoin attention, in the silence that followed he solemnly arose. At a wave of his dexter the steward, all alertness, replenished the glasses.

"Gentlemen," said the Briton, "after a successful voyage, fraught with interesting incidents and excitements, we have anchored upon the soil of battle-worn, grand old Dixie. We come not as mercenary adventurers to enlist under the banner of the Confederacy, but, like true knights-errant, to join as honorable volunteers the standard of the bravest lance in Christendom, that of the noble, peerless Lee. (Cheers, hear, hear!) In gaining this Palestine of our chivalrous aspirations we have successfully encountered the more than ordinary perils of the sea, in storms, the lingering chase, and hazards of the blockade. Through all vicissitudes there was a mind to conceive, a hand to guide, a courage to execute. Gentlemen, I propose the health, happiness, and speedy promotion of the officer who merits these commendations,—our worthy commander."

Mingled with vociferous applause came the customary hip! hip! huzza! hip! hip! huz——

The half-uttered huzza froze like an icicle on the petrified lips of the orator, who,

> "With wild surprise,
> As if to marble struck, devoid of sense,
> A stupid moment, motionless stood,"

as the apparition of a Federal lieutenant appeared upon the cabin stairway.

"Who commands this steamer?" was the Federal's interrogatory.

"I am that unfortunate individual," groaned the unhappy commander, as reminiscences of a long confinement came painfully to his mind.

"You are a prize to Admiral Porter's squadron, and I relieve you from all further responsibility. Gentlemen, as paroled prisoners, you are at liberty to finish your repast."

The withering enunciation of capture blighted like a black frost the hopeful blossoms that had, under the inspiring influence of the sparkling Epherney, bubbled into poetic existence. One by one the lights soon faded in this banquet-hall deserted, their last glimmer falling mournfully on the debris of the unfinished congratulatory repast.

Ere an hour elapsed two more unfortunates, lured by the channel-lights, entered and likewise anchored off the mound, and became a prey to Admiral Porter's fleet.

CHAPTER XXVI

"Strike the Flag!"

ALONE AND HUNTED on the black ocean, John Maffitt was drinking the dregs now. He had given heart, soul, and body to the Confederacy. For what? The South's unconquerable bastion had fallen. Visions of disaster and dissolution trooped through his mind. Below deck lay fifty thousand pounds of bacon, two thousand barrels of flour, salted beef, undeliverable sorely-needed rations for the empty bellies of Lee's hard-pressed graylegs. He knew too well the fate of the three runners, with similar freight, that had raced past him. His cargo could mean life or death. He was cut off from Wilmington, but perhaps Charleston was still accessible. As long as the Confederacy stayed afloat, he read his duty plain. Shaping the *Owl's* course southward and setting a double lookout, he accommodated his speed to make the Charleston bar by ten the next night. Dejectedly, he sought his bunk, only to be aroused at dawn by his irrepressible Irish quartermaster, Murphy, who would have, without quail, tangled with the "divil himself" at Maffitt's bidding.

"Steamer ahead, sir."

"How far off?" asked Maffitt sleepily.

"Foive miles, sir."

"What does she look like?"

"One of them Yankee divils."

"Show them our heels, Pat."

Sunrise found the *Owl* coasting along shiny waterways thick with

Federal constables. Five times during the day Union gallinippers sighted her and gave chase. Yet, as Maffitt phrased it, "a little more coal and stirring up of the fire draft was sufficient to start the *Owl* off with such admirable speed as to convince the Federals that she was the fastest steamer that ever eluded the guardians of the channelways."

Maffitt's timing and navigation were precise. At ten that night the *Owl* stood in for Maffitt's Channel off Charleston. Her cut-water sliced the dark sea silently, as if aware of the nature of her mission. He had discovered this channel back in the 1840's. Now it was serving a purpose he had never envisioned. Up ahead he saw a dim sprinkle of lights indicating the encircled city. He knew the harbor as well as he knew his own face.

Anticipating the possibility of capture, he stowed the undelivered government mail, his private papers, his war journal, and most precious of all, the log of the *Florida*, in two canvas, lead-weighted bags. Dangling them by a stout line over the quarter, he ordered a cool-headed seaman to stand by, hatchet in hand. If capture became inevitable, he was to cut the rope and drop the bags to the bottom.

Running stealthily at low speed, the *Owl* groped over the western tail of Rattlesnake Shoal. Streaks of mist blotted out the stars and the waters just ahead. Over the harbor hovered an absolute hush of nature; not a whisper, not a light on the water. Even the low, precise rataplanplan of the *Owl's* paddles seemed muffled and far away.

Maffitt's nerves were fraying from his long ordeals, but in the clinches they hardened like seasoned hickory. Suspense gripped vessel and crew. Tension held the engine room. The coal passers were ready. Beside the fireboxes were neat piles of Cardiff smokeless, waiting to be shoveled in at the command. Handy, near by, were slabs of bacon whose blaze would be odorous, but hot as hades. In a pinch they could be depended on to raise an extra pound or two of steam in a hurry. The engineer stood at the throttle. Maffitt had personally briefed his twenty-man crew that afternoon. This might, he said, be their last service to the Confederacy. They had to deliver the goods, unless God willed otherwise.

The haze began to lift as the *Owl* came abreast of Sullivan's Island. Off his starboard bow lay Fort Moultrie, invisible and silent.

The *Owl* slackened her speed. It was the old technique. Crawl along as far as you can, and then run like hell for the goal. Maffitt stood at his "battle-station" beside his pilot, who would have steered the vessel into the whole Yankee squadron, had Maffitt asked it.

Suddenly a cleft in the haze revealed a blockader anchored dead ahead. He might have crashed her, gouged out a hole at the water-line, and taken her with him to the bottom. But he had a cargo to deliver—if he could.

"Hard aport! Full speed ahead!" he barked. It was time to run for it. Sheering sharply, the *Owl* almost grazed the blockader, now rearing above the runner like a malevolent Gibraltar. Out of the blackness a voice trumpeted, "Heave to! Or I'll blow you out of the water!"

Threatening words. Deadly implication. How often had he heard them. He knew what to expect. Nor was he disappointed. As the *Owl* veered to port, a point-blank broadside blanketed her with a sheet of flame. The Federal must have been waiting for him. Fired at less than forty feet, the blast doused the *Owl* with acrid smoke. Maffitt could taste the sulphur in his throat. Like a scythe it guillo-tined the *Owl*'s turtle back, riddled the forecastle, clawed at the bulwarks. The runner reeled under the concussion. Splinters rained on deck like hail. Two of the crew were down, bleeding badly. Half dragging them, Maffitt got them to his cabin door and took his station again. He felt a warm trickle down his neck where a piece of iron had nicked him. A fraction of an inch deeper, it would have sliced his jugular clean as a razor.

Magically, it seemed, a hellish glare blossomed above the road-stead. A stupendous chandelier. The blockader moved up fast, measuring the craft for her death shot. She was a big converted riverboat, and lit up now like a church. A second blast slashed over the *Owl*. It was aimed too high, but it shrieked like a thousand fiends. Capture or death! So it looked. Any moment might see Maffitt and his ship blown to smithereens. His pulse beat at his temple like a hammer. Was this the way he was to go out? Stricken like his ship, pounded and lashed with fire? If so, he would at least vanish in a blaze of some glory. What was it Secretary Mallory had urged? "Fire your ship, if capture becomes inevitable." Easy to say, hard to do.

Convinced the *Owl* was done for, Maffitt's hatchetman hacked the rope that held the mail bags. In a wink, as Maffitt would later testify, "the log book of the *Florida* was dropped in fifteen fathoms off Charleston."

Up ahead, two more blockaders came to life, barging in to get a shot. The whole harbor seemed to detonate in a deafening bedlam. Rockets jetted up, Drummond lights flared, signals blinked here, there, on every hand, red, white, blue, like flowers. Clouds of biting smoke eddied over the water and coiled around the runner, bringing tears to Maffitt's eyes, stinging his throat like acid. He was living up to the nickname he disliked. But even a salamander would find this hard going. Hauling this way and that, dodging a rundown, shuddering at each onslaught, the *Owl* kept moving.

"Wear round, if you can," ordered Maffitt to his pilot. "We'll get out somehow."

He smiled as he said it. Somehow, yes, but just how? He knew this: If only the *Owl* could get her head seaward and put on her running shoes, she would get out—barring, of course, a shell in her engine room. He identified one Federal ship, so he thought. The *Shenandoah*, to whom he had twice shown his heels. She yearned for revenge.

Bulking darkly off to port rose the ominous pile of Fort Sumter, silent as a lightless mausoleum. Intense white light glazed the bastion. Where were her gunners? Had Sumter fallen like Fort Fisher? Bombed by everything known to naval gunnery, breached and gashed, the fort still held out. Beauregard had said, "Sumter must be held to the bitter end." This was the bitter end, or damn near it, thought Maffitt. Shorn of firepower, holding on with only the "will which says hold on," Sumter was merely a symbol now. Sumter's name—boasted a Charleston paper—would take its place beside Thermopylae when the war's history was written.

Maffitt fancied he could see the steeples of St. Michael's and St. Philip's. It was only a fantasy. Yonder, below the dark waters, slept the *Keokuk*, harpooned to death like a giant, iron-skinned whale by Sumter's guns. Dark shapes were converging on the *Owl*. Where did they all come from? Maffitt guessed correctly. Porter had hurried the blockaders—no longer needed off Fort Fisher—down to reinforce the Charleston cordon, where runners were still coming and going.

The din was terrific. Shells crackled everywhere. One tore through the *Owl's* stack, leaving a hole big as a rum barrel. Yet in the very cataract of fire lay the *Owl's* hope of escape. Overzealous blockaders, apparently believing the blockade was being run en masse, were firing at shadows. In more peaceful times the commander of a blockader was to confirm this: "We thought that innumerable blockade runners were forcing a passage into the harbor. Hence our indiscriminate broadsides. We were shooting at our own ships in the melee. It had unfortunate results while you scooted to safety under our indiscriminate discharges."

Maffitt's thoughts harked back to a bright September afternoon, off Mobile Bay, when he took the *Oneida's* pounding for two hours and lived to tell the tale. Like those perilous hours, this night would be ineffaceably engraved on his memory. Too often had he walked hand in hand with the grim comrade. It was too late in the game for fear. Nor did he know it now, this man whom the novelist called "the reincarnation of John Paul Jones and Horatio Nelson."

But now it was Fly, *Owl*, Fly, if you can! She did, with waves of destruction pacing her, rattling on her deck like kettle drums.

To his pilot Maffitt drawled, "Sounds like a pack of Kilkenny cats."

Hot smoke stung the gash in his neck; but open water lay ahead, and the *Owl* was dashing for it over Maffitt's Channel. Perhaps his namesake had brought him luck, after all. With shots zipping after, the *Owl* vanished in the night. John Maffitt had in twenty-four hours written a blockade running classic. History books would call it just that.

Days later the *Owl* limped into Nassau harbor. At her masthead, above her shattered decks and bulwarks, flew the familiar ensign. It was an omen for those who saw it. The Confederacy still lived! Or did she? "The *Owl* appeared in the offing," wrote one who saw her, "and ran close past us into the harbor, a shothole through her funnel, several more in her hull, her standing rigging in rags, and other indications of a hot time." The steam whistles and bells of the twenty-odd runners that speckled the roadstead screeched and clangored. But the exultant chorus died on their lips. John Maffitt brought news. Fort Fisher had crumbled! The door that fed Lee's army was slammed shut. The Atlantic seaboard was barred like a prison. Wilmington was battened, and Nassau's gold rush had ended like a blown-out candle. On her docks lay two and a half million pounds of bacon that would rot where it was stacked. The Confederacy's ghost had gone up in the smoke of the Dahlgrens that ground Fort Fisher into an unrecognizable mass.

On February 17 Charleston was evacuated. Of Fort Sumter the victors took over only piles of debris left by four years of bombardment. Chaos and blue soldiers were overrunning the Deep South, liquidating the last pockets of resistance. In Virginia, along the bitter-held lines at Petersburg, Grant's orchestra was crashing out the fire-music for the South's grand exit. The glamor and the glory, the shouts of victory and the keening of bullets, Bull Run, Second Manassas, Chancellorsville, the bright dreams and the flags, the hopes and the rebel yells, the red liquid of life and the decaying bodies—were being shoveled into a common sepulcher, to the wailing and weeping of a people bowed down with grief and misery.

2

Late in March, a letter from Secretary Mallory caught up with Maffitt at Havana. With the *Owl* patched up, he had dashed there, not knowing what it was he hoped for. Even while the pillars of the temple were tumbling over his head at Richmond, Mallory spoke glibly of new and speedier blockade runners building in Britain, of the "expediency of running into Galveston," now that Wilmington and Charleston were no longer runnable.

Fine words. Expediency was right. Had Mallory ever ridden a runner through fire? felt the hot impact of guns fired at forty feet? At Havana the last official emissary from Richmond found Maffitt. He brought a bag of gold to pay off the *Owl's* crew, to buy coal and food, "to keep you going until the Confederacy got back on her feet." Desertion was already whittling down the *Owl's* crew. It was a woebegone company. Six had vanished. Who could blame them? They had starving families at what was left of their homes. Maffitt had sought to hold them with promises, appeals. Twelve others stuck by him. To them he said, "I do not intend to surrender this ship. I'll sink her first."

Secretary Mallory—so Richmond's emissary said—wanted Maffitt to run the *Owl's* cargo up the coast, sneak into Hampton Roads and up the James River to Richmond. It was madness. In the offing at Havana the hounds were tugging at the leashes. The mop-up was on. Bitter-ender Gideon Welles had ordered the last roundup of every Confederate maverick left on the sea. If they refuse to surrender, sink them on the spot. Shoot down anything with the slightest taint of the Confederate Navy. He again promised halters for Raphael Semmes and John Maffitt. They were proscribed for "crimes" on the high seas.

April, 1865. Spring overlaid the South. A loveliness of sweet young blossoms, a beautiful pall covering the torn land. One bright April day the Federal ships hanging off Havana suddenly went berserk. Long and lustily they blew their whistles, while one hundred guns reverberated across the water. Maffitt watched the white puffs in the distance and wondered, though not for long. It came all too soon. Lee had surrendered at Appomattox. *Dies Irae.* He went to his cabin and raised a glass. But the wine tasted bitter.

More news filtered over from the mainland. President Davis and his cabinet were in flight. Maffitt read the Davis manifesto in wonderment: "We have now entered a new phase of the struggle. Let us not despond, my countrymen, but, relying on God, meet the foe with fresh defiance and with unconquered and unconquerable hearts."

How could words stem a tide of a million blue soldiers? Or blow breath into thousands of boys rotting in graves from Gettysburg to Galveston? Call it what one would—conquered, defeated, subjugated—for John Maffitt it added up to the same thing. He had always faced up to the actualities. At long last "Pirate Maffitt" was a man without a country, the *Owl* a ship without a home port. He was on his own, hectored and hounded. Yet, as long as a Confederate flag flew somewhere, he felt bound to it. Galveston still held out. Here General "Prince John" Magruder was staging a last pitiful show, though the ring was closing by land and sea.

By night, the *Owl* glided past the Morro, laughed up her sleeve at the Federals waiting outside, and streaked for the Gulf. But the *Cherokee* picked up her trail and hung on doggedly. Maffitt finally shook her off. The *Owl* had the speed; Maffitt, the seamanship and the tricks. For the last time he performed his uncanny *ruse de guerre* of stripping off sail, stopping his engines, and freezing in his tracks.

Knowing the trickiness of the Galveston approaches, Maffitt decided to run in at dawn while the blockaders, unsuspecting, were still rubbing sleep out of their eyes. But Galveston was no pink tea —they were gunning for him. The American Consul at Havana, divining Maffitt's intentions, had sent a fast express across the Gulf, urging a warm reception for the holdout "pirate."

The *Owl* appeared out of the Gulf mists like the wraith of a ship. In her fireboxes blazed Cardiff coal, whose smoke was a white vapor hardly visible at two hundred yards. Far away, on land, he heard desultory rifle fire. The war was still on, and it was now May, 1865. Galveston was still in Confederate hands. It was heartening.

Now to business. Through the early light he sized up the Federal girdle about the northeast channel. As at Mobile, he went straight into their jaws. Maffitt stood on the bridge. How he slid through he never knew, nor did the Federals ever reveal. The Official Records are barren. Galvestonians, alarmed from sleep by the fleet's gunfire, ran to the housetops to watch and cheer. The best record extant of Maffitt's last run into what was the Confederacy, appeared years later in a Galveston paper:

> One fine morning in the spring of 1865 Captain John Newland Maffitt, formerly commander of the famous Confederate cruiser *Florida*, but then captain of the fast runner *Owl*, ran successfully through the blockading fleet of sixteen vessels, but grounded on Bird Island shoals, just at the entrance to Galveston harbor. It was a most exposed point within range of the enemy, who rained shot and shell around the stranded vessel. In the harbor, under command of Captain James H. McGarvey, was the Confederate fleet, composed of the gunboats *Diana* and *Bayou City*, and the several transports. With a volunteer crew Captain McGarvey went with the *Diana* to the rescue, to find the gallant Captain Maffitt and his crew working to float their vessel, which, with the assistance of the *Diana*, was soon done.
>
> In the face of great danger Captain Maffitt remained at his exposed post on the bridge of the *Owl* directing his men and displaying the greatest calmness and bravery.

The record of the *Owl's* run-out from Galveston through the blockading fleet is buried in the debris of the Confederacy, though an official dispatch from the American Consul General at Havana to Secretary Seward reported the *Owl's* return to the Cuban capital on May 9, 1865.

A faded, undated note in Maffitt's handwriting, found among his papers, vouched: "The last order issued by the Navy Department when all hope for the cause had departed, was for me to deliver the Owl to Fraser, Trenholm & Company, in Liverpool, which I accordingly did."

Those last four words reveal nothing of the epic gantlet he ran to obey the orders that rang down the curtain on his services for the Southern Confederacy. When they reached him, the man who promulgated them, Stephen Mallory, late naval secretary of the prostrate South, was a Federal prisoner on his way to a cell in Fort Lafayette, New York harbor. The war was over, but not for Maffitt. He had determined to carry out these orders. Such was the duty he felt imposed on him. The Owl would not be surrendered.

She had reached the home-stretch of her brief career; but Havana was no place for a homeless Confederate outcast, though he managed, with gold, to wangle coal out of a dealer, who bootlegged it into the Owl by night. Robed in seeming invisibility, she stretched boldly up the Atlantic seaboard for Halifax. Utilizing every trick of the trade, Maffitt ducked in for coal and out again under the noses of Federal cruisers keeping watch off this port. Heartsick, he shaped his course for England, facing a future as uncertain as the North Atlantic over which his ship plowed. Under sail, and sometimes steam, battling a gale-swept ocean, he was thankful each day when night fell and cast her friendly folds over his anxious heart and sturdy ship. By day he kept ceaseless vigil on the bridge, his glasses glued to the horizon for every speck that might herald danger.

Twilight was falling one July day when the Owl picked up St. George's Channel beacon and ran into the Irish Sea. Like her commander, she was weather-stained and footsore. Federal warships still haunted these waters. Gideon Welles had alerted them the Owl might try for England. They must watch for her, sink her, and capture Maffitt. Sliding along close to shore, within quick reach of neutral sanctuary, the Owl picked up a pilot off Holyhead and pressed on into the Mersey. With dragging feet she straggled up to Liverpool to anchor off the Toxteth Docks near a British gunboat. At her masthead rippled colors bearing an outlawed device. Once, in this port, it had been hailed as the guidon of a splendid new nation. But the Southern Confederacy was dead! Long live the

Union! Where were all the well-wishers who had cheered the Confederacy on? Forgotten was Liverpool's role in the blue-gray drama, forgotten her building of the *Alabama* and *Florida* that had wreaked such havoc on Federal shipping, forgotten the gold that poured into her coffers from North and South alike, forgotten the scores of ships that streamed down the Mersey with munitions to keep the battle fires burning across the seas. For this waif of the beaten South there was only silence.

The anchor chain clanked to the bottom. It had the sound of dirt falling on a coffin lid. That night Maffitt and his crew slept soundly. Next morning, July sunlight fell upon the obsequies of John Maffitt's hopes and struggles. He was immaculate in Confederate gray. At noon the boatswain piped all hands aft. Facing his depleted crew, Maffitt spoke:

This is the last time we meet as sailors of the Confederate States Navy. I have chosen to bring our ship to England rather than sail her into a Federal port because I was ordered to.

The Confederacy is dead. Our country is in the hands of the enemy, and we must accept the verdict. Our armies are beaten, our navy at the bottom. I am grateful to you for your loyalty to me and to the South. I had believed God would give us the victory. I was wrong.

Other words wanted out, but his tongue refused to shape them. After an awkward silence, he told his men they were released unconditionally from the ties that bound them to the Confederacy: there was gold enough in the *Owl's* strong box to pay them off in full, and grog enough in the spirits room to splice one last brace for the Confederacy. Then, for each man a personal good-by and a hearty handclasp.

Now to cut the ties forever, to strike the colors that, in his heart, at least, would never be lowered. Liverpool was too busy with its workaday tasks to notice this little ceremony, which closed the book for John Maffitt.

Taking the halliards into his hands, he fingered them nervously. Three ragged cheers, echoes of a dismal, burnt-out past, died quickly on the July air. The starry banner was coming down. Amen. Just before the bunting touched the deck, Maffitt caught it and folded it neatly. It was his sole material legacy of four years of fiery travail.

But branded on his heart would be memories of gun-flashed nights and days . . . yellow jack . . . explosions that made the sea an inferno . . . Drummond lights on the Gulf Stream . . . dashes through Federal squadrons . . . the *Florida*, whose name he had made famous and whose deck he had glorified with courage beyond the call of duty . . . the sting of salt spray . . . dim, threatening shapes on the horizon . . . the crackling flames of the *Jacob Bell* . . . the ladies at Barbados one ineffable night when he walked in glory. One further memento would he carry ashore—a garment, faded but still possessing a sort of sustaining magic, his ancient naval cloak that once a Queen had worn.

With great emotion he unbuckled his sword and laid it on the binnacle. He had unsheathed the blade to fight for what he deemed right. Vanquished it was, but still as honor-bright as the day it first flashed from its scabbard.

CHAPTER XXVII

Moorings

THE FLAGS WERE furled, the last shots fired. The blockaders, the runners, the *Florida*, the *Alabama*—indeed, the whole dream of a Southern republic, had sailed away for the port of lost causes. In a sense, John Maffitt went with them. Pitched in a far lower key was the motif of life ahead of him, yet never could he erase gunfire from his hearing, nor red stabs in the night from his vision. All this would remain vivid in his mind to the very last.

The remnants of the South's armies and the men who manned her pitiful navy were straggling home. For John Maffitt there was no homecoming yet. Awaiting him was trial for war crimes and a possible noose. Chief charges against him were burning Northern merchant vessels, and inhuman treatment of his captives. The first was fantastic. The United States had waged naval war in the same manner in the Revolution and the War of 1812. The second had no basis in fact. Indeed, the contrary was true. Yet Gideon Welles intended seizing him for "piracy." Raphael Semmes was already in irons. For John Maffitt a like fate loomed the moment he set foot on American soil.

But England, which had thrilled at his exploits, gave him refuge. An exile, he might have kissed the rod, but to his daughter he wrote, "My stomach is as yet too delicate to take the nauseous dose, or pardon-asking pill. I must bide a wee." For his ravaged homeland he grieved, "God help the South. The people require

His grace and divine assistance in this their time of sorrow and humiliation."

To make a living, Maffitt returned to the sea. It was his profession, his first love. Old Neptune seemed to welcome him back. Ruefully, he observed, "A man who has been brought up in the navy is not fit for much else." For two years he was master of a British merchantman trading between Liverpool and Brazil, over waters he had once lit up with blazing Yankee ships.

Not until 1868, after President Johnson's general amnesty, did he feel safe to come home. Pausing at New York, he made bold to visit the navy yard he had once proposed raiding. Perhaps shipmates of yore would remember him. Trudging along, he presently heard a step behind him, felt a hand on his shoulder, and a voice exclaiming, "Ha! I have captured the pirate at last!" It was old friend and former enemy George H. Preble, who bore him off to headquarters for a reunion with men who had once deluged him with shot and shell and marveled at his escapes. Four years later, at Preble's earnest request, Maffitt testified before a Court of Inquiry which investigated Preble's handling of the Oneida that memorable September afternoon in 1862 off Mobile Bay. Largely through Maffitt's version of the affair, Preble was restored to his grade in the navy—and to an admiralcy. This re-cemented an old friendship that endured to the end.

On his way south, at Washington, he petitioned Federal authorities for restitution of his property in that city, only to be told it was irrevocably confiscated, an injustice that darkened and impoverished his last years. It was never righted.

Back he came to Wilmington, where a defeated people received him with open hearts and arms. On the sound near Wrightsville beach he purchased a small farm, and called it Moorings. Here he reassembled his lares and penates, his daughters, his sons, one of whom, Eugene, had made the eventful cruise on the Alabama with Raphael Semmes. Many an old blue-water comrade dropped by to swap yarns and listen to his delightful reminiscences of sea and war. But tilling the soil, and raising berries, fruits, and flowers, was pretty tame fare. His merry old laugh still bubbled, but actually his heart was trampled in the wreckage of the Confederacy. Never could he reconcile his life to the new, changed order of things.

On Wilmington streets he became a dignified, honored figure, invariably in cooler weather with his faded naval cloak about his shoulders. He feelingly remarked, "If my old companion was endowed with intelligence and the power of utterance, it could unfold many a tale of no ordinary interest. The Queen of Greece has been encircled in its protecting folds. In Italy, Spain, France, and England, and in Germany, in Palestine, and among the Pyramids, this dear old cloak has served me truly and ever proved a faithful friend."

A visitor from Scotland, David McRae, journeyed shortly to Wilmington to express in person his admiration of Maffitt's adventurous career. Said McRae: "I had heard a great deal about Maffitt in the North where he was regarded by many as perhaps the ablest naval officer who had lent his sword to the Confederacy. It was said by more than one that if he had stood by the North, he would have been in Admiral Farragut's place today."

McRae found Maffitt a cultivated, gentlemanly man, small and spare in figure, but with a finely-cast head and firm mouth that seemed to express the energy and determination of his character. To McRae, Maffitt offered his then much-quoted apologia for the Confederate Navy:

> The Confederate Navy, minute though it was, won a place for itself in history. To the Confederates the credit belongs of testing in battle the invulnerability of ironclads and of revolutionizing the navies of the world. The *Merrimack* did that. And though we had but a handful of light cruisers, while the ocean swarmed with armed Federal vessels, we defied the Federal navy and swept Northern commerce from the sea.
>
> If only the old usage in regard to sea prizes in neutral ports had been still in vogue, we should have done more, and the pecuniary gain to the officers and men and to the Confederate government would have been immense—but a Confederate cruiser out upon the ocean was a lonely knight-errant. Her nationality was unrecognized; her facilities for supply and repairs hampered by neutrality proclamations that affected only her. She had to do everything for herself, live upon the enemy, and contend friendless and alone against the world.
>
> Well, it is all over now.

In 1870, a third marriage—to Emma Martin, sister of his son Eugene's wife—brought him happiness. Inspired by his bride and gifted with apt expression, he took up his pen to relive through memoirs his days of danger and daring. His first production was *Nautilus, or Cruising Under Canvas* (which he considered naming *Adventures of a Midshipman's Cloak*). It recreated his fascinating reefer days on the *Constitution* in the Mediterranean. He projected a book on the cruise of the *Florida* that would do for this historic vessel what Raphael Semmes had already done for the *Alabama*. That was as far as he got with it. His literary output included widely read magazine articles on blockade running and commerce raiding. Unfinished business also was a history of the War of 1812, which he prefaced with his own experiences suppressing piracy in the West Indies.

In 1884 friends sought to have him appointed to a position in the Wilmington Custom House, but President Cleveland refused to nominate him. It was a great shock to him. No longer able to manage his farm, he moved into Wilmington, where the speeding years brought crushing sorrow and hardship. Tragically, his beloved Florie and gallant-hearted Eugene both passed away before him. He never recovered from the double blow.

With the end in sight, his mind went a-roving back to long gone days. "The ship is ready," he said, "the sails are set and the wind is favorable; all we are waiting for is Mr. Lambert to come and ask God's blessing upon us; then we will heave anchor and away on the billows."

In his half-delirium the whole panorama of war flashed before him. Once again he was ordering "Full speed ahead!" down to the engineer as the *Cecile* dashed through hurricanes of crackling shells; or standing on the quarter-deck of the *Florida*, trumpeting "Where away!" up to the lookout who had just sighted a Northern ship in the distance.

On May 15, 1886, he struck his colors to his last enemy. Near the close, his mind cleared.

"Where is my cloak?" he asked. It was brought to him.

At Piraeus, drawn by the fame of the Constitution, came the fairy princess of the Balkans, Queen Amalie of Greece, and King Otho. To Midshipman Maffitt fell the coveted assignment for the royal visit. As Commodore's aide, he would escort the royal pair aboard. On the passage to the frigate the breeze caught the spray from the oars and with unseemly discourtesy sprinkled the royal party in the sternsheets, whereupon Midshipman Maffitt gallantly doffed his blue naval cloak and threw it around her Majesty.

Dusk drifted over the harbor. The muskets of the marines were ranged around the capstan with sperm candles in their muzzles, making a unique chandelier. The quarter-deck was transformed into a fairy ballroom. The ship's band struck up an animated waltz, one the Queen fancied. She gazed wistfully at the Commodore, who gazed embarrassedly back at the Queen. In her eyes he read, "Do let's waltz."

"I am no waltzer, your Majesty," admitted old Bruin, "but I have a number of young gallants aboard. My aide, Midshipman Maffitt, is quite adept at the business." He turned to the enthralled reefer, "Mr. Maffitt!"

The young gentleman's eyes met the Queen's. He bowed, then his arm encircled her waist and they were off with alacrity. Gracefully he whirled her around the deck with as much zest as if she were a señorita at a masked ball at Port Mahon. Soon a dozen couples were spinning about them, but the Queen seemed to prefer her first partner among all those who tried to replace him. The dancing was protracted. The candles in their musket sconces glowed like topaz. The night grew chilly. John Maffitt fetched his naval cloak. Wrapped in its folds she danced on. It was observed that the Queen whispered things to him that only he could hear.

Florida Epilogue

FEBRUARY, 1864. The *Florida* was off again on the long hunt. On a thick, squally night she slid out of the Brest roads like a specter, outwitting the Federal posse that had patrolled the offing for four months. Refurbished and recruited, she bore southwest for her old stalking grounds off Brazil, below the Tropic of Cancer.

Gone from her quarter-deck was the man who had given her fame. No halo of glamor, like that which crowned John Maffitt, ever adorned her new commander, Lieutenant C. Manigault Morris of South Carolina, who, nevertheless, turned in a creditable record. Maffitt had left a score hard to beat. Under his command the *Florida* and her tenders had captured, burned, or bonded fifty-five ships. To the *Florida* John Maffitt had also bequeathed an invaluable officer complement, versed in all the tricks of the raiding trade, and a petty officer personnel who speedily whipped the new Jacks taken on at Brest into first-rate man-of-war's men. Among the newcomers on the berth deck were a score of Garibaldi's former Red Shirts. Seamen by trade, they had temporarily cast lots with the Italian liberator. Now they were back on the sea, on the *Florida*, and loyal Confederates by grace of a mark on a piece of paper. Of calm nights, up from the forecastle, rose a strange medley of chanteys, Neapolitan airs, and *Dixie*, to which the sons of Italia gave a fine operatic finish.

Pausing at Funchal in the Madeiras for coal, the *Florida* met her old nemesis, Commander George H. Preble, whose inglorious try at sinking her off Mobile still rankled. Restored to duty, he was banished to a third-rate command, the sailing sloop of war *St. Louis*. The *Florida* could have demolished her, but Morris felt the start of a cruise was no time to risk a fight, even with the poor old *St. Louis*. He simply ignored her. Preble, on his part, hesitated to tangle with the cruiser.

But prize pickings were slim. Six weeks passed before the *Florida* bagged her first prize, the tall-masted *Avon* of Boston, bound from the North Pacific for Ireland. Morris burned her on the spot, but it was an inauspicious start. Veering away from the Equator, the *Florida* ran into Martinique, where she coaled only to whip northward for Bermudian waters. Prowling about these Federal-infested environs was risky, but the raider seemed to lead a charmed life. For two months she zigzagged around the island. Twice she steamed into the Bermuda anchorage to find that John Maffitt had left an unforgettable imprint. The red carpet was run out, coal run in. Here a letter from Secretary Mallory reached Morris suggesting "a dash at New England commerce."

Up to July 1—four months after leaving Brest—the raider took only four prizes: the *Avon*; the schooner *George Latimer*; the brig *W. C. Clark*; and the bark *Harriet Stevens*, which she burned in sight of Bermuda. On the last-named "lady," the *Florida's* boarders discovered 312 pounds of opium, which was dispatched to Richmond hospitals by way of a passing blockade runner.

On July 8 the *Florida* had a final surge of luck. Bearing up for the Virginia Capes, she caught and fired the whaler *Golconda*, homing from the South Pacific with 1,800 barrels of oil in her hold. Next morning, the *Margaret Y. Davis*, in ballast from Port Royal, came to a blazing end. Late that afternoon, with Cape Henry off the port beam, the lookout sighted the big bark *Greenland*, deep-laden with coal for the Federal blockading squadrons in the Gulf. Towing her was the steam tug *America*, which cast off her companion and made a successful dash for the shelter of Hampton Roads. The *Greenland* was torched off joyfully.

The cruiser now stood directly off the North's vast war base, which Lieutenant Read had hoped to burn. Here, on the threshold of Hampton Roads, on July 10 she staged her most dazzling performance. It was, except for the capture of the famed *Jacob Bell*, the most profitable day of her career. She opened the ball at 3 A.M. in the pre-dawn darkness, thirty miles off the Maryland shore, when the bark *General Berry* hove out of the mist with a cargo of hay for the fifty thousand horses of Grant's army, now investing Petersburg. She made a fine early morning blaze. At sun-up, the bark *Zelinda* peeked over the horizon unsuspectingly. Morris seized and fired her at once. The flames were still rising when a third prize, the schooner *Howard* of New York, obligingly appeared with a cargo of fruit from San Salvador. Bonding her, Morris sent her off to land his prisoners where she could.

That afternoon Morris made a sensational catch, the brig-rigged steamer *Electric Spark* bound from New York to New Orleans with a formidable passenger list. She refused to haul up at the raider's request, and the *Florida* was forced to call on her pivot gun's long arm to convince the fugitive of the futility of trying to run away. While Morris toyed with what to do with his big prize, the English schooner *Lane* sailed past with a deckload of fruit from Central America. Overhauling her, Morris made a deal with her skipper to land the prisoners he had just taken on the *Electric Spark*. For $720 Morris purchased the fruit stacked on the *Lane's* deck, and promptly threw it overboard to make room for the prisoners. The *Electric Spark* was stuffed like a Christmas basket with a variety of merchandise. Out of her safe came $12,000 in United States postage stamps, bundles of greenbacks, twenty-dollar gold pieces, and several dozen watches.

Morris' disposition of the *Electric Spark* matched Maffitt at his best. Instead of burning her, Morris kept the prize near the *Florida* until the *Lane*, bearing off his prisoners, had long vanished into the night. Then he scuttled the *Electric Spark*, and thereby created a mystery that baffled the Federal Navy for months. No flames of her destruction flared on the night sky. Not a clue did he leave on the waters, not even a small boat. He said he wanted to give her passengers "the idea we had carried her off to make a tender of her or to run her into Wilmington."

Meanwhile, at the same hour that the *Florida* was cutting short the flight of the *Electric Spark*, the tug *America*, which had escaped the *Florida*, sped into Hampton Roads and sounded the alarm. At 1:45 that afternoon a telegram from Admiral Lee, naval commandant at the Roads, bounced on the naval secretary's desk at Washington like a hot coal. Repeated was the panicky race-away of pursuit ships reminiscent of the year before, when Lieutenant Read had turned the Navy Department upside down with his fiery performance in the same waters. Telegrams flicked out. The *Florida* was on the loose on the nation's doorstep! She had captured the *Electric Spark* and would no doubt convert her into a formidable tender! She had burned five ships in three days!

But, as by some naval sleight of hand, the *Florida* and the *Electric Spark* had vanished—utterly. Yet, like two werewolves of the sea, the two ships were seen everywhere for the next few months. Skippers of Northern merchantmen apparently saw them all over the ocean, and even in their sleep. First to take the warpath in chase was the fine steam sloop *Shenandoah*, which dashed out to sea immediately, only to crisscross her own track twenty-four times in a fortnight. Attesting the zeal of his search, her captain attached to his report a map depicting the ship's peregrinations. It resembles a jigsaw puzzle. From the Gulf of St. Lawrence came a hot tip that the *Florida* and the *Electric Spark* were lounging on those waters. The big *Vanderbilt* rushed to the scene under forced draft, only to find a few fishing smacks, nothing more. Rumor had the *Florida* in Long Island Sound ensconced in a bay, waiting to waylay a steamer of the Fall River Line. The steam sloop *Wyoming* came limping up the Delaware River after five years of patrolling off the China coast, afflicted with every infirmity that can befall a ship. She was hustled back to sea without a day's rest, only to break down completely off Nantucket. From faraway Cherbourg, France, came a positive report that the *Florida* and *Electric Spark* were ambushed off the Irish coast, waiting to pounce on passing American ships. The American Consul in the Azores vowed he saw the *Florida* burning a ship off those islands.

So it went. Meanwhile, with American shipping dashing for refuge all over the Atlantic, the *Florida* was getting out of the way as fast as steam and sail would permit. Leaving the *Electric Spark* safely in Davy Jones's locker, she headed across the Atlantic for the Madeiras. After coaling at Teneriffe, she doubled back for the happy hunting grounds off Brazil's great hump. Morris had no way of knowing that while he was putting the American coast behind him, the *Florida's* sister ship, *Alabama*, riddled by the guns of the *Kearsarge*, was settling to the bottom of the English Channel.

On September 26 the *Florida* captured the bark *Mondamin*. It was to be her last bonfire.

Morris had freedom to rove where he pleased. He had hoped to pay a "visit" to the fishing fleets off New England, but the escape of the steam tug had disarranged that plan. Sport in the Atlantic was running out. Game was scarce. Northern ships by scores had dashed for refuge to the nearest ports, but the American whaling fleet in the Pacific offered an alluring, untouched target. The *Florida* could have a field day there, but before rounding the Horn, Morris decided to put into Bahia, Brazil, to coal and refit and, most necessary, to give his sea-weary crew a run on shore.

On the night of October 4, 1864, the *Florida* steamed into the great arm of the sea, All Saints Bay. At nine o'clock her anchor rattled down in the harbor of the ancient city of Bahia. The *Florida* had reached the end of her raiding tether. Daylight revealed the Union steam sloop *Wachusett* moored only half a mile distant across the harbor.

On the bridge of the *Wachusett* was able, courageous Commander Napoleon Collins, whose impulsive mind began planning the *Florida's* doom the moment he came on deck that morning and found himself at long last gazing on the will-o'-the-wisp raider he had searched for to no avail. There she was, trim and saucy, as if saying to the *Wachusett*, "You can't touch me in a neutral port. And I'll have a twenty-four hour start on you when I get ready to leave." Napoleon Collins was a dedicated officer, utterly determined to eradicate by every means at his command the enemies of his country—and the destruction of the *Florida* was something he had dreamed of by night and mused on by day. Now, he had caught up with her at last; but, unfortunately, in the harbor of a friendly nation. Here was the sea-wolf that had captured over sixty American merchant vessels.

Brazilian authorities were quick to sense the explosive setting. They wanted no outbreak of gunfire in their harbor. Before sunrise a Brazilian corvette moved up and anchored between the two belligerents. Then, from both Collins and Morris, the Latin officials exacted promises they would engage in no hostilities in Bahia's harbor. Morris meant what he said; apparently Collins did not. At the same time, Brazil accorded to the *Florida* a forty-eight-hour stay with permission to coal and refit.

But Collins was not satisfied with this. If he stood upon the punctilio and exactions of international law, the *Florida* would escape him. And he would never be able to live down the ignominy of it—or so he thought. Before finalizing his course he sent, through the American Consul, a formal challenge to Morris to steam the *Florida* outside the three-mile limit and square off in a finish fight with the *Wachusett* à la the *Alabama-Kearsarge* set-to off Cherbourg. The *Florida* was really no match for the bigger, heavier-gunned *Wachusett*, but this was not Morris' reason for declining the invitation to a duel. He had put in to Bahia for coal and repairs. When those tasks were finished (he said in his reply to Collins) he would leave, "but should I encounter the *Wachusett* outside Brazilian waters I would neither seek nor avoid a contest with her and would use my utmost endeavors to destroy her."

But this was not enough for impetuous Collins, who by now was ready to risk his nation's goodwill in South America, and the loss of his commission, to wind up the *Florida's* career by whatever means he could devise. Unable to lure Morris into a fight, Collins decided to do at once what he had tried to do for months: sink the *Florida* and sink her on the spot, even in the harbor of a friendly, neutral nation. He wasted no time.

At 3 A.M. on the night of October 7, 1864, the *Wachusett* noiselessly slipped her cable. Cutting across the bow of the sleeping Brazilian corvette, the *Wachusett* steamed straight for the unsuspecting *Florida*. At this hour Lieutenant Morris and half his officers and crew were ashore on twenty-four-hour leave. The *Florida's* deckwatch sighted a steamer headed toward the cruiser and gave the alarm, but too late.

Under a full head of steam the *Wachusett* struck the *Florida* a glancing blow on the starboard quarter, cutting down her bulwarks and carrying away her main yard and mizzen mast. At the same time, her marines doused the *Florida's* deck with volleys of musketry, wounding a number of the *Florida's* crew who had hopped out of their hammocks and, seizing what arms they could in the confusion, returned a scattering fire. Had the *Wachusett* crashed the *Florida* head-on amidships, as Collins intended, the raider would have gone to the bottom at once. Discharging two of his broadside guns into the melee on the *Florida's* deck, Collins backed off and demanded surrender "or else." He was answered by Lieutenant Porter, senior officer aboard the *Florida* at the time, who had no recourse but to surrender the ship. Within minutes a hawser was attached to the *Florida*. With the raider in tow, the *Wachusett* headed for the open sea. The Brazilian corvette, whose crew was aroused by the gunfire, promptly steamed up to squelch what sounded like a battle. Ready to open his broadsides on the Brazilian ship if she interfered, Collins promised to desist and do "nothing further," yet he doggedly continued seaward, dragging his captive after him with sixty-nine officers and men aboard.

It was foul play, a gross violation of Brazil's waters, but then, as now, in war might made right. Brazil demanded apologies and the restoration of the *Florida* to her anchorage at Bahia intact with those of her crew whom Collins had captured. Through Secretary of State Seward the United States disavowed Collins' action. To soothe Brazil's wounded pride, Collins was court-martialed and sentenced to immediate dismissal from the navy. In his testimony before the court he said, "My defense is that the capture of the *Florida* was for the public good." Yet the procedure was a farce. Secretary Welles immediately set aside the verdict of the court and restored Collins to his command.

As for the *Florida:* On November 12, 1864, the *Wachusett* towed her captive into Hampton Roads, where Admiral Porter, with a flair for poetic justice, ordered her anchored directly over the spot where the *Merrimack* had rammed and sunk the *Cumberland* two years before. Apparently to avoid the humiliation of returning the *Florida* to Brazil, resort was had to an adroit removal of the white elephant. A few nights later an army transport mysteriously rammed her. She shortly sank at her mooring. Confederate authorities charged the sinking was deliberate.

One evening in 1872 John Maffitt had dinner with Admiral Porter at the latter's home in Washington.

"Admiral, will you give me a true account of the sinking of the *Florida?*" asked Maffitt.

"Certainly," replied the forthright sea dog.

In quoting what Porter said, Maffitt prefaced it with this note of his own: "Admiral Porter in 1872 thus explained to me the strange disappearance of the *Florida* and his participation in the plot by which the United States government was relieved of the necessity of restoring, intact, the *Florida* to her anchorage at Bahia."

Maffitt then briefed Porter's explanation as follows:

> Mr. Lincoln appeared exceedingly mortified and confused on receiving protests from the different representatives of the Courts of Europe denunciatory of this extraordinary breach of national neutrality. Mr. Seward, with his usual diplomatic insincerity and Machiavellian characteristics, prevaricated, while he plotted with a distinguished Admiral as to the most adroit method of disposing of this elephant.
>
> During an interview between Mr. Seward and Admiral Porter the former exclaimed, "I wish she was at the bottom of the sea!" "Do you mean it?" exclaimed Porter. "I do, from my soul," was the answer. "It shall be done," replied Porter. Admiral Porter placed an engineer in charge of the stolen steamer, his imperative instructions being, "Before midnight open the sea cock and do not leave that engine room until the water is up to your chin. At sunrise that rebel craft must be a thing of the past resting on the bottom of the sea."
>
> At daylight the Florida was no longer to be seen. Rumors were incited—an army transport had run into her—an unknown leak had caused the sinking, etc., etc., but in naval circles foul play was openly asserted. Eventually the principal actor avowed the deed as instigated by the Secretary of State to avoid the reparation demanded by Brazil and urged by the diplomatic representatives of Europe.
>
> "To let loose this fearful scourge upon our commerce again would be terrible; it must be avoided," said the higher-law Secretary.
>
> "It shall be done," said the naval commander. And it was done!

So ended the saga of the *Florida*, at the bottom of Hampton Roads. What mattered the protests and indignation of Brazil? No more would the *Florida* scourge the seas. No more would she haunt the slumbers of Northern merchant skippers or light up the night skies with her bonfires. Yet history would bestow on her and her sister ship, *Alabama*, the finest laurels won by the Confederate Navy.

APPENDIX

MAFFITT'S REBUTTAL TO MRS. WILLIAMS' STRICTURES ON HER TREATMENT WHILE A CAPTIVE ON THE FLORIDA

Fifteen years after the war, John Maffitt wrote his friend and Civil War enemy, retired Admiral George Preble, his version of Mrs. Williams' enforced sojourn on the *Florida* after the capture and burning of the *Jacob Bell*. Maffitt refers to her as a missionary. In her controversial book, *A Year In China*, she does not so identify herself.

His letter is now in the "Preble Papers" in the Massachusetts Historical Society at Boston, and is reproduced here by permission of the Society. It reads:

April 11, 1880

My Dear Preble,

Your postal, accompanied by an abusive book, odoriferous with crafty *lies*, arrived this morning.

This emanation of a female missionary, to the celestial ports of China, was not new to me—

Her book was *concocted* for the bitter times, when abuse of the South, was a popular idiosyncrasy among the *vox populi* of the North. Those who nursed a grievance—revenged themselves by fulminating *lies* ad lib—expecting thereby to achieve popularity on the basis of sectional animosity. When the Jacob Bell was captured and learning that females were on board, I issued an order that personal baggage &c should not be tampered with but brought in safety to the Florida. This order was misconstrued and *private freight*, with baggage—to the amount of 30 tons, was conveyed to the steamer and when the passengers left—this mass of property went with them. When the passengers were brought on board of the Florida—*mistaking* Mrs. Williams for a lady, I gave up to her the entire possession of my stateroom and slept on the Qr deck between two guns. Capt Frisbie & family I placed in the full possession of the main cabin and all messed with me, receiving all the hospitality & courtesy in my power to render. In a brief time I observed that there was a decided enmity between Mrs. W. and the Frisbie's—on the first opportunity Capt F. referred to the ill will that existed and said—"She is an awful woman— a perfect *She devil*— In China she is despised and from the first day of her joining the Jacob Bell, has made herself so disgusting & insulting that for 96 days neither my family or I—have exchanged *one word* with her."

This authoress manifested—while on board the Florida—a very decided partiality for me, particularly when endeavoring to enlist my favorable consideration of her *project*—in regard to her War Insurance, which embraced 18 packages. Her views rec'd no favor from me—as I considered them dishonest. She did make up packages, to leave in place of those specified in her War Insurance & took with her what she eventually claimed to have been destroyed by the destruction of the Bell by the Florida. Her rascality display'd *extreme cunning*, not only in her declamation—but in her false book assertions. In her book the *lies* are so numerous that a sweeping denunciation is all that is left for complainers. Eight years ago, a young gent'n—who was a petty officer on board of the Florida—& now resides in Jefferson City got hold of this book and reviewed it in the scathing manner—exposing her character in the most complete & artistic style. The story about the loss of wardrobe, silver &c &c was a *lie* in exact conformity with the general characteristics of her "Year in China."

When leaving the Florida—she absolutely thanked me for my kindness & expressed the wish to meet me in happier days—The Piratical abuse—was an *afterthought*, to render her book *sensational*. No conversation occurred between us, in which I indulged in sectional animosity.

When Capt. Frisbie arrived in N.Y., Herald reporters interviewed him for a statement—very naturally he bemoaned the loss of his splendid ship & some private property—but stated that he & family were kindly treated by the Pirate &c &c. In all my cruising in the Florida—no act of cruelty or wrong was committed by me—prisoners & passengers were always justly & courteously treated and their personal baggage respected even on occasion, when I knew that thousands of dollars were concealed & by the customs of War—was meet for confiscation.

I have frequently met Captains who were once my prisoners and the meetings were decidedly very cordial & friendly. My duties were by no means pleasant—of course, property was destroyed, under *instructions*—baggage never—and every decent person, was messed in cabin or wardroom. My friend, the life I led was detestable and wearing upon the strongest of constitutions.

Of course a vessel burned, became a *theme* for the grossest abuse & monstrosity of lies—

Misstatements & exaggeration seemed—on both sides—to be a part of the war tactical programme and truthful history (yet to be written) will have to disintegrate facts from absurd fiction. I have given you a hasty resumé of the Williams affair—her malicious lies never disturbed my digestion or excited more than a momentary sensation of irritation.

The subject is nauseating and I quit it, after giving you a proper statement of facts—which I would not do—save to an old & sincere friend.

BIBLIOGRAPHY

Alabama Claims Papers, U.S. Government, 1871
Battles and Leaders of the Civil War, 1886
Bell, Herbert C. F., Lord Palmerston, 1936
Boykin, Edward, Ghost Ship of the Confederacy, 1957
Bradlee, Francis B. C., Blockade Running During the Civil War, 1925
Bulloch, James Dunwoody, Secret Service of the Confederate States in Europe, 1884
Carse, Robert, Blockade, 1958
The Case of the United States as laid before the Geneva Tribunal, 1872
The Century Magazine, Vol. LVI, 1898
Chesnut, Mary Boykin, A Diary from Dixie, 1905 and 1952
Confederate Index (a London Weekly), 1861–1865
The Confederate Soldier in the Civil War, edited by Ben La Bree
Cowley, Charles, Leaves from a Lawyer's Life Afloat and Ashore, 1897
Dalzell, G. W., Flight from the Flag, 1940
Davis, Jefferson, Rise and Fall of the Confederate Government, 1881
De Leon, Thomas C., Four Years in Rebel Capitals, 1890
Douglass, Ephraim, Great Britain and the American Civil War, 1925
Durkin, Joseph T., S. J., Stephen R. Mallory, 1954
Frank Leslie's Illustrated Weekly, 1861–1865
Freeman, Douglas Southall, R. E. Lee, 1935
Grant, Bruce, Captain of Old Ironsides, 1947
Harper's Illustrated Weekly, 1861–1865
Hergesheimer, Joseph, Swords and Roses, 1928
Hill, Jim Dan, Sea Dogs of the Sixties
Hollis, Ira N., The Frigate Constitution, 1931
Illustrated London News, 1861–1865
Journal of Charles W. Quinn, Asst. Engineer on the Florida, Confederate Museum, Richmond
London Daily Telegraph, January, 1897
Macartney, Clarence Edward, Mr. Lincoln's Admirals, 1956
John Newland Maffitt Papers, Southern Historical Collection, University of North Carolina Library
Maffitt, John Newland, Nautilus, or Cruising Under Canvas, 1870
Maps and Charts, Coast and Geodetic Survey, Washington, D.C.
Maryland Historical Magazine, Vol. 10, 1915
Merrill, James M., Rebel Shore, 1958
Monaghan, Jay, Diplomat in Carpet Slippers, 1945
Morgan, James M., Recollections of a Rebel Reefer, 1917
New York Herald, 1862–1865

New York Tribune, 1862–1865
Official Records of the Union and Confederate Armies
Official Records of the Union and Confederate Navies
Owsley, Frank, King Cotton Diplomacy, 1931
Photographic History of the Civil War, 1911
Porter, David Dixon, Incidents of the Civil War, 1886
———, Naval History of the Civil War, 1886
George H. Preble Papers, Massachusetts Historical Society
Regimental Histories, North Carolina, Volume V
Reports of the Secretary of the Navy of the United States, 1862–1865
Reports of the Secretary of the Navy of the Confederate States, 1862–
    1865
Richmond Dispatch, 1862–1865
Roark, Garland, The Outlawed Banner, 1956
Scharf, J. Thomas, History of the Confederate States Navy, 1887
Semmes, Raphael, Memoirs of Service Afloat During the War Be-
    tween the States, 1869
Soley, James R., The Blockade and the Cruisers, 1887
South Atlantic Quarterly, Vol. 28, 1929
Southern Historical Papers
Sprunt, James, Chronicles of the Cape Fear River, 1916
Taylor, Thomas E., Running the Blockade, 1912
United Service Magazine, 1880, 1882, 1892
Villiers and Chesson, Anglo-American Relations, 1861–1865, 1919
Washington Star, 1862–1865
West, Richard S., Jr., Gideon Welles, 1943
Wilkinson, John, The Narrative of a Blockade Runner, 1877
Williams, Martha Noyes, A Year in China, 1864
Also various newspapers from Portland, Maine; Wilmington, North
    Carolina; and Bermuda.

INDEX

Index

301